THE 96 INCARNATIONS

Who Are You?

Steven Mark Weiss

STRAIGHTFORWARD COMMUNICATIONS

ISBN:

Address inquiries to: the96incarnations@gmail.com

Dedicated to the people who figure out that there is a calculator for determining their lunation phase at www.the96incarnations.com

Table of Contents

"I adopted the theory of reincarnation when I was twenty-six. Religion offered nothing to the point. Even work could not give me complete satisfaction. Work is futile if we cannot utilize the experience we collect in one life in the next. When I discovered reincarnation . . . time was no longer limited. I was no longer a slave to the hands of the clock. . . . I would like to communicate to others the calmness that the long view of life gives to us."
– Henry Ford (Leo 4)

"I believe that life is basically a process of growth; that we go through many lives, choosing those situations and problems that we will learn through."
– Jim Henson (Libra 3)

"We all return. It is this certainty that gives meaning to life and it does not make the slightest difference whether or not in a later incarnation we remember the former life. What counts is not the individual and his comfort, but the great aspiration to the perfect and the pure which goes on in each incarnation."
– Gustav Mahler (Cancer 6)

"The soul is everlasting, and its learning experience is lifetime after lifetime."
– Shirley MacLaine (Taurus 3)

"I am a firm believer in reincarnation for people who either have more work to do or have so much debt to pay back that they have to be here."
– Prince (Gemini 6)

"In contrast to reincarnation and karma, all other views seem petty and narrow."

– Richard Wagner (Gemini 6)

"I believe in reincarnation, and I believe I've lived quite a few lives."

– Andre Romelle 'Dr. Dre' Young (Aquarius 5)

Please Read This First: How to Determine Your Sun Sign and Your Lunation Phase

In the introduction to this book, which we will get to in a few pages, the conceptual importance of the Sun's zodiacal position along with the phases of the Moon and their interrelated role in reincarnation theory will be explored. Meanwhile, kindly do us both a favor and first make sure you know which one of twelve is your own astrological Sun sign and which one of eight is your personal Moon (aka "lunation") phase. After you are in possession of this knowledge it will be entirely up to you whether it's worth your time to read the somewhat arcane introduction or to get right to the good stuff.

As you have by now doubtlessly surmised, there are 96 possible Sun sign/lunation phase combinations (12 Sun signs x 8 lunation phases). The one that pertains to you will tell you, at least in a mythical way, about where you are in the course of your spiritual evolution and what your soul is likely to be busy doing in this lifetime. If you have an astrological background, or consult an astrologer, you can easily get this data for yourself.

Alternatively, you can perhaps even more easily get this info by connecting to the following web address: www.the96incarnations.com.

Here you will find a link to a calculator that will ask you to input the following information:

- Date of Birth
- Time of Birth
- Place of Birth

The calculator will reveal your Sun sign and lunation phase. Once you have acquired this information, you can do what any normal person would do and go directly to the portion of this book that pertains to you. Pretty good deal, right?

Honestly, no offense will be taken by the author if jumping to your own section is your predilection. In all likelihood, the introduction will still be there when you get around to it.

Prologue: Famous People Rule

It won't take long for you to realize that a really cool thing about this book is its embrace of celebrity. After all, even in a matter as significant as the state of one's evolutionary path, who doesn't want to know what movie stars, pop musicians, athletes and iconic figures in other noteworthy areas of public life have to say? No matter how much insight and sincerity a random astrologer may muster, we live in a time when famous people rule.

At its essence what you will encounter in these pages is an opportunity for you to find, in terms of your soul station, your celebrity cohort. Employing a series of quotes by the famous to elucidate the character keynotes of each Sun sign/lunation phase group, one actually gets a pretty coherent compilation of the range of possible soul states. Hopefully the methodology offered here will match you up with the right cohort and you will be bathed in wonder by the appropriateness of the quotes to your own way of looking at things!

To be honest, that which started out as something closer to a marketing ploy than a book idea actually developed into a pretty compelling proposition. Organized in terms of their Sun/Moon lunation aspects, the groups of famous people collectivized here actually present collective purpose in a convincing manner. Let's avoid being the sort of astrologer who goes around trumpeting "proof" of astrology, but the correspondences within the delineated groups are actually very cool.

Some examples:

Many people are aware that Elvis Presley was a great admirer of Richard Nixon, even when that admiration went against the grain of the anti-establishment times in which Elvis lived. The irresistible attraction may lie in the fact that both are Capricorn 1 soul mates.

Arsenio Hall is the first black American to host a network late night talk show. Toni Morrison is the first black American to win a Nobel Prize in literature. Jackie Robinson is the first black American to play baseball in the major leagues. What gives? All are Aquarius 1.

It's hard to quickly catch the connection between them, but both Shirley Temple and Madeleine Albright served as U.S. delegates to the United Nations. It must be a Taurus 2 thing.

Dame Nellie Melba and Barbra Streisand, both Taurus 3's, are essential vocal icons of their respective times. Then again, so are Aretha Franklin and Chaka Kahn who share the third lunation phase and the Sun sign Aries.

Have you ever noticed the similarities in the world view of Newt Gingrich and Donald Trump? How interesting that they are both Gemini 4.

Mike Tyson and Michael Phelps are world-famous athletes associated with dominance and the mutual nickname "Iron Mike." They also share the Cancer 4 path.

Gillian Anderson and David Duchovny were unforgettably paired as FBI special agents in 'The X-files.' Although they portrayed somewhat opposing personality types, how curious that they should both be Leo 5.

Kanye West and Kendrick Lamar are giants of modern music who have collaborated on dozens of successful projects. It probably helps that they are both Gemini 6.

Oddly, famed modernist poet T.S. Eliot and famed comedian Groucho Mark had great respect for each other's work and pursued a long epistolary relationship. Both are Libra 6.

Tough guys known for their iconic relationship to motorcycles and for starring as the title character in the movie 'Papillon,' Steve McQueen and Charlie Hunnam share an Aries 7 connection.

Thomas Edison, Jennifer Aniston and Michael Jordan may be as diverse as a group can get, but all three nearly drowned as children and grew up fearful of water. All are Aquarius (The Water Bearer) 7.

Phil Knight, Michael Dell, Herb Kelleher and Rupert Murdoch are all famous capitalists who made their mark catering to emergent consumer tastes in the late 20th Century. All of them are Pisces 7.

For those who like their political philosophy a bit on the blood-spattered side, the Taurus 8 collection of Robespierre, Idi Amin, Pol Pot, Karl Marx and Malcolm X should suffice very nicely.

If one wishes to roll sex appeal and a cheerful personality into some tabloid fame, it might be helpful to be a Cancer 8. Just ask Jessica Simpson, Sophia Vergara and Khloe Kardashian.

There are dozens more of these correspondences and the hope here is that you will enjoy discovering them for yourself. It is further compelling to note the connections among famous collaborators who simply share a lunation phase, perhaps indicating an evolutionary resonance that goes far beyond the mere limitations of personality as expressed by a Sun sign. Robert/Redford Paul Newman (LP1), Johnny Carson/Jimmy Fallon (LP 2), Freddie Mercury/Rami Malek (LP3), Vin Diesel/Paul Walker (LP4), Robin Williams/Pam Dawber (LP 5), Daniel Radcliffe/Rupert Grint (LP6), Jordan Peele/Keegan Michael Key (LP 7), and Patrick Swayze/Jennifer Grey (LP 8) are just a handful of the inextricably bound creative pairs who emerge in this study.

Truly an argument can be made that a full examination of the sort of synchronicities indicated above would have made a better (i.e. more marketable) book than the one you have here. The argument against such a book, though, is that such a book would tend to crowd out the reader as an equal participant in the revelatory potential of that which is presented here. This work is, for good or less than good, consecrated to the purpose of the reader participating in something quite personal and revelatory rather than merely observational.

In all honesty, I'd really rather you accept this book is about you than them.

As for our celebrity guests, I thank and honor them one and all. Let me here acknowledge that the sparse biographical notes included here for each of them are hardly worthy of their complete stories. Each of these well-known folks could have an entire book written about them and, frankly, most of them do.

I should also recognize here that I might have some bad information on a birth date or two. Hopefully the instances are very few and the cause for regret quite manageable. I make no claims to rigorous scholarship, only a desire to look upon life in a state of wonder.

Introduction: We're All Going Through A Lunation Phase

So this is a work of astrology and it seems somehow righteous that here at the outset I should confess that I am making stuff up. I was going to write *simply* making stuff up, but simple doesn't really do it justice. I'm ready to grant *capriciously* and to a certain extent *irrationally*, but neither of those admit the fact that herein exists an earnest attempt at creating something meaningful.

I happily concede that astrology is no science, but it is far more than a lunatic belief in the power of sky objects to make things happen on Earth. In some ways it is astrology's misfortune to be an art based upon astronomy and mathematics. This dependence makes it seem to rationalists as if astrology is attempting to establish its bona fides in a linear causality rather than accessing the ephemeral truths of a spiritually oriented imagination. (Admittedly, there is a long tradition of mercenary fortune telling, but that probably has as much to do with the foibles of human nature than the conceptual inadequacies of astral geometry).

Be that as it may, it is easy to get away from the fact that astrology is unquestionably an art. If there is any causation to it, it is most often akin to the visceral epiphany one may encounter in the symphony hall or in the feeling of synchronicity one experiences when faced with an unexpected connectedness in coincidental events. While one is certainly free to make one's own judgments regarding the genuineness of predictive techniques, scientific process as precisely understood by rationalists is not the concern here.

A lifetime of interest has led me to think that astrology is best characterized as a great mythology. On one level it is a collection of magical/allegorical descriptions of human events rendered via astronomical allusions involving gods and goddesses and the ancient heroes with whom they interacted. On another, as noted by the eminent psychoanalyst Carl Jung, astrology is a sort of primitive psychology whose symbols and classifications articulate fundamental personality traits and conditions common to all mankind.

Whichever track one takes, what becomes apparent about astrology after even short exposure is that it is an exceedingly complex field of study. It is not hyperbolic to label it as a theory of everything...a richly imagined timing mechanism for all of history that includes every possible nuance and manifestation of human personality and experience. Its descriptions, techniques and segmentations are, like the heavens themselves, endless.

So it is of course frustrating to serious students of the art that many (most?) people consider astrology to be wholly circumscribed by the daily-dozen list of behavioral advisements that appear, deservedly, on the newspaper comic pages. “If you are an Aries, today is not a good day for eating rocks.” Well then, thank your lucky stars that you are some other Sun sign and may chow down at the quarry!

Even in this slightest of astrological activities, however, there is something of great import. For the Sun sign analyses that are generally one’s first encounter with astrology are the baby steps that gets the whole journey started. They are the mythic ‘in the beginning.’

Sun sign analyses introduce both the symbolism and the segmentation that are core to astrology. Astronomical bodies symbolize types of energy. Signs are the segmenting lenses through which the energy is filtered.

In meeting the Sun’s energy we symbolically encounter no less than the spring of life in human existence. Other planets and astronomical features symbolize many other powerful things, but there is no existence without the Sun. Passed through the personalizing lens of an astrological sign, the Sun's energy becomes our identity...our ego...our "I am."

Thus in this present work, which endeavors to describe the purpose one embodies in a human incarnation, it is impossible not to consider the Sun. In a way this is almost a cautionary observation for those who would enter the deep dark woods of astrology. However far one's astrological journey may take one, there is no light, nor enlightenment, without a primary consideration of the Sun and the qualifying effects of its placement in the zodiac.

It is also true that humanity's other great light, the Moon, the reflective side of personality, is of extraordinary consequence in this exercise, particularly in its waxing/waning relationship to the Sun. Even as a potent evolutionary marker though, a claim central to this analysis, the Moon takes its luminosity from the star in the middle of our human paradigm. "Who am I?" is a necessary precursor to "Where did I come from?; Where am I going?; and What's the point?"

Considering all the celestial input available to astrologers, it's extraordinarily easy to search for the wisdom beyond our own modest star and the humble reflective rock that orbits our earth. There is a whole lot of universe out there and, astrologically speaking, it all invites speculation. Why just stick to celestial vanilla and chocolate?

The answer to that, as already alluded to, is that our aptly named "lights" are obviously humanity's prime markers. Their saturation of our daily awareness addresses something fundamental in our being. Their position in the sky at one's birth is cosmically foundational.

Taken as a unit, the Sun and Moon speak to the dynamic passage of an ego and soul through an earthly incarnation. If you will allow such a bold assertion, then you might also accept a further implication of the cyclicality of this never-ending (for all intents and purposes) Sun/ Moon sky dance. It is a phenomenon that is spectacularly less limited and finite than a human life span and one that at least visually teases a case for something like reincarnation.

Now again, with due respect to the outraged rationalists, we are still speaking in terms of an artistic conceit. Do we actually reincarnate? I don't know.

Truly, though, the apparatus of astrology...its inherent bias towards epic structure...benefits mightily from an evolutionary thread. What does the art of astrology tell us about a life's ultimate purpose? Well, perhaps that one lives a given life in training to come back to live a better life, or at least one that is somehow more evolved.

Astrology has quite a few devices for injecting the thread of incarnation into its tale, many of them having to do with the Moon. The lunar nodes, an intersection of the Moon's orbit and Earth's celestial equator, are familiar to astrologers in this regard. Here, though, we are going to consider the lunation phases.

Phenomenologically, a lunation phase describes the angular relationship at any given time between the Sun and the Moon. There are, by tradition, eight of these phases in a lunar cycle: new Moon (1); waxing crescent (2); first quarter (3); waxing gibbous (4) ; full Moon (5); disseminating/waning gibbous (6); last quarter (7); and balsamic/ waning crescent (8). The thrust of the argument here is that the particular phase during which one is born has great significance in describing one's karmic status in a chain of incarnations...the later one is born in the lunar cycle the further one has travelled down one's evolutionary path.

Now here it is important to point out that this is not "my" concept. I was first introduced to the lunation phases by the wise and influential astrologer Marc Roberts, whom I was privileged to encounter early in my own formal astrological education during the late 1970's. At a seminar in Chicago, Roberts gave a memorable talk on the significance of each of the lunation phases in terms of the soul's growth...and the kernels of his rich insight are amply reflected in this present work.

It wasn't until years later that I fully came to realize that Roberts' work, as well as that of other significant astrologers interested in psycho-spiritual Moon lore, was predicated on the work of the incomparably important astrologer Dane Rudhyar. Anyone who would like to explore the roots of the thinking behind the significance of the lunation phases would do well to consult Rudhyar's seminal work 'The Lunation Cycle.' In all honesty, there is little in modern spiritualist astrology that does not derive some of its purest essence from Rudhyar's contributions, although the specificity of that influence here regarding lunation phases must be especially acknowledged.

Thus it is entirely fair to give credit to Messrs. Rudhyar and Roberts for the conceptual underpinnings of my own work, in particular with regard to the lunation phases as a progressive system of reincarnation. Indeed, the changes in the Moon's aspects are as compelling as any astronomical phenomenon available for humankind's observation, and well worth a place in the sacred mythology regarding humanity's evolutionary path. Here's to Messrs. Rudhyar and Roberts for noticing.

Of course, the Moon itself is by nature a changeling and therefore a philosophical challenge to hard-edged observation. Mesmerizing to an extraordinary degree, the Moon manages to absorb attention away from the defining power of its illumination source. As already has been mentioned in these paragraphs, though, the establishing principle of identity for a Moon phase or a human being is the Sun.

The aim of this current work is to bring the Sun back to its rightful place in matters of personal experience, even when considering a matter as profoundly grand and abstract as the soul's path through multiple lifetimes. It may be, for example, that anyone in a fifth lunation phase lifetime will confront the spiritual importance of relationships. Yet what this means for a Sun sign Aries versus a Sun sign Libra or Capricorn is certainly worthy of emphasis and exploration.

This brings us to famous people and the fact that, thanks mostly to the Internet, we know just about everything there is to know about them, including everything they have ever said to anyone ever. This repository of direct authority is boundlessly helpful in personalizing the lunation phases, and in bringing a little pizzazz to what might otherwise seem merely theoretical. The key here is that while the lunation phase emphasizes the act of spiritual evolution, the Sun emphasizes the actor.

So it is that the majority of this book is given over to well-known people collected into their respective Sun sign/lunation phase categories who will share their wisdom in their own words. Authorial analysis has been kept to a minimum because, frankly, these quotes will either resonate as lucid collections or they won't. Having the opportunity to judge is hopefully the kick you will get out of exploring this book.

Perhaps the truly alarming part of this effort is that I may have ultimately written another (yawn!) Sun sign astrology book, although I will maintain that in its emphasis on a soul's growth makes it a bit more than that. Perhaps I falsely flatter myself when I invoke my own formative literary encounters with great modern mythologists such as Carl Jung and Joseph Campbell, but I'd like to think they would have a little empathy for this well-meaning effort at placing every person among the many persons in a collective and cyclical pageant, however theoretical, of human evolution.

Please just don't let the made up parts distract you from any insight that all of this may engender. Or maybe we can just agree that while you are here you will simply try to have a good time. Thank you.

1st Lunation Phase/New Moon

Moon 0 degrees to 45 degrees ahead of the Sun

Keyword: Ego

The new Moon soul is anything but a weak soul. There is the cry of unfettered creation as in the arrival of a newborn. "I am here, damn it, and life must attend to me."

The LP1 lifetime is one in which the emotional tides of the Moon have yet to establish province in the spirit. The pure Sun energy reigns unchallenged and supreme. The soul's purpose in this lifetime is to create a wholly self-referential identity—-ego is not merely a condition of character; it is the objective.

For students of astrology, it is worth noting that LP1 individuals are those most fully representative of their Sun sign. The key here is that with a great degree of frequency LP1 individuals have the Sun and Moon in the same astrological sign. This lack of separation between Sun and Moon energies and the recognition that the Moon is at the very beginning of its developmental cycle are the reigning mythic principles in an LP1 life.

One can identify an LP1 Individual by such factors as curiosity and will. Life is a brand new coloring book and the box of freshly scented crayons has yet to be opened. The spiritual mantra is "let me at it."

There is often a hint of naiveté in these individuals, but their innate drive is second to none. Extraordinary success comes to LP1's who are able to consecrate themselves to a purpose. Failure resides in not deciding what one wants to be when grown up.

Aries 1

For an Aries in the first lunation phase, life is an invitation to do something without the reflective restraints one encounters in what might be described as soul-searching. Please understand, the Aries 1 can be an extraordinary individual and may develop into a skilled artisan or a deep thinker or virtually anything at all, but the root energy is the expression of an unfettered will. Here, more than in any other incarnation, there is the experience of the great and uncompromised energy of an unquestioning and explosive bias towards action.

Indeed, those in the immediate realm of an Aries 1 may be forgiven a certain amount of fatigue. If the first lunation phase is the newborn phase of the soul, the Aries 1 is its squalling embodiment. The Aries 1 life partakes of energy that commands attention even when the dial is set to instinctual, because well, it's sort of impossible to ignore.

There's really not a whole lot else to say about Aries 1. Act. Do. Enjoy the ride. Be moderate only when in peril. These guides don't always lead to success, but they do lead somewhere...and an Aries 1 definitely will be, quickly and unreservedly, headed somewhere.

Aries 1 is here? There they go.

"Enjoy life. There's plenty of time to be dead."

– Hans Christian Andersen, world-famous Danish author of classic fairy tales; emerged from an impoverished upbringing to become one of the most honored writers of his time

"Listen, smile, agree, then do whatever you were going to do anyway."

– Robert Downey, Jr., award-winning American actor/producer/singer; famous for the role of Tony Stark/Iron Man for which he has earned in excess of $250 million

"Live for each second without hesitation."

– Elton John, iconic British pop singer/musician/theatrical composer; a Grammy Legend winner; knighted by Queen Elizabeth for his contributions to British pop music and AIDS research

"I was always drawing racing cars and rockets and spaceships and planes, things that were very fast that would take me away."

– Gary Oldman, Oscar-winning American actor; famous for complex characters ranging from Dracula to Lee Harvey Oswald; first lead role was punk rocker Sid Vicious in Sid & Nancy

"Okay, okay, okay. I understood that pushing the elevator button over and over again would not make the elevator appear sooner. But I couldn't help myself."

– James Patterson, prolific American novelist; holder of the Guinness record for the most #1 'New York Times' bestsellers by any author; his favorite book as a child was 'Peter Pan'

"I'm pretty sure I could outrun the whole Dallas Cowboys team."

– Adrian Peterson, legendary American football running back; nicknamed "All Day" by his father because of his drive; was considered an athlete who could go directly from prep ball to the NFL

"I have a lust for life."

– Diana Ross, world famous American singer and actress; leader of The Supremes...the most successful female vocal pop group in history; recipient of Grammy Lifetime Achievement Award

"Don't be afraid of making an ass of yourself. I do it all the time and look what I got."

– William Shatner, Emmy-winning American actor/singer; famous as Captain James T. Kirk of the U.S.S. Enterprise; appeared in all 79 broadcast episodes of 'Star Trek; fond of Dobermans

"Music can be all things to all men. It is like a great dynamic Sun in the center of a solar system which sends out its rays and inspiration in every direction... It is as if the heavens open and a divine voice calls. Something in our souls responds and understands."

– Leopold Stokowski, famed English orchestral conductor; known as "the bad boy" of classical music; linked with the Philadelphia Symphony/Disney's innovative animated classic 'Fantasia'

"Don't wait for the stars to align, reach up and rearrange them the way you want...create your own constellation."

– Pharrell Williams, Grammy-winning American singer/songwriter/ record producer; famed for the song 'Happy;' in 2003 his company produced 43% of the songs released on American radio

"Sure, Kill Bill is a violent movie. But it's a Tarantino movie. You don't go to see Metallica and ask the fuckers to turn the music down."

– Quentin Tarantino, Oscar-winning American filmmaker/actor; known for violent nonlinear movie plots; has described being a sports spectator as "boredom at its most colossal"

"If you ask me what I came into this life to do, I will tell you: I came to live out loud."

– Emile Zola, Nobel-nominated French author; founder of the "naturalist" literary movement built upon Darwinian evolutionary theory; famed for his "J'Accuse..." defense of Alfred Dreyfus

Taurus 1

Much has been written by astrologers about the Taurus connection to life as something material and sensorial and essentially *real*. There are losses and gains. There are joys and sorrows. Time is a friend and then it is an enemy and then, perhaps, a friend again.

Although some may ascribe a plainness or lack of complexity to such a life, the Taurus 1 is more appropriately observed as an archetype of admirable strength. Enduring the pressures and setbacks of a real world existence, the best of them become nigh unto imperishable and as precious as diamonds. Day by day they take life at its conflicted word and work to thrive in steady pursuit of whatever may seem a tangible worthy objective.

This is not meant to create the impression that a Taurus 1 is simply saddled with a yoke of drudgery. Artists, thinkers, builders, athletes, and other exceptionally spirited people dot their ranks. It's just that their talents rarely rely on the ephemeral, and are far more prone to being the result of an investment in reality and conscientious prolonged effort.

Ultimately, in a Taurus 1 life reality simply has the right of way and one does the best one can to negotiate and, as necessary, endure it. Genuine talent, hard work and discipline tend to win out over a more ragtag approach. Humor often helps...and painkillers.

"You have to have faith that there is a reason you go through certain things. I can't say I'm glad to go through pain, but in a way one must, in order to gain courage and really feel joy."

– Carol Burnett, beloved American actress/comedian/singer/author; the queen of television sketch comedy; famous "ear tug" sign-off acknowledges loss of grandmother and daughter

"Some people see things that are and ask, 'Why?' Some people dream of things that never were and ask, 'Why not?' Some people have to go to work and don't have time for all that."

– George Carlin, groundbreaking American comedian/author; plagued by heart disease and drug issues; much of his money taken by the IRS on tax evasion charges

"Life's too short to be a pushover."

– Kelly Clarkson, Grammy-winning American singer/songwriter/actress/TV personality; known for winning first season of 'American Idol;' abandoned by her father at age six

"I hold a little fundraiser every day. It's called going to work."

– Stephen Colbert, Emmy-winning American comedian/writer/producer/actor/television host; known best for acid political commentary; his father and two brothers died in a plane crash

"One day, in retrospect, the years of struggle will strike you as the most beautiful."

– Sigmund Freud, world-renowned Austrian neurologist; the father of psychoanalysis and talk therapy; his addiction to tobacco resulted in 33 cancer surgeries

"It's not what you start in life, it's what you finish."

– Katharine Hepburn, legendary American actress; four-time Academy Award winner; denied role of Scarlett O'Hara in 'Gone with the Wind' as the producer said she "lacked sex appeal"

"Age is such a natural progression. You shouldn't fight it."

– Ann-Margret, award-winning Swedish-American actress/singer; rose to fame in 'Bye Bye Birdie;' a stage fall at the age of 31 fractured her face and knee and led to a time of alcoholism

"Nursing is an art: and if it is to be made an art, it requires an exclusive devotion as hard a preparation as any painter's or sculptor's work."

– Florence Nightingale, celebrated English social reformer; key figure in the evolution of professional nursing; contracted fever during Crimean War and lived much of life as an invalid

"If you are always allowed to stop training whenever you feel discomfort, you will find it too easy to give yourself permission to quit."
– Jet Li, globally acclaimed Chinese actor/ writer/director/producer/martial artist; became a national martial arts champ at age 11; retired early due to hyperthyroidism and spinal problems

"You don't need people's opinion on a fact. You might as well have a poll asking: 'Which number is bigger, 15 or 5?' or 'Do owls exist?' or 'Are there hats?'"
– John Oliver, Emmy-winning English-American comedian/writer/producer/ political commentator/actor/ television host; known for HBO's 'Last Week, Tonight;' notoriously modest

"I enjoy writing, I enjoy my house, my family and, more than anything I enjoy the feeling of seeing each day used to the full to actually produce something. The end."
– Michael Palin, honored English comedian/actor/writer/culturist; a member of 'Monty Python;' was president of the Royal Geographic Society; knighted for service to television and geography

"I plead with you—never, ever give up on hope, never doubt, never tire, and never become discouraged. Be not afraid."
– Pope John Paul II, charismatic Polish cleric; the first non-Italian pope in over 400 years; a vocal human rights advocate; survived an assassination attempt in 1981; canonized as a saint in 2014

Gemini 1

In the Gemini 1 life one witnesses the birth of thought as life's salient mode. What is perhaps most noteworthy at this point in the evolutionary path is that the extraordinary brain apparatus that regulates one's thinking is metaphorically a sort of blank slate. Thus, the Gemini 1 faces a constant primal preoccupation regarding "what is one to think?"

Without ingrained filter or predilection, in a consciousness that has an extraordinarily flexible syntax, the answer that keeps recurring is "it depends." No matter how closely something is observed, or how ingrained a matter might seem with an air of permanence, the Gemini 1 comes to the conclusion that accurately observing anything almost always comes with a dose of perceptual bias. Refusing to stipulate to black and white, the Gemini 1 mind awakens to the glories of mutability and grayscale and the breadth of the possible.

This is not a put down or a joke. Gemini 1's are astute observers of the panoply of matters that are of interest to them, and many spend their whole lives sharing those observations. They have a real passion, and often great skill, when it comes to reporting the tricky relationship between observation and the observable.

Just don't expect the Gemini 1 to suddenly show up with a pledge of allegiance or a homegrown version of the Ten Commandments. Unfettered Intellectual dynamism is their bag. Certainty and homogeneity of thought are to be located in a different spiritual department.

"You know the thing that interests me about 'Unsolved Mysteries?" It's because there are people out there, people who know something, who may have one final clue."

– Raymond Burr, Emmy-winning Canadian-American actor; known for solving mysteries as 'Perry Mason' and 'Ironside; into viniculture, hybridized orchids and seashells

"I am convinced of the validity of contradiction. There are many worlds. Each is true, at its time, in its own fashion."

– Errol Flynn, award-winning Australian actor; famous as a romantic swashbuckling action hero; his autobiography, 'My Wicked, Wicked Ways,' was hailed as a first-rate literary work

"We color and mould according to the wants within us whatever our eyes bring in."

– Thomas Hardy, renowned English novelist/poet; nominated 11 times for a Nobel he never won; he was a successful architect before devoting himself full time to his literary career

"Everything is temporary if you give it enough time."

– Jewel, Grammy-winning American singer-songwriter/musician/producer/actress/author; her first album 'Pieces of You' went 15-times platinum; stars in a Hallmark Channel mystery series

"The difficulty lies not so much in developing new ideas as in escaping from old ones."

– John Maynard Keynes, legendary English economist/political essayist; produced breakthrough work on the broad economic effects of unemployment and governmental deficit spending

"If you are possessed by an idea, you find it expressed everywhere, you even smell it."

– Thomas Mann, Nobel laureate author/critic/philanthropist; considered one of the leading intellects of his age through subjects ranging from spirituality to aesthetics to social justice

"I just can't help but see things differently."

– Kylie Minogue, award winning Australian soap actress/pop star; prolific and talented lyricist; the name "Kylie" translates as "boomerang" in Australian aboriginal dialect

"The universe was born restless and has never since been still."

– Henri Rousseau, celebrated French avant-garde artist; self-taught; sometimes considered "the godfather of modern art;" spent most of his working life as a toll collector in a customs office

"Have faith in your own thoughts."

– Brooke Shields, award-winning American actress/model/author; famous for beauty/sexuality commercially exploited at a very tender age; a French lit major at Princeton University

"I wasn't allowed to grow as an artist. My albums were nicer to look at than to listen to."

– Nancy Sinatra, award-winning American singer/actress; associated with the hit song 'These Boots are Made for Walkin';' works as the creator/steward of the Sinatra family website

"To listen is an effort, and just to hear is no merit. A duck hears also."

– Igor Stravinsky, Grammy HOF Russian composer/pianist/conductor; one of the most influential artists of the 20th Century; self-described as "an inventor of music;" authored two memoirs

"The important thing is not what they think of me, but what I think of them."

– Queen Victoria, reigning British monarch for six decades; presided over the largest empire in world history; an assiduous diarist who wrote an average of 2.500 words per day

Cancer 1

There is a 'lunacy' to a Cancer 1 life that is impressive even by Cancer standards. In astrology, the sign Cancer is said to be ruled by the Moon; and here are folks born while the Sun is in the sign of Cancer and the Moon (in the sky) is essentially nowhere to be found. The result is an incarnation in which feelings, sometimes irrational ones, have to be expressed (out loud and sometimes fiercely) by the ego.

Remarkably, it is this inflexible quest to discover and express one's own deeply encrypted emotional yearnings that makes these folks pretty close to indomitable. Deep down A Cancer 1 has only a vague tolerance for the rights, opinions and feelings of anyone who may be lined up against them. Apology is rarely in their vocabulary, and they have no dial to modulate the fierceness with which they love, hate or complain about life's unfairness.

Lest this sound like harsh criticism, let it be immediately said that an unleashed Cancer 1 can truly be the greatest of heroes. Lacking a bias towards reserve or contemplation or general notions of appropriateness, and as true believers in whatever tribe they may end up inhabiting, the Cancer 1 is the archetype of the faith defender. While their motivation may be mammoth uncertainty about what it is they are feeling, they are paradoxically uncompromising in making sure their feelings about what should be are granted respect.

Ultimately, in Cancer 1 what one encounters is a collection of unremitting strivers, scrappers, rule breakers and amassers of things who have little sense when it comes to ducking a fight or a fling. They are absolutely astonishing in their emotional relentlessness, almost as if enduring life's pain and ending up with stuff is the only possible route to self- validation. Consider yourself warned.

"Fortune always favors the brave, and never helps a man who does not help himself."

– P.T. Barnum, American showman; founder of Barnum & Bailey circus; catered to the gullibility of crowds via a long list of freak shows, hoaxes and other exploitative entertainments

"I don't care about the rules. In fact, if I don't break the rules at least ten times in every song, then I'm not doing my job properly. Emotion is much more important than making mistakes, so be prepared to look like a chump. If you become too guarded and too processed, the music loses its spontaneity and gut feeling."

– Jeff Beck, Rock & Roll HOF English musician; considered one of the all-time greatest "maniac guitarists;" obsessed with vintage hot rods; has been in three major car crashes

"You don't learn to walk by following rules. You learn by doing, and by falling over."

– Richard Branson, highly-honored honored British businessman/author/philanthropist; created the Virgin business empire, famous for risky daredevil exploits and personal style eccentricities

"As a kid, when I got to the edge of a cliff I wanted to jump off. I didn't want to kill myself. I wanted to fly."

– Tom Cruise, award-winning American actor/producer; a Hollywood legend; known for action films such as 'Mission Impossible' and 'Top Gun;' a genuine daredevil; battled severe dyslexia

"When I was a young fellow I was knocked down plenty. I wanted to stay down, but I couldn't. I had to collect the two dollars for winning or go hungry. I had to get up. I was one of those hungry fighters. You could have hit me on the chin with a sledgehammer for five dollars. When you haven't eaten for two days you'll understand."

– Jack Dempsey, American world heavyweight champion boxer; famous for his punching power and savage fights; arguably the wealthiest and most popular sports hero of his times

"You may get real tired watching me, but I'm not going to quit."

– Harrison Ford, American actor; a Hollywood superstar, immortalized as Han Solo and Indiana Jones; bullied as a school boy; he is a pilot, motorcycle collector and master carpenter

"If it wasn't hard, everyone would do it. It's the hard that makes it great."

– Tom Hanks, Oscar-winning American actor; one of only two actors to win consecutive best actor Academy Awards; before acting he was a bellman who once carried Cher's bags

"I wish I was beautiful or at least wise, but I'm simply mad and violent."

– Courtney Love, infamous American singer/actress, grew up on a commune; became a stripper at age 16; famous for 'wild girl' antics and for being married to grunge superstar Kurt Cobain

"Most people give up just when they're about to achieve success. They quit on the one yard line. They give up at the last minute of the game one foot from a winning touchdown."

– Ross Perot, billionaire American businessman; two-time independent U.S. presidential candidate; famously eccentric—-described by Sen. John McCain as "nuttier than a fruitcake"

"I have been criticized and ridiculed for turning to astrology, but after a while, I reached the point where I didn't care."

– Nancy Reagan, American actress; best known as the First Lady during the Ronald Reagan administration; famous for her anti-drug stance and bringing astrology into the White House

"You got to pay your dues if you want to sing the blues...And you know it don't come easy."

– Ringo Starr, R&R HOF British musician/singer-songwriter/actor; best known as the drummer for the Beatles, played left-handed on a right-handed kit; a germaphobe; allergic to pizza

"I never thought I'd be successful. It seems in my own mind that in everything I've undertaken I've never quite made the mark. But I've always been able to put disappointments aside. Success isn't about the end result; it's about what you learn along the way."

– Vera Wang, American fashion icon; famed for bridal gowns; previously a figure skater and youngest-ever editor of Vogue, has a room devoted to a collection of more than 1,000 t-shirts

 Leo 1

Among the mythic qualities of the Moon is its representation of the deep connection one has to a cultural identity. The Moon represents the awareness that we are somehow part of a collective that preconditions anything our personalities may hope to accomplish. Our heritage is a link to our emotions, says the Moon, and therefore much of who we are is steeped in the glow of reflected light.

The key to a Leo 1 life is that they could not possibly relate less to the preceding cosmological observation. Born at a time of no Moon these avatars of the primal ego energy inherent in the Sun are here solely to radiate their own personal heat and light, and that will be quite enough thank you. There is no apology, and arguably not even much awareness, with regards to an empathic sense of otherness...although they will magnanimously tolerate being adored by their fans

Selfish as this may sound, begrudging the Leo 1 their particular personality mode would be somehow akin to criticizing the rooster crowing at dawn. The Leo 1, unblemished by a sense of externally imparted participatory requirements, is proudly consecrated to the ever present potential of a (their?) new day. Whatever the outcome of their acts, they are comforted by the personal purity of their intent and the fact that the Sun will almost certainly be back tomorrow.

In truth, the only real fear a Leo 1 has is being diminished by a sense of personal confinement. Many of them will eventually have a story, or several, about how they survived a cloudy day and reinvented themselves. Shine on Leo 1, shine on.

"The place in which I'll fit will not exist until I make it."

– James A. Baldwin, award-winning American novelist/playwright/essayist/poet/activist; a leading voice of the civil rights movement; challenged mythic qualities of collective identity

"You can't always do that which you can do in your sleep. That doesn't fulfill an artist. You're looking for places where you can grow, in some way, whether it's a large way or a small way. I want to grow as an artist, as a person and as a woman. I want to enjoy myself and my life and the company that I'm keeping. I want to bring something to the table that's different than anything else would bring, but that has its place and value, and then keep moving."

– Angela Bassett, Golden Globe winning actress, Yale University MFA, famous for playing socially significant black women; rejects scripts in which "the character is just a device"

"You were born to be / You only have to see / You are the Sun / You are the Sun"

– Belinda Carlisle, American pop singer and wild child; best known as lead vocalist for the Go-Go's; addiction problem; post-addiction achieved second stardom internationally; Buddhist

"Being a superhero is a lot of fun."

– Chris Hemsworth, award-winning Australian actor/philanthropist; best known as the Avengers hero Thor; a 'People' Sexiest Man Alive; an avid surfer and supporter of marine ecology

"There's a rebirth that goes on with us continuously as human beings. I don't understand, personally, how you can be bored. I can understand how you can be depressed, but I just don't understand boredom."

– Dustin Hoffman, Oscar-winning winning American actor; famous for sympathetic portrayals of the marginalized and vulnerable; mistaken for a window cleaner during 'The Graduate' audition

"You don't need to be accepted by others. You need to accept yourself."

– Bindi Irwin, Australian actress/singer/wildlife activist; daughter of wildlife icon Steve Irwin; grew up at the Australia Zoo; 2015 'Dancing with the Stars' champion

"I am my own experiment. I am my own work of art."

– Madonna, world-renowned American singer/actress/writer/business-woman/style icon; nicknamed the "Queen of Pop;" the best selling female recording artist of all-time

"I was seen in earlier years by family members and people of authority as somebody wasting his time. I had trouble with the restrictions of conformity. It made me edgy."

– Robert Redford, American movie legend, director/producer/businessman; founder of the Sundance Film Festival; attended college on a baseball scholarship; pursued a fine arts career

"If you are on an honest journey to find yourself, you'll find God."

– Martin Sheen, acclaimed American film/television actor particularly known for political roles; devoted to a variety of liberal activist causes, he has been arrested at protests over 70 times

"In this life, if you don't celebrate yourself, nobody will."

– Kevin Smith, award-winning American filmmaker/actor/comedian/author; best known for creating the stoner characters Jay & Silent Bob; became a vegan after suffering a heart attack

"My sign is Leo. A Leo has to walk with pride. When he takes a step, he has to put his foot down. You walk into a room and you want people to know your presence, without you doing anything."

– Wesley Snipes, award-winning American actor/director/producer/martial artist/author; but known best for action and sports films and as the superhuman Marvel character 'Blade'

"I'm normally drawn to something I haven't done and seen before."

– Gus Van Sant, award-winning American producer/director/screenwriter; interested in iconoclastic topics ranging from homosexuality to new age spiritualism to mental abnormality

 Virgo 1

Like other souls in the first lunation phase, a Virgo 1 is open to life as a source of creative wonder. Where they depart from the pure thrill of encountering the sunny possibilities of existence, however, is in their relentless obsession with clouds. It is simply any Virgo's lot to spend a good deal of their life force in an analysis of how energy and fulfillment may be blocked and how obstructions may be made to pass.

Thus Virgos do have a tendency to be moralists although they usually stop short from being scolds, which they would tend to describe as a behavioral flaw. This is particularly true of Virgo 1's, who may project their findings onto society but who are essentially concerned with honest self-appraisal. Insofar as they are concerned with generalized human virtue and the keys to righteous living they are even more keenly concerned with bringing it down to the level at which it matters and works on a personal level.

So it is that the tales of Virgo 1 lives are rather like personal diaries in which practical data has been amassed, catalogued and ranked in utility. For a Virgo 1 the basic ability to read and to intellectually discriminate among everyday choices is often a large part of who and what they are. If life is a search for one's kernel of worth, a Virgo 1 enjoys nothing so much as eliminating the chaff.

For the Virgo 1's who succeed at life, it generally comes down to a respect for nature, healthy habits, skill development, hard work, curiosity, honesty, and self-deprecation. A strong ego, a Virgo 1 would argue, is one that is inclined to idle in the background. Simplicity and purity are much better grounding than a star on the Walk of Fame.

"One must accept the fact that we have only one companion in this world, a companion who accompanies us from the cradle to the grave–our own self. Get on good terms with that companion–learn to live with yourself."

– Agatha Christie, world-famous English author; her two famous murder-solving detectives, Miss Marple and Hercule Poirot, were essentially pacifists; her mother opposed her learning to read

"My first big break came when I was five years old. It's taken me more than seventy years to realize that. You see, at five I first learnt to read. It's that simple and it's that profound."

– Sean Connery, Oscar-winning Scottish actor/producer; famous as the first cinematic James Bond; competed in the 1953 Mr. Universe contest; worked as a milkman and a nude model

"I used to like to dig myself a hole just to see how long it took to get out of it."

– Buddy Hackett, popular American comedian/actor; guest with the most historical appearances on the 'Tonight Show starring Johnny Carson;' animal lover and sanctuary builder

"Actors are not a great breed of people, I don't think. I count myself as something of an exception. I grew up in the theater, and my values were about the work, and not being a star or anything like that. I'm not spoiled in that way, and if I fight for something, it's about the work, not about how big my trailer is."

– Amy Irving, award winning American movie/television/stage actress; acting since babyhood; nominated for a best (Oscar) and a worst (Razzie) award for the same performance in 'Yentl'

"What we want is to destroy our false, inorganic connections, especially those related to money, and re-establish the living organic connections, with the cosmos, the Sun and earth, with mankind and nation and family."

– D.H. Lawrence, highly influential 20th century British author; writing is concerned with emotional health and human vitality in an era of growing modernity and industrialization

"Embarrassed journalists ask me embarrassing questions, and they get embarrassing answers, and then hand out embarrassing stories to the embarrassing editors, who put them to the front pages of newspapers. When is this going to end?"

– Yao Ming, Chinese-born HOF pro basketball star/executive/philanthropist; lauded for his humble public deportment and his broad charitable undertakings; founded a California winery

"I never wanted all this hoopla. All I wanted was to be a good ball player and hit twenty-five or thirty homers, drive in a hundred runs, hit .280 and help my club win pennants. I just wanted to be one of the guys, an average player having a good season."

– Roger Maris, American major league baseball player/actor; best known for breaking Babe Ruth's 34 year-old record of 60 home runs in a season; ran a beer distributorship after baseball

"I don't do divas. I don't do entourages. I don't do the Hollywood crap."

- Tyler Perry, award-winning American actor/writer/producer/comedian/director; best known for his tough/ethical elderly black woman character, Madea; conquered an abuse history

"Get in the game. Do the best you can. Try to make a contribution. Learn from today. Apply it to tomorrow."

– Cal Ripken Jr., American HOF baseball player/philanthropist; famous for breaking Lou Gehrig's major league streak of consecutive games (2,632); established foundation for at-risk youth

"Listen, I was the first black manager in baseball and there was incredible pressure. I don't blame anyone else. I was too tough . . . I lack patience. I probably got on guys a little too hard, with the wrong tone of voice."

– Frank Robinson, American HOF baseball player; only player ever to win the MVP in both the American & National leagues; first MLB black manager; known as exacting/fiercely competitive

"Real wisdom is not the knowledge of everything, but the knowledge of which things in life are necessary, which are less necessary, and which are completely unnecessary to know."

– Leo Tolstoy, essential Russian novelist and moral philosopher; most famous works are 'War and Peace' and 'Anna Karenina;' meticulous about personal habits; a "self-improvement junkie"

"I wish my parents had spent more time worrying about my education than me being a star."

– Shania Twain, Grammy-winning Canadian singer-songwriter; best-selling female artist in country history; hits include 'That Don't Impress Me Much' and 'Man! I Feel Like a Woman!'

Libra 1

If one tracks the progression of zodiacal signs as an evolutionary tale, the Libra life represents the moment when consciousness fully crosses the divide from "me" to "we." It's not that qualifying the world in terms of personal perspective come to an end. It's just that Libras are emphatically willing to concede that living has a lot to do with an appreciation of individuals who are not us.

Thus one invariably finds Libra 1, a spiritually unsullied representative of Libra energy, measuring worth via the effects people have on other people. The greatest good in all areas of endeavor is constructive relatedness. Failure invariably stems from an overly self-referential disposition that fails to allow for contrasting points of view.

Unsurprisingly, these souls gravitate to matters of ethics and aesthetics, principled behavior and disciplined creativity that facilitate a positive collectivity among people who chose to meet one another's awareness on a constructive human plane. In simple terms, Libra 1's are primarily invested in matters relating to how people do or do not abide co-existence. One-on-one relationships are essential here, communal considerations indispensible, and love is life's brass ring.

For the rest, it is hard not to correlate Libra 1's with the concept of peace. These newborn souls are beings who orient themselves to the philosophies and phenomena that make us pass through life in harmony with our fellow souls. God bless them, even the strange ones, you know?

"Be a part of all that is decent and be an ambassador for the kind of world that you want to live in."

– Julie Andrews, Oscar/Grammy HOF/Emmy-winning English actress/singer/author; best known as the nanny in 'Mary Poppins' and 'The Sound of Music;' adopted two Vietnamese daughters

"Anyone who ever gave you confidence, you owe them a lot."

– Truman Capote, acclaimed American author; celebrated for 'Breakfast at Tiffany's' and 'In Cold Blood;' known for his elite high society social status; openly gay in a repressive era

"One of the most serious problems that our country has inherited is an unwillingness to talk to anyone who disagrees with us or who won't accept, before a discussion, all the premises that we demand."

– Jimmy Carter, 39th president of the United States; U.S. Naval Academy grad; Nobel Peace Prize laureate; admired for his post-presidential life as philanthropist/head of Carter Foundation

"That's why I'm so successful because peace is my main thing, it's not about money. It's about making sure everybody is having a good time and loving and living and enjoying life."

– Snoop Dogg, iconic American rapper/actor; most Grammy nominations (17) of any music artist in history without winning one; first A-List celebrity to brand a line of cannabis products

"To be true to one's own freedom is, in essence, to honor and respect the freedom of all others."

– Dwight Eisenhower, 34th president of the United States; WWII Supreme Allied Commander of NATO but hated war and never experienced combat; sponsored first modern U.S. civil rights bill

"You can't see the world through a mirror."

– Avril Lavigne, award-winning Canadian pop-punk singer/composer/musician/actress; created the Avril Lavigne Foundation to support children with serious illnesses and disabilities

"I'm dragging the audience to hell with me."

– Jerry Lee Lewis, R&R HOF American singer/songwriter/piano player; 'wild man' stage persona engendered nickname 'The Killer;' married seven times including once to his 13 year-old cousin

"Who cares who gets the last shot or scores the most points? Who cares who gets the credit? If we win, we're all winners."

– Paul Pierce, American pro basketball player/TV analyst; 10-time all-star; nicknamed 'The Truth;' charitable foundation active in a wide array of programs serving disadvantaged youth

"The life of a rock & roll band will last as long as you can look down into the audience and see yourself."

– Bruce Springsteen, Grammy HOF/R&R HOF American singer-songwriter/humanitarian; nicknamed "The Boss;" fronted the E-Street Band; admired for connection with his fans

"Don't judge me. You could be me in another life."

– Sting, Grammy/Emmy-winning British singer/songwriter/musician/actor/activist; founding member of The Police, best known for album 'Synchronicity;' co-creator of The Rainforest Fund

"You need the villain. If you don't have a villain, the good guy can stay home."

– Christoph Waltz, Oscar-winning German-Austrian actor/director; big break was the anti-Nazi film 'Inglorious Basterds' in a performance that won 27 awards; a men's health activist

"It's very easy to be judgmental until you know someone's truth."

– Kate Winslet, Oscar-winning British actress; known for relationship films such as 'Titanic' and 'Eternal Sunshine of the Spotless Mind;' co-founder of Golden Hat Foundation to fight autism

 Scorpio 1

To put it a little indelicately, a Scorpio 1 usually seems to be looking for a fight. Unless there is a dose of Libra in their chart, they tend not to have that peacekeeper mechanism that lets perceived aggression go quietly unchallenged. If you crowd their plate they relish spotting a fast ball up high and tight.

Despite the absence of the Moon's emotive force in their makeup, personal vindication is ratcheted up to a pretty passionate level in the life of a Scorpio 1. These are folks who identify life not as a chance to build bridges, but as a life-or-death contest engendered by the necessity to compete with other folks for the world's resources, power and public acclaim. Scorpio 1 is motivated, rather than daunted, by confrontation and obstructionism; not compromising their ambitions in the face of challengers nor suffering being anyone else's puppet or fool.

Due to their extraordinary willpower and wholly opportunistic natures Scorpio 1's are capable of great success in the worldly pursuits, and they will often fight their way to fame and fortune. These are not blithe spirits but, rather, test-seeking souls who engage life to beat back both their demons and your conflicting ambitions. The only finality of which they are really certain is death, better yours than theirs.

If you boil it down to a single concept, the Scorpio 1 is really the embodiment of an unfiltered passion for victory. It doesn't really matter if they compete in the world's great arenas or if they are hell bent on amassing a collection of stamps more valuable than the next guy's. They kind of thrive on people telling them they can't prevail.

"There are moments in business and in life when you have to say, 'Failure is not an option'."

– Donny Deutsch, noted American advertising executive/TV personality; stridently political he publically called Donald Trump a "coward" and challenged him to a "schoolyard fight"

"Suffering in life can uncover untold depths of character and unknown strength for service. People who go through life unscathed by sorrow and untouched by pain tend to be shallow in their perspectives on life. Suffering, on the other hand, tends to plow up the surface of our lives to uncover the depths that provide greater strength of purpose and accomplishment. Only deeply plowed earth can yield bountiful harvests."

– Billy Graham, American Christian evangelist; preached to millions in stadium "crusades;" friend of many U.S. presidents; holds record for mentions on Gallup "most admired" list (61)

"Someone asked me once what my philosophy of life was and I said some crazy thing. I should have said, 'how the hell do I know?'"

– Rock Hudson, iconic American actor; 'leading man' known for roles in 'Giant,' 'Pillow Talk,' and 'McMillan & Wife,' bisexual; first major Hollywood actor known to have died from HIV-Aids

I'm a firm believer in taking risks in life, because you'll never get anywhere unless you do, and the more risk involved the greater the outcome–or the worse, but you never know so you've got to go for it."

– Famke Janssen, award-winning Dutch actress/model; work includes 'X-Men,' 'How to Get Away with Murder,' and 'Blacklist;' often a character with strange powers and/or a dark streak

"Les Misérables is one of my favorite stories."

– Larry King, quintessential American talk show host; conducted over 40,000 "street" interviews (simple direct questions); his eight wives included two Playboy bunnies and his h.s. sweetheart

"If you can believe in something great, then you can achieve something great."

– Katy Perry, American pop superstar; hits include 'I Kissed a Girl,' 'Firework,' and 'Roar;' brought up in a strict Christian household and as a child was not allowed to listen to any secular music

"I've been absolutely terrified every moment of my life–and I've never let it keep me from doing a single thing I wanted to do."

– Georgia O'Keeffe, award-winning American artist; "the mother of American modernism;" famed for flowers/landscapes; painted in any weather and continued working after going blind

"Go and do the things you can't. That is how you get to do them."

– Pablo Picasso, massively influential Spanish-expatriate artist; co-creator of Cubism; best known for 'Guernica;' carried a pistol loaded with blanks that he would fire at "boring people"

"If it can be destroyed by the truth, it deserves to be destroyed by the truth."

– Carl Sagan, best known American scientist of his generation; a popular media/literary figure; railed against 'nuclear winter' and 'global warming;' considered a narcissist by detractors

"My father left me with a saying that I've carried my entire life and tried to pass on to our kids: 'Tough times don't last, tough people do.'"

– Curt Schilling, all-star American baseball pitcher/analyst/entrepreneur; famed for the "bloody sock" game; staunch right-wing political activist; fired by ESPN for transphobic social media post

"There are only two places in this league, First Place and No Place."

– Tom Seaver, American HOF baseball pitcher; known to fans as 'Tom Terrific' and 'The Franchise;' credits being a Marine with teaching him the value of discipline

"I don't sing for anybody. I wouldn't sing for the Queen dear."

– Joan Sutherland, legendary Australian operatic soprano; known as 'La Stupenda' for her vocal power and range; reigned for 30+ years in top form due to meticulous personal care

Sagittarius 1

If the first lunation phase is a spiritual crib of sorts, the Sagittarius 1 is particularly ill-suited for the metaphor. Sagittarians are simply not inclined to tolerate enclosures, real or symbolic. In the case of the raw Sagittarian energy of the first lunation phase, well, even a steel cage, factual or figurative, has probably met its match.

The zodiac's true Universalists, Sagittarians are consecrated to an unbound journey of discovery. It may seem a bit paradoxical, but they hunt an understanding that transcends all denominational borders while simultaneously being the wisdom at the core of all things. Easy classifications are not for them, as their paths are defined by the search for large truths that might abet all of mankind.

In the actual living, a Sagittarius 1 life is generally experienced as a high octane adventure with an enormous number of interesting roadside attractions. In assimilating these into some sort of universal theory, the difference between open-mindedness and broad-mindedness comes to the fore. The Sagittarius 1 tends to eschew the former, which implies an unfiltered acceptance of everything, preferring a lens of righteousness in an idealized search for foundational wisdom...even if their path sometimes veers through the craziest and most painful of places.

Fortunately, most Sagittarius 1's are blessed with optimism and a great sense of humor. They know that some of their byways must inevitably lead to dead ends; they accept life's absurdity when they encounter it; and they are more than willing to give false starts and pratfalls their comic due. In the end it's all good, although a human proclivity towards deceit and hypocrisy can feel sort of feel like the penitentiary in a world full of better possibilities.

The Sagittarius 1 knows that some things are hard to laugh at no matter how hard one tries.

"I just want to thank everybody I have ever met in my entire life." (Oscar acceptance speech)

– Kim Basinger, Oscar/Golden Globe/SAG winning American actress/model; first "Bond Girl" to go on to win an Oscar; said the constraints of a modeling life felt to her like a "choking"

"The only way to define your limits is by going beyond them."

– Arthur C. Clarke, eminent British SF writer/futurist/inventor; famous works includes 'Childhood's End' and '2001: A Space Odyssey;' the "father" of geostationary satellites

"I salute the light within your eyes where the whole universe dwells... for when you are at that center within you and I am at that place within me, we shall be one."

– Crazy Horse, Sioux Chief and folk hero; fierce defender of Native American territory and tradition; said to have a near-mystical power of avoiding injury in battle

"There are very few things that surprise me."

– Judi Dench, Oscar-winning British actress; equally well-known for her work in Shakespearean drama and James Bond films; celebrated her 81st birthday with a "carpe diem" tattoo

"There is no Democratic or Republican way of cleaning the streets."

– Fiorello H. La Guardia, American congressman and popular three-term mayor of New York City; operated independently of both major parties; crusaded against "bossism" in politics

"The end of all learning is to know God, and out of that knowledge to love and imitate Him."

– John Milton, 17th Century English epic poet best known for the classic 'Paradise Lost;' his 'Areopagitica' is one of the great tracts in defense of free speech and freedom of the press

"I like to write my lyrics on clay tablets."

– Randy Newman, Oscar/Grammy/Emmy-winning American singer-songwriter, called "king of the soundtracks" for films such as 'Ragtime' and Toy Story;' nominated for 22 Academy Awards

"I see people as the nucleus of a great idea that hasn't come to be yet."

– Richard Pryor, Grammy HOF/Emmy-winning American actor/comedian; all-time great stand-up comic; iconic commentator on the American racial divide; Mark Twain prize winner

"As soon as a woman is old enough to have an opinion and have a voice and be unafraid, she's very much encouraged by all sorts of people to crawl under a rock and die. And it's so weird. My crime is not dying."

– Sarah Silverman, edgy "politically incorrect" American comedienne/writer/actress; won a writing Emmy for her HBO special 'Sarah Silverman: We Are Miracles;' a lifelong vegetarian

"I am inspired by thinkers. I am inspired by rebellion. I am inspired by children. I have been inspired by love. I have been inspired by heartbreak. I try to take everything that comes at me in life. There have been times in my life that I didn't handle things... right. But even though you stumble, you still kind of get through it."

– Nikki Sixx, American heavy metal bassist/songwriter/photographer; best known as co-founder of the band Mötley Crüe; infamous for wild behavior related to substance addiction

"You just have to keep trying to do good work, and hope that it leads to more good work. I want to look back on my career and be proud of the work, and proud that I tried everything. Yes, I want to look back and know that I was terrible at a variety of things."

– Jon Stewart, Grammy/Emmy-winning American comedian/satirist/producer/activist; best known as host of 'The Daily Show;' his production company also created 'The Colbert Report'

"I've just been really lucky to not be too much of a stereotype."

– Marisa Tomei, Oscar winning American actress; known for her roles in 'My Cousin Vinny,' 'The Wrestler,' and 'Spiderman;' practices yoga, Tai Chi, and belly dancing; has an Eye of Ra tattoo

Capricorn 1

Rarely has a Capricorn 1 ever been charged with possessing too much humility. Quite the contrary, these are folks who more often than not are marked by boundless and proud worldly ambition and a capacity for tooting their own horn. Through all lunation phases the Capricorn bias is towards ascent, and these emotionally uncompromised first lunation phase Capricorn souls find particularly little helpful in the qualities of minimalism, modesty, and standing back in the crowd.

While of course there are exceptions, most Capricorn 1's quite sincerely long to be the apotheosis of something culturally enviable. They crave honor and acknowledgment and wealth and influence and power; they need to set the tone and be in charge. Lest this sound too much a negative indictment be assured that a Capricorn 1 is willing to outwork everyone to fulfill their ambitions. Their aspirational nature pushes them to the sort of effort, and even the risk of notoriety, that would make lesser mortals cringe.

When you get right down to it, the truth is that Capricorn 1's is tend to view themselves, unabashedly and often publically, as God's Chosen Ones. Yes, they can thus come off as pushy and horribly egocentric. Yet they will also stridently challenge anyone, often successfully, to prove that they are wrong.

Take your time. The Capricorn 1 is highly unlike to run off and hide.

"I am the greatest. I said that even before I knew I was."

– Muhammad Ali, legendary American heavyweight boxing champion/social activist; widely considered one of the most charismatic and influential sports figures of the 20th Century

"What is one to think of those fools who tell one that the artist is always subordinate to nature? Art is a harmony parallel with nature."

– Paul Cezanne, preeminent French post-Impressionist artist; credited for the foundations of much of modern abstract art; described by Picasso as "the father of us all"

"I acted like Cary Grant for so long that I became Cary Grant."

– Cary Grant, acclaimed English film actor; started from humble beginnings and created the suave Hollywood persona that he eventually came to inhabit in his public and private lives

"Turn your nightmares into your dreams. Some dreams don't turn out the way you want them to...then wake up and turn them around in your favor."

– Salman Khan, extraordinarily successful Indian actor/producer/singer/philanthropist; topped the 'Forbes India' chart in terms of fame and revenues; 'People India's' "Sexiest Man Alive"

"Even though all these obstacles keep coming at you, you just have to keep going through them...because it's worth it to do something in your life, as opposed to fantasizing about doing something."

– Diane Keaton, Oscar-winning American actress/director; famous for early work in 'The Godfather' and Woody Allen films; frequently cast as a rom-com matriarch in latter film career

"When you're that successful, things have a momentum, and at a certain point you can't really tell whether you have created the momentum or it's creating you."

– Annie Lennox, iconic British singer/humanitarian; co-founder of The Eurythmics; most successful female artist in British music history

"Only if you have been in the deepest valley, can you ever know how magnificent it is to be on the highest mountain."

– Richard Nixon, 37th president of the United States; his career first defined the possibilities and pitfalls of politics in the media age; only president to ever resign in the face of scandal

"The only limit to the height of your achievements is the reach of your dreams and your willingness to work hard for them."

– Michelle Obama, much admired American lawyer/administrator/writer; iconic First Lady of the United States; culture creator/style setter; has appeared three times on the cover of 'Vogue'

"Whatever I will become will be what God has chosen for me."

– Elvis Presley, iconic 20th Century singer/musician/actor; the "King of Rock and Roll;" sold over a billion records; also starred in 31 movies mostly playing variations of his own public persona

"We represent our constituents. And so they don't get to dictate policy."

– Jeff Sessions, American politician and U.S. Attorney General; intractable supporter of extreme right wing causes and political policies

"God had to create disco music so I could be born and be successful."

– Donna Summer, Grammy-winning American singer-songwriter; the "Queen of Disco;" also enjoyed financial and critical success as a painter

"Put God first in everything you do ... Everything that I have is by the grace of God, understand that. It's a gift ... I didn't always stick with Him, but He stuck with me."

– Denzel Washington, Oscar-winning actor/director/producer; famous for roles displaying extraordinary strength of character; he is a devout and active Christian

Aquarius I

It is tempting to just describe Aquarius 1's as crazy. In truth, they sort of are. With their unpredictable Uranian personalities flashing full force in a symbolically Moonless sky, even the most sane and successful among them have a capacity for willful eccentricity that is simply off the charts.

Some may describe Aquarius 1's as mind gamers. They can usually read motives and solve puzzles better than the average homicide detective. It's rarely peaceful, and often somewhat threatening, to have an Aquarius 1 running around inside your head.

On the other hand, it is equally valid to stipulate the primacy of the Aquarius 1 capacity for outside-the-box brilliance in service to humankind. Nobody catches an oncoming cultural vibe, projecting its future implications and potential cultural benefits, like an Aquarius 1. These folks often seem to be so strange because they so purposefully and seamlessly divide their time between today and tomorrow, with a seeming telepathic capacity for knowing future predicaments and solutions in advance of their real world occurrence.

Perhaps the fairest way of piercing their essence is to just characterize them as 'originals.' Aquarius 1's are idiosyncratic groundbreakers sprinkled with the fairy dust of human potential. Fortunately, most of them come to the conclusion that humanity's fate is ultimately dependent on a bias towards brotherhood and at least a conditionally optimistic sense of tomorrow.

To be sure, they do become quite discouraged sometimes. Their personal existence has a roller coaster quality and occasionally they jump the tracks or wander off, for years sometimes, to deal with existential bedlam. But one thing you can count on with an Aquarius 1 is that in their wholly unique and unprejudiced way they are working on moving every last one of us along.

"Life is like therapy–real expensive and no guarantees."

– Garth Brooks, American Country Music HOF singer/songwriter; best-selling American recording artist in history; took a decade-long break from touring/ recording mid-career

"I have always felt comfortable tapping into my inner idiot."

– Isla Fisher, award-winning Australian actress; known primarily for quirky character roles in movies such as 'Wedding Crashers' and 'Definitely, Maybe;' married to Sacha Barron Cohen

"Most people think they know the answer. I am willing to admit I don't even know the question."

– Arsenio Hall, award-winning American actor/comedian/writer/producer; first black host of a syndicated late night talk show; a winner of Donald Trump's 'Celebrity Apprentice'

"Chickens are a symbol of chaos. Wherever you stick a chicken, unless it's a chicken farm, it's just chaos."

– Ed Helms, award-winning American actor/comedian/singer; known for his roles in 'The Hangover,' 'The Daily Show' and 'The Office;' into the "cool gear" of disaster preparedness

"You get your chips your way. I'll get my chips mine."

– Phil Ivey, Hall of Fame American pro poker player/spokesperson/humanitarian; nicknamed "The Phenom" and "The Tiger Woods of Poker;" known as a great reader of opponent tells

"If there is a God, his plan is very similar to someone not having a plan."

– Eddie Izzard, Emmy-winning British comedian/actor/marathon runner/transgender activist; self-described as "a lesbian trapped in a man's body;" self-identified as a transvestite at age 4

"The function of freedom is to free someone else."

– Toni Morrison, Nobel-laureate American novelist/professor; best known for the 'Beloved' trilogy about the life of an escaped slave; first African American woman to win a Nobel Prize

"The best thing you can give yourselves...is the gift of possibility. And the best thing you can give each other is the pledge to go on protecting that gift in each other as long as you live."

– Paul Newman, legendary American actor; often played an outsider challenged to deal with abnormal societies; founder of company that donates all profits to charity; a racecar driver

"There's not an American in this country free until every one of us is free."

– Jackie Robinson, American HOF baseball player; famously broke the major league "color barrier;" also was first black to be a VP of a major U.S. company with Chock Full O' Nuts

"I don't even know my own phone number."

– Axl Rose, iconic American rock musician; charismatic founder/lead singer of R&R HOF band Guns N' Roses; notorious for clinically manic-depressive behavior; became a mid-career recluse

"There are two contrary impulses which govern this man's brain-the one sane, and the other eccentric. They alternate at regular intervals."

– Franz Schubert, celebrated Austrian composer; bridged the Classical and Romantic eras; famed for melodies; wrote 600 pieces before death at age 31; called "a genius" by Beethoven

"I'm not lost; I'm just in between places I recognize."

– Cybill Shepherd, American beauty queen and actress; her autobiography is titled: "Cybill Disobedience: How I Survived Beauty Pageants, Elvis, Sex, Bruce Willis, Lies, Marriage, Motherhood, Hollywood, and the Irrepressible Urge to Say What I Think"

"Follow the path of the unsafe, independent thinker. Expose your ideas to the danger of controversy. Speak your mind and fear less the label of "crackpot" than the stigma of conformity."

– Thomas J. Watson, American businessman; chairman and CEO of IBM; known as "the greatest salesman in the world;" famous for the slogan "THINK" he trademarked 14 years before "IBM"

Pisces 1

A Pisces 1 life is about the relationship a newborn soul is capable of establishing with a greater Spirit. This is a conceptually exotic and deeply personal state of affairs, and to describe it from the outside requires forbearance and a healthy reliance on guessing. To those not living this incarnation (almost all of us), the phrase "you could not possibly understand" is entirely appropriate.

Despite the limitations of language for describing this incarnation, it probably works to describe the Pisces 1 life as a quest. There is a tendency here to believe that in the chaos that is the human condition there just might be, in conference with the creative forces of the universe, the reward of a divinely assigned animus. Finding this one... and yes, holy... purpose is the jackpot of this incarnation.

Alas, finding the Answer can entail an arduous growth process. There is often deep pain, physical and emotional, in the Pisces 1 story. Encountering Sprit can come at a price and is not the sort the thing one can accomplish half-heartedly.

Unsurprisingly, considering their remote focus, a Pisces 1 can often seem to outsiders as vague and distracted, skittish and strange, even visionary and mad. The world of the ordinary is somehow alien to them. They have more trouble than most in relating to the behaviors and beliefs that others would call normal.

At their best, though, evolutionary innocence combined with mammoth spiritual aspiration allows the Pisces 1 to rise to a special level of fulfillment. There is great potential for serenity in knowing who and what one really is. Wherever they go Pisces 1's cast a compelling spell.

"From then on, I realized this is what I want to do, what I'm supposed to do: Giving energy and receiving it back through applause. I love it. That's my world. I love it. I enjoy it. I live for it."

– Erykah Badu, Grammy-winning American singer/songwriter/actress; called "the queen of neo-soul;" controversial political activist but claims her core position is seeing "good in everyone"

"I think if people are passionate about something, it could be real estate or biochemistry, and that spark gets turned on in them, everyone's beautiful in that zone."

– Cindy Crawford, arguably America's most famous fashion model/spokesperson/entrepreneur; has appeared on 600+ magazine covers; majored in chemical engineering at Northwestern

"I feel I am blessed that I have found my stride and relaxed into my life's purpose."

– Taylor Dane, award-winning American singer-songwriter/actress; successful in every major contemporary music genre; majority of her hits have "love" or "heart" in the title

"All I want to do, ever, is play chess."

– Bobby Fischer, U.S.-born chess legend; first American player to win the World Chess Championship; a troubled and eccentric genius, secluded for two decades; citizen of Iceland

"The only way to do great work is to love what you do."

– Steve Jobs, legendary American technology entrepreneur; a pioneer of the personal computer age; co-founder/CEO/chairman of Apple, chairman of Pixar; almost became a Buddhist monk

"I'll never take for granted the opportunity to put on a Dodger uniform."

– Clayton Kershaw, all-star MLB baseball player; winner of the Cy Young award; famous for his work ethic and his curve ball; lauded for his "Christ-centered" life and humanitarian work

"We are what we are."

– Kesha, popular American singer/songwriter/rapper/actor; musically-oriented from infancy; harassment/assault trial versus the producer who built her career led to song 'Praying'

"When I was onstage doing the work, adrenaline killed the pain because I never hurt in front of an audience."

– Jerry Lewis, iconic American comedian/singer/actor/producer/director/humanitarian; world-famous "funny man" known for broad slapstick humor; raised $2.8 billion for MDA

"The only love affair I have ever had was with music."

– Maurice Ravel, popular French composer/conductor/pianist; began formal education at the Paris Conservatoire at age 14; most famous for 'Bolero' and 'Daphnis et Chloe'

"I became the butterfly. I got out of the cocoon, and I flew."

– Lynn Redgrave, award-winning British actress; famous for her role as a sympathetic "fatty" in the film 'Georgy Girl;' noted for one of the entertainment industry's messiest-ever divorces

"Work lovingly done is the secret of all order and all happiness."

– Pierre-Auguste Renoir, world-renowned French Impressionist painter; one of the most highly regarded artists of his time; painted with severe arthritis for last three decades of his life

"I rarely know exactly what I want to do, but always know exactly how I want it to make me feel. Feeling always leads the sound!"

– Rihanna, Grammy-winning Barbados-born international pop star/actress; iconized for her vixen image; known for trauma in her personal life including domestic abuse

"The real joy in life comes from finding your true purpose and aligning it with what you do every single day."

– Tony Robbins, American author/entrepreneur/philanthropist/life coach; known for his self-help books/seminars/infomercials; named the "high priest of human potential" by the NY Times

2nd Lunation Phase/Crescent Moon

Moon is 46 to 90 degrees ahead of the Sun

Keyword: Attachment

The crescent Moon soul is faced with a conundrum. Think figuratively of an infant who has become just old enough to inhabit an unattended crib with the side down. Reasonable explanations can be offered both for staying and for going.

Generally the LP2 lifetime is marked by upbringing in a collectivized tradition, often organized around the prospects of familiarity, safety and, for better worse, adherence to a proscribed set of behaviors. The cultural status quo thus has a strong grip on the LP2 native, but it is not enough to satisfy the soul's search for liberating personal experience. The mantra becomes "do I stay or do I grow?"

It's not meant to sound ignoble, but this is the fly and flypaper life. Here one must summon the strength to be elsewhere, to be free of the past, to be different than what has been assigned, to not settle down in the muck of limited perception. These are individuals whose spirits can be easily trapped by what they cannot grow beyond.

Even more than the development of the will, here one wrestles with the prospect of developing faith in oneself. Bending without breaking, or perhaps stretching without tearing, is the supreme accomplishment of the LP2 life. Here is the lifetime in which the young soul gets out of bed to retrieve, without parental permission or assistance, its own glass of water.

Aries 2

When one considers the essential Aries urge to unbridled acts of will, it is easy to see the dilemma of the Ram in the second lunation phase. Think of a rocket firing while bolted to its gantry or a sprint through a jungle heavily pocked with quicksand. The uneven firing of the Aries 2 engine is exhausting and the psychological toll of a restricted ride quite palpable.

Often the central issue of an Aries 2 life is whether one must tear out one's roots to independently thrive or to find fulfillment in willful attachment. It is a dilemma that tends to breed great conflict and a wavering battle between punching up and settling down, leading to no shortage of commitment and abandonment issues in their experience and character. Aries 2 histories are laden with poignant tales of disappointment and reclamation, separation and return, escape and homecoming.

Not surprisingly, many truly first-rate actors are found in the Aries 2 incarnation. Their artistic explorations are invested in an examination of the primacy of identity, often in roles featuring a potent mix of aggression and attraction. The quintessential character question in much of their work is whether granting legitimacy to others is a route to symbiotic nurturing or a slide into desperately unhappy entanglement.

Oh well. It's likely a conundrum for the Aries 2, but it does make great popcorn fodder for the rest of us.

"If one does not attach himself to people and desires, never shall his heart be broken. But then, does he ever truly live?"

– Jackie Chan, world-famous Chinese actor/director/producer/philanthropist; inventor of the "kung-fu comedy;" Communist advocate; abandoned by parents, disinherited his own children

"I always say I am a realist, and my mom says, 'No, you just have anxiety'."

– Jessica Chastain, award-winning American actress; known for strong-willed feminist roles; anxiety-filled childhood included father abandonment/sister suicide; mental health advocate

"Basically I believe the world is a jungle, and if it's not a bit of a jungle in the home a child cannot possibly be fit to enter the outside world."

– Bette Davis, legendary Oscar-winning American actress; known for unsympathetic/cutting characters; father disliked children and divorced doting mother; married four times

"It was the only ambition I ever had–not to be a dancer or Hollywood movie star, but to be a housewife in a good marriage."

– Doris Day, iconic American singer/actress/humanitarian; "the queen of romantic comedy;" parents separated early; lost only child to cancer; bankrupted by husband; divorced four times

"I think all of us have our inner 13 year-old a lot closer to the surface than we're willing to admit, even to ourselves."

– Jennifer Garner, award-winning American actress/humanitarian/spokesperson; a beauty known for "kick-ass" roles; conservative upbringing, but became a liberal devoted to rural poor

"The greatest escape I ever made was when I left Appleton, Wisconsin."

– Harry Houdini, Hungarian-born magician/entertainer/auteur; history's most famous escape artist; father was a Jewish rabbi; he was a vigorous combatant of psychic spiritualism

"A lot of times in cinema today the women are overly sentimental, so I constantly try to do the opposite. I like strident women."

– Keira Knightley, Oscar-nominated British actress/spokesperson/humanitarian; known equally for romances and action roles; born into a family of dramatists, had an agent by age six

"We're actors at the end of the day. I don't take it home with me. My experience outside of work, I love... when I hear wrap, it's the most exciting part of my day. I'm the first to have my make-up off, in the car, out. I've gotta go home. I want to get back to my life. I love it back there."

– Heath Ledger, Oscar-winning Australian actor; famous for pushing the cultural envelope in movies such as "Brokeback Mountain" and "The Dark Knight;" died from drug overdose

"My goals have changed throughout my life. At one time it was winning awards, selling out concert dates, selling more albums than anyone else. Now, my goals are to see my grandchildren grown, live a long and healthy life with my family and friends and travel the world."

– Reba McEntire, Oklahoma-born country singing legend known as "the Queen of Country;" also a successful actress/entrepreneur; capitalized on genuine "rowdy rodeo-girl" upbringing

"I was with a friend of mine recently who was dying and while he was lying there with his family around his bed, I just knew that was it, that was the best you can hope for in life–to have your family and the people who love you around you at the end."

– Ewan McGregor, popular British actor; known for a broad range of roles from a heroin addict in 'Trainspotting' to Jedi master Obi-Wan Kenobi in 'Star Wars;' a UNICEF ambassador

"(Hollywood) gave me glory, but it gave me loneliness also...and a lot of missing my own land, my own people and my own country."

– Omar Sharif, award-winning Egyptian-born actor; featured in epics 'Lawrence of Arabia' and 'Dr. Zhivago;' multi-ethnic and poly-lingual; world-renowned contract bridge player

"I do think that despite my best efforts to resist it, I am now a grown-up. It's due to lots of very difficult decisions that you make over a long period of time–about motherhood, wifehood, and work, and all the things that one has to make decisions about."

– Emma Thompson, Oscar-winning British actress; known for witty and enigmatic roles in period dramas and literary adaptations; born into a family of actors; an environmental activist

 Taurus 2

Taurus is far from uncomfortable in the second lunation phase. The Taurus 2 identity completely resonates with the notion that a good life expresses a firm foundation and a willingness to build rather than detach. Having embraced one's mind/spirit/body platform, a good life is a matter of extending preparation and perseverance into a lifetime of conscientious practice.

Put plainly, a Taurus 2 is marked as uniquely capable of taking both responsibility and the long view. The foundations and designs of history, both personal and universal, matter. The best demeanor one can summon to one's existence is, from a Taurus 2 perspective, an awareness of origin, rolled up sleeves and a sense of gravitas.

Certainly, Taurus 2's are only towards the beginning of their karmic evolution and the wagon they always seem to be pulling can sometimes appear to be a bit wobbly and overloaded. Fortunately, as they tend to be well aware of their inner strength and earnest sense of purpose, they are not incapable of a begrudging acceptance when they grind to a temporary halt. Their spiritual reserves make them far more adept at powering up than surrendering and they are far more suited to the role of master than the mastered.

Ultimately, the overarching need of the Taurus 2 is to be taken seriously by others...and considering the effort they make to build themselves into something worthy, why wouldn't we take them seriously?

"I was taught to strive not because there were any guarantees of success but because the act of striving is in itself the only way to keep faith with life."

– Madeleine Albright, Czech-American politician/diplomat/educator; family fled from Nazis; became U.S. Ambassador to the United Nations; first female U.S. Secretary of State

"Be brave and clear. Follow your heart and don't be overly influenced by outside factors. Be true to yourself."

– Shirley Temple Black, celebrated child actress; brought cheer to many during the Great Depression; later ran for Congress and served as U.S. Ambassador to the United Nations

"When you really have the preparation time and things start taking the shape that they need, you have a beautiful feeling that comes from the hard work."

– Penelope Cruz, Oscar-winning Spanish actress/model; studied classical ballet for a decade at Spain's National Conservatory; has diverse international philanthropic interests

"I literally wake up and try to tackle every day the best I can and do my best to try to make life as productive and positive as I can."

– John Cena, professional American wrestler/actor/hip-hop artist; 16-time world champion; known as 'The Prototype;' renowned for his work with the Make-A-Wish foundation

"There's an old saying about those who forget history. I don't remember it, but it's good."

– Stephen Colbert, charismatic American television host/author; known for political commentary and satire, winner of Peabody/Emmy/Grammy awards; a generous philanthropist

"I need to behave in a way that will cause people to take me seriously."

– Megan Fox, American actress/model; best known for 'Transformers' and 'Mutant Ninja Turtle' film series; raised in strict Pentecostal household; crusader against sex-symbol objectification

"My only goal is to look back at the end of each year and see that I have improved."

– Jim Furyk, esteemed American pro golfer; winner of the FedEx Cup and Player of the Year; Ryder Cup captain; only coach was his father; runs a charitable foundation for needy families

"You have no right to go before a public without an adequate technique, just because you feel. Anything feels–a leaf feels, a storm feels–what right have you to do that? You have to have speech, and it's a cultivated speech."

– Martha Graham, American dancer/choreographer; known as the "mother of modern dance;" influenced by doctor father who cured with movement techniques; famed for intense style

"Whatever there is of greatness in the United States, or indeed in any other country, is due to labor. The laborer is the author of all greatness and wealth. Without labor there would be no government, no leading class, and nothing to preserve."

– Ulysses S. Grant, 18th U.S. president; commanding general of the Union Army during the Civil War; dismantled the KKK during Reconstruction; memoirs are considered a literary masterpiece

"As adults we try to relax from the never-ending quest for reason and order by drinking a little whiskey or smoking whatever works for us, but the wisdom isn't in the whiskey or the smoke. The wisdom is in the moments when the madness slips away and we remember the basics."

– Willie Nelson, Grammy HOF American "outlaw" singer/songwriter/actor/activist; his 'Stardust' album of American standards charted for a decade; devoted to farm and environmental causes

"With three boys in the house, my mother was always on us when growing up about keeping our faces clean, washing behind our ears, and brushing our teeth. So I still take my morning routine seriously."

– Cam Newton, American football star; only person to ever receive the Heisman Trophy, win a collegiate championship and be drafted first by pros in the same year; father a Baptist minister

"Contemporary architects tend to impose modernity on something. There is a certain concern for history but it's not very deep. I understand that time has changed, we have evolved. But I don't want to forget the beginning. A lasting architecture has to have roots."

– I.M. Pei, world-renowned Chinese-American architect; famous projects include JFK airport, the Louvre Pyramid, and the Rock and Roll Hall of Fame; has won every major architectural honor

 Gemini 2

The inherent stickiness of the second lunation phase is often an obstacle in a Gemini incarnation. A Gemini is born to perceive and communicate, actions most easily taken on a kind of free flowing mental highway. While most natives of this sign easily motor past an encyclopedic range of impressions, insights and assorted roadside attractions, it is the vexing lot a Gemini 2 to rather frequently encounter civilization's tar pits, demolition zones and out-of-date maps.

Many a Gemini 2 is somehow mired in the past, a place well-suited for germinating perplexity and directional confusion if one tries to find a cogent connection between past and present. Of course, Gemini is an intellectually versatile sign and there are those who can turn this retro fixation/examination into insight, art and a signature form of dry observational wit. The other side of the coin is expressed by Gemini 2's living in a perpetual state of anxiety and annoyance because what are people thinking and what the heck does anything really mean?

It is usually the lot of a Gemini 2 to wrangle with the issue of what it feels like to be a free thinker in the clutches of unpremeditated circumstances. After all, how does one think freely when life or culture or history, acting independently of personal direction, alternately lifts you up and then forces you to a knee? And what is the impact on anything as inflexible as 'truth' when cultural and personal circumstances are so drastically and quixotically mutating?

As befits the Gemini reign over duality, the answers to such things can be both cynical and sublime...in the life of a Gemini 2, often both at the same time.

"It took me so many years to move out. I'm definitely a bit of a Peter Pan, reluctant to grow up. It all seemed really nice at home-why change it? Part of me would prefer not to have any responsibility whatsoever."

– Helena Bonham Carter, award-winning English actress; famous for her genre versatility; often plays eccentric characters; does not like to watch her own performances

"The guys who won World War II and that whole generation have disappeared, and now we have a bunch of teenage twits."

– Clint Eastwood, Oscar-winning American actor/director/producer/musician/politician; iconic conservative tough-guy; served as mayor of Carmel-by-the-Sea; meditates twice a day

"It's really a wonder that I haven't dropped all my ideals, because they seem so absurd and impossible to carry out. Yet I keep them, because in spite of everything I still believe that people are really good at heart."

– Anne Frank, famous German-Dutch victim of the Nazi holocaust; her diary translated into 60 languages is one of the most famous journals of all time; died in a concentration camp at age 15

"I have come to an unalterable decision–to go and live forever in Polynesia. Then I can end my days in peace and freedom, without thoughts of tomorrow and this eternal struggle against idiots."

– Paul Gauguin, famed post-Impressionist French painter; self-taught; drawn to indigenous cultures and spiritual themes; eschewed formal society; referred to himself as a "savage"

"Some might consider me an unlikely advocate for gun rights because I sustained terrible injuries in a violent shooting. But I'm a patriot, and I believe the right to bear arms is a definitive part of our American heritage."

– Gabrielle Giffords, Arizona-born U.S. congresswoman; debilitated survivor of a politically motivated assassination attempt; a major supporter of mental health causes

"You hope that your teenage self would like and forgive your 50-year-old self."

– Hugh Laurie, award-winning English actor/director/musician; best known for his role as the brilliant but arrogant Dr. Gregory House; a virtuoso on five different musical instruments

"It's not unusual for writers to look backward, because that's your pool of resources."

– Paul McCartney, world-famous British singer-songwriter; co-founder of The Beatles; plays over 40 musical instruments; a highly regarded painter; twice failed an audition as a choir boy

"I would never wish my upbringing on anyone... but I wouldn't take it back for the world."

– Mary-Kate Olsen, American actress/entrepreneur; famous with Gemini twin sister Ashley as child stars on TV's 'Full House;' with Ashley has built a vast fashion/media empire (Dualstar)

"Cannibalism is a radical but realistic solution to the problem of overpopulation."

– Prince Philip (Mountbatten), Greek-born English noble; a decorated soldier; husband of Queen Elizabeth for over 70 years; mother institutionalized for schizophrenia; famously frank

"Ideas, like young wine, should be put in storage and taken up again only after they have been allowed to ferment and to ripen."

– Richard Strauss, renowned German composer/musical director; famous for his tone poems and operas; complicated relationship with Nazi Germany; wrote 140 pieces by the age of 18

"If I cared deeply about what people thought of me, I probably would have never made it out of Compton, California."

– Venus Williams, American tennis star/entrepreneur/author; won multi Grand Slam titles and an Olympic gold medal; learned to play on public courts; pro at age 14; gender equality activist

"People are part of my music. A lot of my songs are the result of emotional experiences, sadness, pain, joy, and exultation in nature and sunshine and so on...like 'California Girls' which was a hymn to youth."

– Brian Wilson, Grammy-winning California-born musician/composer/producer; co-founder and creative force of The Beach Boys; abused as a child; treated for serious stress-related disorders

Cancer 2

A Cancer in any lunation phase experiences life most satisfactorily as a member of a clan. How well suited they are then to life in the second lunation phase, one in which attachment is the base assumption. Even though the phase also predicates a need to escape one's conditioning, it is the Cancer 2 who is most likely to shrug off any urgency in this regard.

What Cancer 2's tend to have most in common is a deep feeling dive into the essence of empathy. A Cancer 2 draws life force from a preternaturally strong resonance with familiarized others as they participate in the collective cultural environment. Recognizing that growth is a factor in any living spirit, they just prefer that the out flowing waves move everyone in their particular boat towards a commonly defined shore.

To be sure, this sort of cultural collectivizing is not always a success in broad terms. What makes a tribal bond strong is the ethos that separates it from its rivals. Although the resultant potential for hostility can sometimes be dissolved by the wisdom of peace-oriented sages, it's also true that the world has more than its share of small-minded jerks who are hell-bent on demonstrating that a culturally defined empathy does not always lead to the most sanguine of universal outcomes.

What might be kept in mind is that this Cancer phase, emblemized by a very slight sliver of Moon, is still rudimentary and searching. All Cancers crave an emotional in-kind investment with others, but a Cancer 2 most often has yet to master the techniques of behavioral discrimination, personal patience and attitude modulation. Strength of spirit is rarely compromised in a Cancer 2 life, but outcomes are unsettled and highly variable.

"I don't think there's anything immature about fighting for the underdog and fighting for people who don't have a voice. I have an intense desire to protect people who can't protect themselves."

– Kristen Bell, award-winning American film /television actress/humanitarian; frequently plays a duck out of water heroine; diagnosed as depressive during childhood; a mental health activist

"I don't think you can bring the races together by joking about the differences between them. I'd rather talk about the similarities, about what's universal in their experiences."

– Bill Cosby, legendary American comedian/television personality; at height of his career known as "America's Dad;" PhD in education; late in life convicted as a "violent sexual predator"

"I love theaters. I love the event of going there and seeing a movie with a lot of people. I like the community coming around the story."

– Willem Dafoe, prolific award-winning American actor; known best for intense 'outsider' and 'oddball' roles; raised by "horny" sisters; expelled from high school for making an adult film

"To me, YouTube isn't just, 'Watch my videos!' It's, 'Let's have a conversation and get involved in each other's lives.' I want to make [my fans] feel like they have a reason to have a YouTube account because they can comment and have a voice."

– Shane Dawson, American actor/author/comedian/director/musician; one of the first people to rise to fame as a YouTube content provider; raised by an abusive alcoholic father; LGBQT icon

"The more we care for the happiness of others, the greater is our own sense of well-being."

– Tenzin Gyatso, Chinese sage; the 14th Dalai Lama; Nobel Peace Prize laureate; in Buddhist tradition the living personification of compassion

"I think I'm getting there, but it's very hard to perform at my absolute peak when an awful lot of people come just to make their presence known, when the lights go down and all you can hear is people screaming."

– George Michael, Grammy -winning English singer/songwriter/producer; "most played" British artist 1984-2004; first Western pop star to tour China; LGBQT icon; scandal-plagued life

"We have a strict 'no a-hole policy' at SpaceX. And we fire people if they are. I mean, we give them a little bit of warning. But if they continue to be an a-hole, then they're fired."

– Elon Musk, iconic South African/American entrepreneur; founder of Tesla and SpaceX; maintains that humanity must become a multi-planet species; charged with fraud by SEC

"There's no substitute for rolling up your sleeves and working with the people who can make a difference. They get the benefit of your participation and you gain a direct understanding of the real problems and potential solutions, which makes you a more informed giver."

– Michael Milken, infamous American financier; known as the "junk bond king;" imprisoned for racketeering and securities fraud; later life devoted to irreproachable charity work

"I think empathy is a beautiful thing. I think that's the power of film though. We have one of the most powerful, one of the greatest communicative tools known to man."

– Michelle Rodriguez, iconic American "action" actress; best known for work in the 'Fast & Furious' series; expelled from five high schools; criminal traffic citations; forthrightly bisexual

"Don't divide the world into "them" and "us.""

– Donald Rumsfeld, American political figure; four-term congressman; Secretary of Defense under presidents Ford and G.W. Bush; controversial architect of 2003 Iraq war

"I've never lived in the visual world. I live very much in an emotional-contact world."

– Richard Simmons, iconic American fitness guru/media personality; known for flamboyant and energetic style; self-described "clown prince of fitness;" reclusive in later life

"There is no energy in matter other than that received from the environment."

– Nikola Tesla, renowned Serbian-American engineer/physicist; an electrical transmission pioneer; sought to develop a global communications network; lifelong mental health problems

 Leo 2

In the second lunation phase one has to reconcile oneself with environmental definition. This can be a literal environment or a cultural one, but the key is that one is starting from a place of strong conferred identity. Luckily the Leo 2 does not mind being defined by the construct of the native jungle...as long as there is no argument about who gets to step on the big rock and be king.

Rising above the crowd is no mere metaphor for a Leo 2. They tend to have both a figurative and literal thing about heights. There is a compulsion to look down...on the earth and particularly on other (lesser) souls.

In any lunation phase a Leo, represented by the Sun, is a guardian of the power of ego. The catch in the second lunation phase is that there is just enough of a Moon to project a whisper of a social compact. A Leo 2 life is one that finds an individual's sense of identity snagged on the horn of a slight crescent of collective consciousness.

To combat this situation the Leo 2 tends to take life by the creative/inventive horn. There is a constant declaring of individualized talent and intent, even in the most mundane of activities. Be the subject art or food or sex or whatever, the Leo 2 will be there to tell you how they intend to do it bigger and better and more compellingly than anyone else has ever managed to do it.

With Leo 2 it's truly hard not to think of a cat that has gained the high ground. Perhaps you become its prey...or maybe you are just an audience. Either way, one can't help but to look up and blink a little.

"My mother always accused me of being in love with the sound of my own voice. When we went on road trips, she'd be like, 'Stop singing. Be quiet, you're talking just to hear yourself speak.' It was probably true. I like to ramble on, which is probably why I'm well suited to interviews. You know, there's no other forum where you're literally supposed to sit down and just talk for hours about yourself. I love it."

– Ben Affleck, Oscar-winning American director/actor/screenwriter; often plays arrogant/ruthless characters; tallest actor to ever play Bruce Wayne/ Batman

"There are definite pleasures in scale."

– Joe Baum, famed New York restaurateur; president of Restaurant Associates; created 167 restaurants including The Four Seasons and the food complex at the World Trade Center

"I am someone who's been in politics for 43 years and I know what I'm doing and what I should do. Have no doubt that I know how to tell the truth and to do so elegantly."

– Fidel Castro, Cuban president; pursued Communist doctrine yet amassed a great personal fortune; launched revolution from the Sierra Maestra Mountains—-the highest range in Cuba

"People say my ego is grand. I think it's in proportion to me."

– Wilt Chamberlain, HOF American basketball player; known as 'Wilt the Stilt' and the 'Big Dipper,' nearly mythical strength and stamina; titled his autobiography "A View from Above"

"Celebrity has its uses. I can always get a seat in any restaurant."

– Julia Child, iconic American chef/author/television personality; introduced French cooking to the American mass market; rejected from military service due to her height (6'2")

"Never let anyone define you. You are the only person who defines you. No one can speak for you. Only you speak for you. You are your only voice."

– Terry Crews, American football pro /actor/activist; specializes in action/comedy roles; a talented artist; gained fame as a pumped up spokesman in a series of Old Spice commercials

"If I won't be myself, who will?"

– Alfred Hitchcock, legendary British film director; said his own movies were too scary for him to watch; several of his films including 'Vertigo' and 'North by Northwest' deal with fear of heights

"I'm a sucker for a compliment."

– Meghan Markle, American actress; the Duchess of Sussex; prior to royal marriage known for role on TV legal drama 'Suits;' a passionate foodie; almost always wears stiletto heels in public

"I believe in equality, equality for everybody. No matter how stupid they are or how superior I am to them."

– Steve Martin, award-winning American actor/comedian/writer/producer/musician; a "wild and crazy guy;" first comedy album was 'Let's Get Small;' memoir is titled 'Born Standing Up'

"Every star has that certain something that stands out and compels us to notice them."

– Maureen O'Hara, Irish-American actress/singer; famous redhead known for passionate but sensible roles; called "Queen of Technicolor;" frequently paired with leading man John Wayne

"I don't want to follow the herd."

– Alain Robert, French-born rock and urban climber; death-defying climbs of skyscrapers and landmarks earned him the nickname "The French Spider-Man;" arrested 100+ times

"If we all worked on the assumption that what is accepted as true is really true, there would be little hope of advance."

– Orville Wright, American inventor; he and his brother Wilbur developed the world's first successful airplane

 Virgo 2

Virgos are mostly analytical souls. Their enthusiasm resides in a bias towards examining concrete form and rational structure in all of life's experiential phenomena. The revelation of a practical utilitarian truth generally holds far greater appeal than the random unhinged epiphanies one may encounter in the realms of magic, chance or chaos.

So it is that the second lunation phase is a fairly comfortable incarnation in which to be a Virgo. There is meaning and purpose in being part of a tribe and in consciously grooming one's link to a supportive culture. Virgo 2's embrace the value of bringing their personal skill to the marketplace, and they enjoy the real-world benefits to be gained in honing their connection to the world at large.

Where things get a little fuzzier for Virgo 2 is in the truth that life is rarely an unbroken procession of expertly-engineered high-functioning links. In the course of a human lifetime shit happens. Pain, setbacks, and the occasional outright catastrophe come with the existential territory.

Happily, where Virgo 2's tend to shine brightest is in their reasonably blithe acceptance of disappointment and conflict as inescapable aspects of the human condition. In Virgo 2 phase there is a tendency to see imperfection as a building block rather than an obstacle. Failure, at least the kind that can eventually be surmounted, is almost treated opportunistically with a fond embrace as the thing that guarantees improvement.

The result is that there is something ineffably decorous and witty and admirable about most Virgo 2's. They get that the cosmos plays jokes all the time, and that sometimes the joke is on them. And then, with the application of clear thinking, it's not.

"I think I'm a mama's boy who wanted to be a hockey player, who failed, and had to become a singer. I think that I'm a generous, impatient, kind, jerk."

– Michael Bublé, Grammy-winning Canadian singer; known for classic jazz standards coupled with pop influences; credits grandfather's music collection for his song preferences

"No matter how great the talent or efforts, some things just take time."

– Warren Buffett, iconic American investment guru; founder of Berkshire-Hathaway; the "Oracle of Omaha;" personally frugal despite immense wealth; spends most of his time reading

"Many a man has fallen in love with a girl in a light so dim he would not have chosen a suit by it."

– Maurice Chevalier, award-winning French café singer/actor; known best for playing debonair characters in 1930's musical comedies; learned English while a POW in a WW1 prison camp

"Thank you hard taco shells for surviving the long journey from factory, to supermarket, to my plate and then breaking the moment I put something inside you. Thank you."

– Jimmy Fallon, Grammy/Emmy-winning American television personality/actor/writer/producer; host of the 'Tonight Show with Jimmy Fallon;' an SNL alum; as a child wanted to be a priest

"To be aware of limitations is already to be beyond them."

– Georg Wilhelm Friedrich Hegel, canonical German philosopher; leading figure in the early 19th Century Idealism movement; advocated for rational synthesis of conflicting perspectives

"Work hard, don't quit, be appreciative, be thankful, be grateful, be respectful, also to never whine ever, never complain, and, always, for crying out loud, keep a sense of humor."

– Michael Keaton, award-winning American actor/director/producer; successful in comedic and dramatic roles; breakthrough role was wiseacre spirit in 'Beetlejuice;' lives on a Montana ranch

"It's hard to let go. Even when what you're holding onto is full of thorns, it's hard to let go. Maybe especially then."

– Stephen King, renowned American author; a master of horror/fantasy; has sold 350M+ books; purchased the van that injured him in a near career-ending accident; writes 2,000 words/day

"If everything was perfect you would never learn and you would never grow."

– Beyoncé Knowles, Grammy-winning American singer/dancer/actress; rose to fame as lead singer of 'Destiny's Child;' on tour a favorite pastime is visiting local museums

"It is well to cultivate a friendly feeling towards error, to treat it as a companion inseparable from our lives, as something having a purpose, which it truly has."

– Maria Montessori, Italian physician and educator; best known for educational philosophy that bears her name; a lifetime social activist; first woman ever to attend an Italian medical school

"I would never have felt good if I hadn't experienced losing, because losing is part of your life. And it is something that if I could teach people to understand that, I think it could help them a lot."

– Arnold Palmer, venerated American pro golfer; nicknamed "The King;" first great charismatic golfer of the television age; a major pediatric hospital and a golf museum bear his name

"How can you have any pudding if you don't eat your meat?"

– Roger Waters, award-winning British rock musician; best known as singer/bassist/lyricist and conceptual guru for the legendary Pink Floyd; studied architecture at university level

"You got to have smelt a lot of mule manure before you can sing like a hillbilly."

– Hank Williams, legendary American country singer/songwriter; widely considered country music's first superstar; excruciating spina bifida led to alcoholism; died at the age of 29

 Libra 2

Considering what most astrology texts have to say about the peaceful, justice-oriented, aesthetically-attuned sign of Libra, it's disconcerting to encounter the hard edge one often finds in a Libra 2 life story. As in other Libra incarnations, the Libra 2 native places a premium on doing some good in the world and getting along with the rest of humanity. With these Libras, however, there is clearly a point where the experience of cultural suffocation is genuine, and all that is left for the sake of one's sanity is to open the damn truth window or to simply throw down.

Assuredly, even in conflict the Libra 2 is an idealist. Here, though, one encounters little of the natural Libra temperance as the native strongly recoils from the most restrictive aspects of accepted social conditioning. Attempting to pioneer a reasonable equanimity and a little grace in all affairs, Libra 2's find themselves mightily antipathetic to the rigid rituals and questionable base principles that exist in the dark forest of human tribal connection.

So the Libra 2 is the Libra that finds it necessary to strike back at what they experience as an amalgam of inflexibility, lack of talent, ethical degradation and hostility. They are at odds with a world that proclaims it is sane and civilized but often manifests as anything but. The Libra 2 mission remains steadfastly to envision a better life for all, but their starting point is most often picking a fight with the consensus reality.

It's a genuine cross to bear. Peacefulness comes hard when one is being pushed towards the quicksand of cultural inertia. Radical attempts at extrication are sometimes all that there is.

Ultimately, the Libra 2 can achieve much in the throes of this energy dynamic, but don't expect them to turn a cheek just for the hell of keeping the peace.

"I keep my family out of my public life because it can be an awful nuisance to them. What's my mother going to tell strangers anyway? That I was a cute baby and that she's terribly proud of me? Nuts. Who cares?"

– Montgomery Clift, Oscar-nominated American actor; famed for his good looks and holistic approach to his movie roles; bisexual and free-spirited; became an abuser of pills and alcohol

"In every single way that was just everything I hate."

– Simon Cowell, British music producer/television personality; famous as judge on 'Pop Idol' and 'American Idol;' best known for his scathing comments about competitors' performances

"Find inner peace? I looked; it wasn't there."

– Bob Geldof, award-winning Irish singer/songwriter/producer/author/activist; best known as organizer of charity efforts Band Aid and Live Aid; ex-wife and daughter died of drug overdoses

"I didn't invent the hamburger. I just took it more seriously than anyone else."

– Ray Kroc, iconic American businessman; the corporate founder of McDonald's; a TIME "most important person of the century;" described as "cunning"/"ridiculously competitive"

"If slaughterhouses had glass walls, everyone would be vegetarian. We feel better about ourselves and better about the animals, knowing we're not contributing to their pain."

– Linda McCartney, influential American photographer/author/musician/social activist; spouse of Beatle Paul McCartney; co-wrote all of Wings hits; died from cancer at age 56

"Remember this: No one is looking at your imperfections; they're all too busy worrying about their own."

– Isaac Mizrahi, superstar American fashion designer/media personality; known for personal flamboyance and wit; went from bankruptcy to hugely successful collaboration with Target

"You have your way. I have my way. As for the right way, the correct way, and the only way, it does not exist."

– Friedrich Nietzsche, iconic German philosopher; explored the nature of good and evil and the role of religion in modern society; essentially a nihilist but identified with "super-man" concept

"And that is my definition of democracy, the right to be in a minority and not be suppressed"

– Lee Harvey Oswald, infamous American assassin; ex-U.S. Marine; defector to Soviet Union; presumed assassin of American president John F. Kennedy; murdered while in police custody

"Either you decide to stay in the shallow end of the pool or you go out in the ocean."

– Christopher Reeve, American actor/director/producer/screenwriter/author/activist/ equestrian; best known for role as 'Superman;' paralyzed in horse riding accident

"I love iconoclasts. I love individuals. I love people that are true to themselves, whatever the cost."

– Tim Robbins, Oscar-winning American actor/director/producer/writer/activist; known best for his role as a wrongly convicted murderer in 'The Shawshank Redemption;' very vocal politically

"I can't stand satisfaction. To me, greatness comes from that quest for perfection."

– Mike Schmidt, American HOF baseball player/broadcaster; played 18 seasons with Philadelphia; named as best third baseman of all time; cancer survivor and health activist

"Make a choice of what you want, who you want to be and how you're going to do it. The universe will get out of your way."

– Will Smith, iconic Oscar-nominated American film actor; began as Grammy-winning rapper "The Fresh Prince;" successfully moved into television; had a mid-life crisis at career peak

 Scorpio 2

Whether a Scorpio always loves a challenge is debatable. Human beings, even Scorpios, are arguably not designed to savor an endless battle of wills with hostile competitors or celebrate a constant tearing away from perceived captivity. In the case of Scorpio 2, though, there is certainly a bias towards flexing one's fiercest mojo if not always loving the process.

In truth, anyone who has ever had to summon excessive force to challenge resistance has had a glimpse into the soul of a Scorpio 2. What if you were really that fly whose survival depended on escape from that flypaper? How much passion could you summon to the life or death struggle for freedom?

To be sure, Scorpio 2 is not always at a life moment that calls for such dramatic description. If one cares to understand them, though, it needs to be accepted that a Scorpio 2 almost always feels that they are at such a crisis moment. On the battlefield or the buffet line, there is a constant 'winner takes all' gleam to their spirit.

Understandably, things can go very badly for a Scorpio 2. In the desire to challenge (or occasionally cement) people and predicaments that seem totally untenable (or unstable), there's a pretty strong propensity for them to break things...not least of all themselves. The flip side is that a highly functioning Scorpio 2 can manifest so much strength of consciousness that followers and an entirely new cultural order may be left in the wake of their efforts.

In all things a Scorpio 2 life is one that is predicated on the testing of will versus established conditions. It's not just a matter of dominant perspective; it's a test of actual domination. The fallout is often considerable.

That's about it. You've been warned. And whatever you do, don't take the last of roast beef if you don't want a Scorpio 2 fork in the back of your hand.

"The talk you hear about adapting to change is not only stupid, it's dangerous. The only way you can manage change is to create it."

– Peter Drucker, Austrian-American business guru; considered "the father of modern management;" stressed the role of managers in leading knowledge-based business/society

"Women sometimes go too far, it's true. But it's only when you go too far that others listen."

– Indira Gandhi, first woman prime minister of India; a childhood revolutionary; successfully led India in war versus Pakistan despite U.S. disapproval; assassinated by Sikh bodyguards

"If the day should ever come when we must go, if some day we are compelled to leave the scene of history, we will slam the door so hard that the universe will shake and mankind will stand back in stupefaction."

– Joseph Goebbels, infamous German politician; minister of propaganda for the Nazi Third Reich; "hard" and "brutal," killed family and himself in Hitler's bunker at end of WWII

"I don't feel like I would be a good mentor. I don't know what I have to offer in that respect. I do this for pretty selfish reasons."

– Ryan Gosling, Golden Globe-winning Canadian actor/musician/humanitarian; known for psychologically intense romantic roles; was a child star on the Mickey Mouse Club

"I hope to bring people to God with my songs."

– Mahalia Jackson, all-time great American gospel singer/civil rights activist; famous for her vocal power and spiritual dedication; divorced husband who wanted her to sing secular music

"I'm so happy after such a long struggle to be living my true self."

– Bruce/Caitlin Jenner, celebrated American athlete/reality television star; set world record as winner of the 1976 Olympics Decathlon; transgender; announced becoming Caitlin on Twitter

"Some believe there is nothing one man or one woman can do against the enormous array of the world's ills... Yet many of the world's great movements, of thought and action, have flowed from the work of a single man."

– Robert Kennedy, American statesman; served as U.S. Attorney General and as a U.S. Senator; fought against organized crime and for civil rights; assassinated during presidential campaign

“Most of us have compromised with life. Those who fight for what they want will always thrill us.”

– Vivien Leigh, Oscar-winning Indian-born Irish/British actress; iconic roles were Scarlett O’Hara and Blanche Dubois; known for scandalous love affairs and for suffering from bipolar disorder

“I’m Jesus Christ, whether you want to accept it or not, I don’t care.”

– Charles Manson, convicted American mass murderer; messianic leader who orchestrated cult killings of Hollywood celebrities; associated with ‘Helter Skelter’ apocalyptic vision of history

“This telegram is a work of art if I say it is.”

– Robert Rauschenberg, seminal American painter/graphic artist; his non-traditional multi-material work anticipated the pop movement; rebuked the inward-facing definition of art

“I am strong, I am invincible, I am woman.”

– Helen Reddy, Australian pop singer/songwriter/activist; described by Alice Cooper as “the queen of housewife rock;” best known for her Grammy-winning feminist anthem ‘I Am Woman’

“It’s better to burn out than to fade away.”

– Neil Young, R&R HOF Canadian singer/guitarist/songwriter; polio and epilepsy survivor; considered the “Godfather of Grunge;” bans use of his music in commercials; political activist

Sagittarius 2

A Sagittarius 2 recognizes that the human condition comes with a great deal of cumbersome cultural adhesive. Nevertheless, as with others of their Sun sign, this does stop them from looking beyond local conditions to the personal and communal prospects of a felicitous enlightenment somewhere 'out there.' Frankly, this lends no small amount of comedy to the Sagittarius 2 situation given that their dynamic is a little bit like what happens when a tethered dog make an ill-advised lunge for a passing rabbit.

Still, whatever forms an abiding culture takes in delimiting their personal circumstances the Sagittarius 2 drive inclines towards an honest and fundamentally optimistic pursuit of human righteousness and universal awareness. Even when conditions limit access, education and adventure are highly prized by these folks. Reflecting an outlook that accepts there is a world of things worth knowing and doing, even a Sagittarius 2 bound by external circumstances is the sort of individual who will look up and attempt to get up before giving up...most likely making a joke or wry observation through it all.

Ultimately, planted in a specific time and place like every second lunation phase being, a Sagittarius 2 uniquely anticipates that there is wisdom dangling at a tantalizing distance just out of one's farthest reach. It may be frustrating, as it is often comical, to try and stretch oneself fully in that direction. But even if wisdom must be pursued on a figurative level and for the edification of a culture that reluctantly flexes its senses of humor and inclusion, the Sagittarius 2 is fairly comfortable with making books, well-worn road maps and smiles into umbrellas.

"Far away there in the Sunshine are my highest aspirations. I may not reach them, but I can look up and see their beauty, believe in them, and try to follow where they lead."

– Louisa May Alcott, famed American novelist/nurse/activist; best known for 'Little Women' which she described as "moral pap;" wrote sensationalistic melodrama under pseudonyms

"I don't know what I'm doing, but my incompetence has never stopped my enthusiasm."

– Woody Allen, iconic Oscar-winning American screenwriter/director/actor/comedian; multi-genre auteur; known for a complex and scandalous personal life; also a talented jazz clarinetist

"Don't be a jerk. Try to love everyone. Give more than you take. And do it despite the fact that you only really like about seven out of 500 people."

– Judd Apatow, Emmy-winning American writer/director/producer/comedian; best known for developing offbeat "bromantic" movie comedies such as 'Superbad' and 'Knocked Up'

"I used to love the feeling of running, of running too far. It made my skin tingle."

– Larry Bird, HOF American pro basketball player/coach/executive; three-time MVP of the NBA; grew up poor with an alcoholic father; "loved" being a municipal garbage man for a while

"There is a power under your control that is greater than poverty, greater than the lack of education, greater than all your fears and superstitions combined. It is the power to take possession of your own mind and direct it to whatever ends you may desire."

– Andrew Carnegie, Scottish-born American industrialist; foundational figure of the 19th century steel industry; retired as "world's richest man;" donated 90% of his wealth to philanthropies

"Let us learn to live with kindness, to love everyone, even when they do not love us."

– Pope Francis, Argentine-born 266th Pope of the Catholic Church; often referred to as "the people's pope;" crusader against social inequality; progressive reformer of church dogma

"The most beautiful people are all in the library."

– Caroline Kennedy, American author/attorney/diplomat; child of assassinated president John F. Kennedy; U.S. ambassador to Japan; Carnegie Corporation board member

"People often tell me I could be a great man. I'd rather be a good man."

– John F. Kennedy Jr., American attorney/publisher; charismatic baby brother of Caroline Kennedy; athletic/adventurous; a 'People' "sexiest man alive;" perished in private plane crash

"Be winged arrows aiming at fulfillment and goal."

– Paul Klee, iconic Swiss-German modern artist; sometimes called "the Father of Abstraction;" fascinated by the subconscious and mysticism; a voracious reader and a gifted violinist

"Imagine how asleep or utterly unperceptive and clueless you would have to be not to see yourself as absurd for the most part."

– John Malkovich, award-winning American actor/director/producer/fashion designer; known for playing offbeat and creepy characters; protean interests; curates personal authenticity

"If you don't know the guy on the other side of the world, love him anyway because he's just like you. He has the same dreams, the same hopes and fears. It's one world, pal. We're all neighbors."

– Frank Sinatra, iconic American singer/Oscar-winning actor; hailed as the "Chairman of the Board;" leader of the showbiz 'Rat Pack;' tombstone reads "The Best Is Yet to Come"

"I don't like defining myself. I just am."

– Britney Spears, American pop superstar; six of her seven first albums reached #1; career doldrums due to tumultuous personal life; comeback included fame as a Las Vegas headliner

Capricorn 2

Mountain goats at their core, all Capricorns are about climbing and the desire to find purchase at the heights of human endeavor. What differentiates the Capricorn 2 is their particularly involved relationship with the situation from which they start out. Eyes focused on an exalted goal, they appreciate that taking the very first step engages as much of their stamina and personal focus as the final exhausted stride that puts them on top.

Again, as with other second lunation phase natives, there is a need to pull at something very hard to loosen the root attachment. Actually, to be honest, sometimes a Capricorn 2 will excavate the entire culture from which one has sprung, place it on their back, and attempt to carry the whole shebang to higher ground. Either way, there is usually a mighty effort to end up at the pinnacle and to be identified as the hero responsible for the successful ascent.

Alas for the rest of us, this often results in a persona that is casual about what the rest of us groundlings may desire. A Capricorn 2 is easily put off by the rules and boundaries that have been established for everyone else to live by, with a sense of special privilege and a lack of guilt over sketchy tactics hardly out of bounds. While they are too serious in their goal seeking to be considered frivolous, they will not recoil from the employment of a dash of mayhem and a smidgen of dirty dealing of if it allows them to separate and rise.

Most Capricorn 2's would take umbrage if you pointed any of this out as a failing. Theirs is not a democratic bias, and they know far better than you the sort of effort it will take to get us all started towards higher ground. Be grateful, and if you can't do that at least don't be a rat.

"The characteristic feature of all ethics is to consider human life as a game that can be won or lost, and to teach man the means of winning."

– Simone de Beauvoir, renowned French writer/thinker/existentialist; author of 'The Second Sex,' the book credited with laying the intellectual foundation for the feminist movement

"A smile can get you far, but a smile with a gun can get you further."

– Al Capone, infamous American gangster; ran the liquor trade in Chicago during Prohibition; nicknamed 'Scarface;' associated with extreme gang violence; finally jailed on tax evasion

"Hey, it's hard work."

– Heidi Fleiss, notorious American businesswoman; best known for the upscale prostitution ring she ran as the 'Hollywood Madam;' jailed for tax evasion

"Justice is merely incidental to law and order."

– J. Edgar Hoover, legendary American political administrator; director of the F.B.I. for 48 years; fiercely patriotic and institutionally authoritarian; famed for ruthless investigative tactics

"The entire United States is within range of our nuclear weapons, and a nuclear button is always on my desk. This is reality, not a threat."

– Kim Jong-un, "supreme leader" of North Korea; military dictator; accused of extensive human rights violations and mass political executions; much of his story shrouded in secrecy

"I question and soul-search constantly into myself to be as certain as I can that I am fulfilling the true meaning of my work, that I am maintaining my sense of purpose, that I am holding fast to my ideals, that I am guiding my people in the right direction."

– Martin Luther King, Jr., hugely influential American Baptist minister and social activist; leader of the American civil rights movement; Nobel laureate; known for "I Have a Dream" speech

"I think the actor has a tribal role as the archetypal story teller. I think there was a time when the storyteller, the priest, the healer, were all one person in one body. That person used to weave stories at night around a small fire to keep the tribe from being terrified that Sun had gone down."

– Ben Kingsley, Oscar-winning English stage and film actor; famous for playing inspirational leaders such as Gandhi and Moses; once a talented young musician encouraged by The Beatles

"Show me a guy who can't pitch inside and I'll show you a loser."

– Sandy Koufax, American pro baseball pitcher; famous for his dominating fast ball and wicked curve; first pitcher ever to win multiple Cy Young awards; youngest player ever elected to HOF

"My father always told me, 'Don't waste energy worrying about things you can't control. Spend your energy focusing on solutions'."

– Jared Kushner, controversial American businessman; became CEO of family business when father convicted of tax evasion; senior White House advisor to his father-in-law Donald Trump

"I played Luke Skywalker. Every time we played, I was Luke Skywalker. Nobody else could be Luke Skywalker."

– Ricky Martin, Grammy-winning Puerto Rican pop singer/actor/philanthropist; 'Livin' La Vida Loca' was breakthrough English hit; child-welfare activist; autobiography is titled 'Me'

"Acknowledge all man as fellow creation, but don't follow him."

– Patti Smith, groundbreaking American writer/artist/actress/singer; rose to prominence as a performance poet; her 1974 'Piss Factory' is widely considered the first true punk song

"The most improper job of any man, even saints (who at any rate were at least unwilling to take it on), is bossing other men. Not one in a million is fit for it, and least of all those who seek the opportunity."

– J. R. R. Tolkien, internationally acclaimed English fantasy writer/scholar; best known for the Middle Earth realm of 'The Hobbit' and 'Lord of the Rings;' famously skeptical of his fans' sanity

 Aquarius 2

An Aquarius 2 lives a life that teeters on an edge between the most aspirational form of utopianism and the purest sort of silliness. Sure they know that earthly life is one in which some contact with an established reality is sort of a stipulated condition. They just tend to act like there is nothing imperative in today's laws of physics, scientific or cultural, holding sway tomorrow.

In living a life that is marked by nothing so much as liberated thinking, the Aquarius 2 by turns makes the world laugh, then cry, then rise up in admiration. Part of the issue is that there tends to be a whiff of the fool in an Aquarius 2. They seem always to have a thought about life that is delivered while one's fly is opened or shoelace is untied.

On the other hand, if you really listen to them, Aquarius 2's really do have a line on how human beings can extricate themselves from all of today's random troubles and tar pits. Their strength is partly in thinking themselves out of a hole and partly in accepting the principle that the hole was only in their mind in the first place. Viewed from the outside they can seem quite confused but it's mostly that they are on a wavelength that's a little quicker and a whole lot different.

Inventive as all get-out, and with a predisposition towards buoyancy, Aquarius 2's are ultimately defined by their humanitarianism. They would prefer if everyone tagged along on their hopeful and somewhat futuristic ride. They sometimes get clobbered by reality, of course, but these are truly brave little engines of human potential that can generally intuit solutions before the rest of us see the problem.

They think, they can.

"The possible is constantly being redefined, and I care deeply about helping humanity move forward."

– Paul Allen, American entrepreneur/investor/philanthropist; co-founder of Microsoft; his autobiography is titled 'Idea Man;' half of his $19B wealth is pledged to philanthropy

"I do like taking stuff seriously that a lot of people look at as nonsense. I enjoy the insanity of that. And I like the commitment that is needed for that."

– Christian Bale, Oscar/SAG/Golden Globe-winning English-American method actor; known for eclecticism of roles and body-altering to fit character; thoughtful and politically outspoken

"Human beings only use ten percent of their brains. Ten percent! Can you imagine how much we could accomplish if we used the other sixty percent?"

– Ellen DeGeneres, Emmy-winning American stand-up comedian/actress/TV host/author; humanitarian/animal activist; LGBT rights advocate; recipient of Presidential MOF

"I feel like a little boy who is constantly offered new toys."

– Placido Domingo, Spanish singer/conductor/director; one of the most famous tenors of all time; known as "King of the Opera;" Presidential Medal of Freedom winner and a British knight

"Never, ever, let anyone tell you what you can and can't do. Prove the cynics wrong. Pity them for they have no imagination. The sky's the limit. Your sky. Your limit. Now. Let's dance."

– Tom Hiddleston, award-winning British stage/screen/television actor; breakthrough role was Loki in 'Thor;' honor graduate of Cambridge University; actively involved in multiple charities

"The riskiest thing we can do is just maintain the status quo."

– Bob Iger, renowned American businessman; CEO /Chairman of the Walt Disney Corporation; considered a business visionary for his corporate acquisition of Pixar, Marvel and Lucasfilm

"You are so much more than your orientation, you know it and I know it."

– Adam Lambert, Grammy-nominated American singer; breakthrough was 'American Idol;' big vocal range/glam-rocker style; toured with the band Queen to raise money for AIDS awareness

"God made the angels to show Him splendor, as He made animals for innocence and plants for their simplicity. But Man He made to serve Him wittily, in the tangle of his mind."

– Thomas More, English lawyer/philosopher/author/statesman/saint; best known as author of 'Utopia' (1516); beheaded by Henry VIII for religious views; canonized by the Catholic Church

"I'm funny how, I mean funny like I'm a clown?"

– Joe Pesci, Oscar-winning Italian-American actor; frequently plays a volatile extrovert with an acid sense of humor; famous films include 'Goodfellas' and 'My Cousin Vinnie'

"There are no constraints on the human mind, no walls around the human spirit, no barriers to our progress except those we ourselves erect."

– Ronald Reagan, 40th President of the United States/movie star; presided during the end of Cold War with the Soviet Union; identified with trickledown economics and "shining city" image

"Remember that your perception of the world is a reflection of your state of consciousness. You are not separate from it, and there is no objective world out there. Every moment your consciousness creates the world that you inhabit."

– Eckhart Tolle, famous German-Canadian spiritual advisor; books include 'The Power of Now' and 'A New Earth: Awakening to Your Life's Purpose; "discovered" by Aquarian Oprah Winfrey

"Be truthful, and the result is bound to be amazingly interesting."

– Virginia Woolf, distinguished British modernist writer; wrote both fiction and non-fiction; fond of stream-of-consciousness narration; pioneering feminist; had long battle with bipolar disorder

 Pisces 2

All Pisces are in on a private joke with the universe. Natives of this Sun sign truly do not experience existence as something defined by tangible boundaries. Given that the prevailing condition of the second lunation phase is an attachment to pre-existing conditions, well the joke in a Pisces 2 incarnation tends to get that much funnier.

Like other members of their fish tribe (school?), Pisces 2's are abstract souls, visiting dimensions that are just beyond the accessibility of other mortals. As far as they engage with reality they do so from a starting place that has more in common with a deep ocean trench or an alien planet than a neighborhood backyard. Spiritual awareness, artistic passion, intense physical regimen, sudden inspiration, copious ingestion of chemical substances, you name it; the Pisces consciousness can hardly be defined as a creation of the easily recognizable.

What perhaps sets the Pisces 2's apart is that they are not yet examples of fully evolved Pisces. Oh, they are plenty Pisces enough when it comes to their predilections and talents, but their somewhat childlike consciousness has a particularly fishlike tendency to take capricious and odd routes to an objective. For the most part a destination is where they eventually end up, not a place at which they have chosen to arrive.

Unlike the firm hold that life places on other signs in this incarnation, the Pisces 2 tends deal with the slippery rather than the sticky. If there is any foundation beneath their spirit it is simply that all life is built upon an ever flowing tidal mutability that sometimes lets you encounter God and sometimes lands you in jail...all in the same lifetime, sometimes on the same day.

Oh well, that's oceanic consciousness for you.

"It's no good saying, 'hold it' to a moment in real life."

– Antony Armstrong-Jones, world-renowned British photographer/ documentarian; 1st Earl of Snowdon; husband of Princess Margaret; life shrouded in scandal; activist for the disabled

"I conclude that there is as much sense in nonsense as there is nonsense in sense."

– Anthony Burgess, prolific English writer/poet/composer/critic; best known for dystopian novel 'A Clockwork Orange;' spoke ten languages; frank opinions had a tendency to "piss people off"

"Losing my mind sounds so pessimistic. I prefer the term winning my insanity."

– Dane Cook, award-winning American stand-up comedian/actor, his album 'Retaliation' (2005) was top comedy album in 30 years; said his style sometimes veers towards "blabbering retard"

"When I sing, I try to live the song or live the emotion of the song. The space I'm in doesn't exist. It's another world."

– Roger Daltrey, Hall of Fame British rocker/actor; lead singer of 'The Who; played pinball wizard 'Tommy' in film of the rock opera; awarded CBE for contributions to music and charity

"One of the most predictable things in life is there will be change. You are better off if you can have a say in the change. But you are ignorant or naive if you don't think there will be change, whether you want it to or not."

– Julius Erving, legendary HOF American professional basketball star; nicknamed 'Dr. J;' known for elegant soaring moves past defenders; tribulations in personal life with women and children

"So I came to the realization: Nothing in life is unfair. It's just life."

– Rob Lowe, popular American actor; rose to fame in heartthrob roles; later TV work included acclaimed drama and comedy series; career notoriously interrupted by sex tape scandal

"Ain't no boundaries, ain't no limits."

– Floyd Mayweather, Jr., all-time great American boxer; won championships in five different weight divisions; complicated and sometimes violent family life

"People are genuinely excited about taking the country in another direction."

– Mitch McConnell, influential American politician; U.S. Senator and Senate Majority Leader; began career as a pro-abortion rights/pro-union moderate before moving far to the right

"After a while, you can't get any higher. It's like your head is in a wind tunnel–everything is vibrating."

– Method Man (born Clifford Smith), Grammy-winning American rapper and actor; member of the famed Wu-Tang Clan; "Method" derives from a New York street term for marijuana

"A God who fits within the confines of our conception is useless. God cannot be comprehended by man's conception or logic. God is an eternal being who transcends the framework of man's limited logic."

– Sun Myung Moon, iconic Korean religious leader/businessman/activist; converted from Confucianism to Christianity at age 10; members of his Unification Church known as "Moonies"

"How wonderful opera would be if there were no singers."

– Gioachino Rossini, renowned Italian composer/artistic director; wrote 39 operas including 'The Barber of Seville' and 'William Tell;' known for both great wit and clinical depression

"In fact, I'm softer than I've ever been, including that unfortunate semester in high school when I simultaneously discovered Krispy Kreme and pot."

– Olivia Wilde, popular Irish-American actress/director/activist; board member of several charities and activist organizations; self-proclaimed 'Trekkie;' often described as "enigmatic"

3rd Lunation Phase/1st Quarter Moon

Moon is 90 to 135 degrees ahead of Sun

Keyword: Volatility

There is no better figurative image of the LP3 soul than that of an active child wrestling with an extraordinarily large collection of building blocks and action figures. The natural predisposition is to build something extraordinary and to have it inhabited by exceptional beings. The limiting factor is that skills and perceptions are not yet fully developed, coupled with the fact that one tends to be intellectually and emotionally volatile and self-absorbed.

So it is that despite the nascent grandeur of one's intentions the pitfalls of the LP3 life have largely to do with a world that manifests in the guise of chaos, or at least the unexpected. The LP3 soul does not accept the fall of his block tower or the rebuff of assigned characters passively. There is often immaturity in the face of disappointment that may manifest as aggression, noise, sullenness or any other manner of acting out.

And yet there are certainly many great lives among the legion of LP3 souls. It sounds odd, but a lot of this just seems to have a basis in dumb luck. While there is no monopoly on good fortune in this incarnation, there is a curious tendency in the LP3 life to have that fairy godmother moment or to at least pull that winning card on the river.

The secret may well be that the temperament of the LP3 soul is not one that is inclined towards running out of energy. For other souls the collapse of a tower might simply be a signal to put the toys away. For the LP3 soul this "failure" is simply an invitation to try and try again.

In the LP3 life the mantra is "pick it up." What chaos at first conquers, perseverance may yet reward. There may be some whining along the way, but so may there ultimately be winning and a glimpse of the animating spirit in all things.

 Aries 3

The general chaos of the third lunation phase is entirely acceptable to most of its Aries natives. All Aries have a proclivity towards running into, over and through life's obstacles. An Aries 3 just seems to get an extraordinary amount of opportunity to put a headstrong personality into practice.

The phrase "ready to rumble" comes to mind. Bad outcomes hurt like they would for anyone else, but the key to an Aries 3 life well lived is fearlessness in the face of engagement. Commotion cravers and culture rockers, they seem to have a special appreciation for the surprisingly upbeat outcome that may materialize via a willing acceptance of confrontation.

Ultimately, Aries 3 tend to be reality-accepting and confident. They are willing to get up into life's grill. Being bitten sometimes, or even losing an ear, comes with the incarnation territory.

"I think there can always be beauty in struggle."

– Patricia Arquette, Oscar/Emmy-winning American actress; has played a wide mix of offbeat characters; known as "the original 90's cool girl;" deeply involved in Haiti earthquake relief

"Life has but one true charm: the charm of the game. But what if we're indifferent to whether we win or lose?"

– Charles Baudelaire, famous French poet/critic; best known for his poetry volume 'The Flowers of Evil' featuring themes of death and depravity; lived a life of debauchery, debt and addiction

"Let the world be as it is and learn to rock with the waves."

– Joseph Campbell, eminent American mythologist; famous for "monomyth" idea that all heroic journeys are essentially the same; considered both progressive and reactionary; a maverick

"I sing to the realists; people who accept it like it is."

– Aretha Franklin, legendary American singer; the "Queen of Soul;" winner of 18 Grammies, Presidential Medal of Freedom, NAACP Vanguard Award; first woman inductee in R&R HOF

"The trick is not how much pain you feel—but how much joy you feel. Any idiot can feel pain. Life is full of excuses to feel pain, excuses not to live, excuses, excuses, excuses."

– Erica Jong, influential American author/poet; best known for "The Fear of Flying,' a frank portrayal of female sexual desire; described good and evil as "flip sides of the same human coin"

"I would have been an archaeologist or something, maybe a historian. There are a lot of things I would have liked to have done differently, but everything that happened to me made me the person I am today. No matter how negative it seemed at the time or whatever hardship it seemed to have been at that time, I'm just the sum of all those amazing experiences."

– Chaka Khan, esteemed American singer/songwriter; the "Queen of Funk;" won 10 Grammies; civil rights activist/philanthropist/Black Panther; autobiography titled 'Through the Fire'

"But life is a great school. It thrashes and bangs and teaches you."

– Nikita Khrushchev, Russian statesman; Premier of the Soviet Union during the Cold War era; told Western leaders "we will bury you;" famed for brandishing shoe in disapproval at U.N.

"As long as you're fierce and you have that inner confidence with yourself, you can get through anything."

– Mandy Moore, popular American singer/actress; broke through with platinum-seller debut album 'So Real;' avid philanthropist; voice for Dove's women's self-esteem campaign

"In the studio, I always put on National Geographic for inspiration. (I like) looking at lions eating gazelles, all that type of stuff."

– Big Sean, award-winning American rapper; outstanding lyricist who embraces topics from sexuality to stress to spirituality; created foundation to help kids in hometown Detroit

"The art of life is not controlling what happens to us, but using what happens to us."

– Gloria Steinem, iconic American journalist/activist; key leader of the Women's Liberation movement; 1st editor of Ms. Magazine; celebrated for undercover Playboy Bunny expose'

"Life is unfair, but remember that sometimes it is unfair in your favor."

– Peter Ustinov, Oscar-winning English actor/writer/director/journalist; known for intelligence and ready wit; a modern Renaissance man; a goodwill ambassador for UNICEF; knighted

"What am I in the eyes of most people–a nonentity, an eccentric, or an unpleasant person–somebody who has no position in society and will never have; in short, the lowest of the low. All right, then–even if that were absolutely true, then I should one day like to show by my work what such an eccentric, such a nobody, has in his heart."

– Vincent Van Gogh, immortal Dutch painter; one of the most influential and popular artists in history; sold one painting during his lifetime; institutionalized for mental illness

Taurus 3

Of all the astrological signs Taurus is the one that speaks most clearly to the principle of endurance. Success resides in the process of outlasting life's chaos and pain. Talent, strength, and one heck of a stubborn streak are the tools that are required for the job.

For a Taurus 3, the touchstone is often the sheer amount of chaos and pain that must be negotiated in a lifetime. Developing one's abilities and holding fast in the onslaught of such an incarnation is a rather Herculean task. A lot of one's life can be spent in spiritual/emotional/ intellectual recoil to the way the big bad world presents itself.

While worldly wounds may be inflicted, though, the upside of refusing to be sanguine about the shaky and ephemeral nature of things is a life in which accomplishment is tied to longevity. Not going down without a fight is the Taurus 3 mantra. Classic prima donnas and unrepentant takers may arise from such circumstances, but so do people of extraordinarily enduring worth.

"It doesn't matter how you travel it, it's the same road. It doesn't get any easier when you get bigger, it gets harder. And it will kill you if you let it."

– James Brown, Grammy HOF American singer/songwriter/dancer/producer/ bandleader; hugely influential funk/ R&B artist; the "Godfather of Soul;" recipient of Kennedy Center Honors

"Men say they love independence in a woman, but they don't waste a second demolishing it brick by brick."

– Candice Bergen, Emmy-winning American actress/model/spokesperson/ photographer; best known for her role as outspoken journalist/unwed mother 'Murphy Brown'

"The world is not the most pleasant place. Eventually your parents leave you and nobody is going to go out of their way to protect you unconditionally. You need to learn to stand up for yourself and what you believe and sometimes, pardon my language, kick some ass."

– Queen Elizabeth II, longest reigning monarch in British history; known for great resilience in handling decades of state affairs; credited with the modernization of the monarchy

"We have resolved to endure the unendurable and suffer what is insufferable."

– Emperor Hirohito, Japan's longest reigning emperor; given the name "Showa," meaning "enlightened peace;" best known for Japan's WWII surrender; helped rebuild post-war Japan

"Maybe wars aren't meant to be won; maybe they're meant to be continuous."

– Rami Malek (as Eliot Alderson); award-winning American actor; rose to fame as hacker who breaks the global economy in 'Mr. Robot;' hailed as Freddie Mercury in 'Queen' biopic

"I've gotten crankier in my old age."

– Shirley MacLaine, Oscar-winning American actress/singer/dancer/activist/author/spiritualist; known for multi-genre success over seven decades; key personality note is forthrightness

"You won't be famous until people start saying the worst things they can about you. Don't worry! It's a good sign!"

– Dame Nellie Melba, world-renowned Australian operatic soprano; known for her charisma and imperious temperament; arguably the most popular diva of the Victorian era

"No matter how well you perform, there's always somebody of intelligent opinion who thinks it's lousy."

– Laurence Olivier, internationally-acclaimed British-born theater/film actor/director; best known for classic dramatic roles; directed himself in Oscar-winning 'Hamlet;' acted into his 80's

"I'm a Taurus. To the bone."

– Michelle Pfeiffer, award-winning American actress/singer/painter/producer/philanthropist; known for beauty and sensitivity; works include many genres; animal rights activist, vegan

"The secret to happiness is to face the fact that the world is horrible."

– Bertrand Russell, Nobel laureate British philosopher/mathematician/humanist; imprisoned for anti-war activism by British government; founding CEO of Campaign for Nuclear Disarmament

"Part of our society kills what it loves, despises what it's created. It really hates success."

– Barbra Streisand, legendary Oscar, Emmy, Tony and Grammy-winning singer/actress/director; only recording artist ever to have #1 album in six different decades; staunch liberal activist

"Life's a bitch and so am I."

– Pete Townshend, iconic British rock musician/composer/philanthropist; known best as the guiding force of Hall of Fame band 'The Who;' prone to fierce guitar-smashing performances

Gemini 3

The most important thing to know about a Gemini 3 is that they are living an incarnation in which any certainty is extraordinarily low probability. Thrown into a lifetime most clearly delineated by chaos, their agile minds are incapable of/resistant to processing life into a firm conclusion. In fact they often tend to fall in love with or at least embrace the practical benefits of the mutable, the contrary, and the outright crazy.

While Gemini 3's are truly capable of amazingly refined intellectual work, it is not surprising to find many moral relativists and opportunists among this cadre. Their signature epiphany is that, in a universe of vague intent, adeptly applied cleverness can yield a much greater real world reward than consistency. For them the best facts are delicate creatures that are both negotiable and fungible.

Needless to say, these people are extraordinarily capable of pissing off a lot of other "types." Despite a capacity for charm, it's hard to be the most popular person in the room when all connectivity is somehow relative and exploiting an intellectual conceit is the neatest trick in the book. A Gemini 3, even when well-intended, possesses the capacity for making others feel at best inconsequential and at worst victimized.

For all of the preceding, though, a Gemini 3 can lead a most successful life. The value of adaptability cannot be discounted, and there is always some coin to be revealed in their bright and entertaining observations. Even when their path negotiates the aggressive and the self-destructive, life is always interesting around them.

And by the way, their gift of gab and free-floating convictions make them extraordinary politicians. Some Gemini 3's even grow up to become president. Good ones.

"Always remember that as long as other people are gullible, there's no limit to what you can achieve."

– Scott Adams, award-winning American newspaper cartoonist; best known for his satirical office-worker strip 'Dilbert;' also a trained hypnotist and an acclaimed expert in persuasion

"A fact looked at from the standpoint of humanity may not be a fact from the standpoint of a Master."

– Alice A. Bailey, well-known British writer/teacher/occultist; wrote 24 books on theosophical subjects; coined the term "New Age;" claimed books were dictated to her by a Tibetan Master

"Never trust nobody. Your moms will set your ass up."

– Notorious B.I.G., all-time great American rapper; central figure in East Coast – West Coast hip hop rivalry; dark lyrics focused on crime and gang life; famously murdered in drive-by shooting

"I'm conservative, but I'm not a nut about it."

– George H. W. Bush, 41st president of the U.S.; successful as a politician, oilman and academic; father of the George W. Bush; combat pilot in WWII; co-created Bush-Clinton charity relief fund

"Acting is something that we all practice at some time in our lives. We're different people to our mothers, fathers, our friends, people that we hung out together with, people that didn't like us or we didn't like them. We readjust ourselves."

– Tony Curtis, iconic American actor; known for good looks and genre versatility; performed 'Dr. Jekyll and Mr. Hyde' at breakthrough audition; difficult upbringing and relationship history

"I do know something; just not with any certainty."

– Anne Heche, prolific American film & television actress/screenwriter/director; raised in a conservative religious household; famously bisexual; memoir is titled 'Call Me Crazy'

"The one unchangeable certainty is that nothing is unchangeable or certain."

– John F Kennedy, 35th president of the U.S.; born to wealth & privilege; war hero; first telegenic president; famed for strength in foreign crises and ambitious domestic vision; assassinated

"If that's all there is, my friends, then let's keep dancing."

– Peggy Lee, famed American pop and jazz singer/songwriter/actress; "the queen of intimate nightclubs;" tragic childhood; noted for egocentricity/dishonesty/self-destructive behavior

"I'm as honest as I can be."

– Macklemore, Grammy-winning American rap artist; his lyrics tend to be atypically anti-swagger; breakthrough album named "The Heist;' suffered from fame/addiction problems

"Let's not get too precious about it: actors are not heart surgeons or brain surgeons. We are just entertaining people."

– Malcolm McDowell, award-winning English film/television/voice actor; gained fame for 'A Clockwork Orange;' frequently plays wryly sadistic villains; battled substance addictions

"I'm a Gemini, so I change my mind every day."

– Natalie Portman, Israeli-born Oscar-winning American actress; iconic roles include disturbed ballerina, hit man apprentice, space queen, and Thor's girlfriend; psychology major at Harvard

"All universal moral principles are idle fancies."

– Marquis de Sade, French nobleman/revolutionary/philosopher/writer; best known for his raw pornography; spent 32 years in prisons and asylums; the term "sadism" derives from his name

Cancer 3

Life tends to be a very serious proposition for a Cancer 3. The world shakes mercilessly and there is a need to find purchase. Only two things help: 1) the will to get up after you've been knocked down; and 2) participatory membership in a community with deep roots.

This is not a matter of rational decision making for Cancer 3. A far more necessary ingredient is passion. For a Cancer 3 the world is really in full-on earthquake mode and hanging on is not something you read up on in the library...it's far more a matter of finding one's courage and fearlessly fighting for the collective.

Unsurprisingly, it is often difficult for others to sync with the Cancer 3 worldview. One encounters a marked propensity for self-righteousness and behavioral excesses and a fair number of faith-based delusions. You are either with them or against them and there is little shyness on their part about keeping score.

To be fair, the urgency of their spirits can make them fantastic captains and comrades. They will go where they have to go and they will lead you through the storm. If this means sailing the whole shebang off the edge of the world, at least they will owe no apology for not caring.

And, like a hero of myth, the Cancer 3 just might get you past the witches and the whirlpools and the Klingons to get you home.

"I've always liked working on stories that combine people who are relatable with something insane. The most exciting thing for me is crossing that bridge between something we know is real and something that is extraordinary. The thing for me has always been how you cross that bridge."

– J.J. Abrams, Emmy-winning American screenwriter/director/producer; broad success in both movies and television; helmed 'Star Wars' and 'Star Trek' projects; created TV series 'Lost'

"Start where you are. Use what you have. Do what you can."

– Arthur Ashe, pioneering American tennis star; only African-American to win Wimbledon and U.S. Open; wrote 'A Hard Road to Glory' history of black athletes; advocate for health causes

"This way of life is worth defending."

– George W. Bush, American businessman/politician; 43rd president of the U.S.; at various times held the historically highest and lowest approval ratings; religious; avid golfer, painter, bicyclist

“If you’re passionate about something then it will definitely work out for you. You should never stop believing in something, and you shouldn’t listen to anyone who tells you otherwise. Never give up on something you love.”

– Ariana Grande, Grammy-winning American singer/songwriter/actress; breakthrough came as young star on Nickelodeon show ‘Victorious;’ founded ‘Kids Who Care’ charity at age 10

“You know, what is team chemistry? My opinion is when you have enough people who care about winning and enough people who losing affects. That’s what chemistry means to me. It doesn’t necessarily mean you’re going to win, but you’re going to have enough people on the same page. It’s almost impossible, I think, to get everyone on the same page, but it’s gotta mean something to you.”

– Derek Jeter, all-time great American baseball player; famed for his consistency in clutch situations; most hits ever for a shortstop; most playoff games; NY Yankee captain for a decade

“If you’re gay and you can’t hold hands, or you’re black and you can’t catch a taxi, or you’re a woman and you can’t go into the park, you are aware there’s a menace. That’s costly on a psychic level. The world should be striving to make all its members secure.”

– Tony Kushner, Pulitzer-winning American dramatist/screenwriter; famed for his ‘Angels in America’ masterwork about gay life and the AIDS crisis; wrote ‘Munich’ and ‘Lincoln’ film scripts

“People can save the world by the way they think and by the way they behave and what they hold to be important.”

– Cyndi Lauper, Grammy/Tony/Emmy winning American singer/songwriter/actress/activist; famed for vocal range and unconventional appearance; tireless advocate for gay rights

"Do not judge me by my success, judge me by how many times I fell down and got back up again."

– Nelson Mandela, Nobel-laureate South African statesman; famed for his work in ending policy of apartheid; spent 27 years in prison for his beliefs; elected president after release

"Every champion was once a contender that refused to give up."

– Sylvester Stallone, award-winning American actor/director/writer/producer; one of the most popular action stars of all time; creator of the legendary 'Rocky' and 'Rambo' series

"People want to be part of something larger than themselves. They want to be part of something they're really proud of, that they'll fight for, sacrifice for, that they trust."

– Howard Schultz, prominent self-made American businessman; best known as CEO/Chairman of Starbucks; supporter of humanitarian causes; earnest advocate of "the American Dream"

"When you're entrusted with a tradition, you've got to protect it."

– George Steinbrenner, prominent American businessman; best known as N.Y. Yankees owner; notoriously media-oriented and meddlesome; hired/fired team manager Billy Martin five times

"I've often reflected on this in the past weeks as I've been following the presidential campaign: Very often, I thought it would have been great for both of these guys to sit down and be force-fed a couple of dozen episodes of Star Trek."

– Patrick Stewart, award-winning British stage and screen actor; Captain Picard in 'Star Trek: the Next Generation;' domestic violence victim/activist; knighted for contributions to drama

Leo 3

All Leos, in any incarnation phase, tend to behave as if they are as incandescent. Say what you will about the dangers of ego, Leos know that they are put on the earth to shine. It's their job.

A Leo 3 life is particularly fascinating because of the implicit murkiness of this incarnation. How does one proceed when down and up, left and right, forward and back and the like are so vague and fluidly randomized. Well, if you are a Leo 3, the first thing you do is take stock of the situation and try and find the light switch.

In truth, one knows these 'cats' because they are inexorably searching for the rheostat or because they have, after a few experiences with strange turns and blind alleys, found it. The real beauty of a Leo 3 is that they are accepting of both states. They have the sort of spiritual and emotional intelligence that allows them to have an appreciation for the bumps and scrapes of looking as well as the reward of finding.

Their strength is that they really have no doubt that they, whether they are strapped to a single triple-A battery or a night-shattering rocket engine, will go on to illuminate something someday. Meanwhile they are capable of a circumstantial sense of humor and, rather unexpectedly, even a touch of modesty. Such grace comes from knowing that the dark does not become one.

"I think we're going to the Moon because it's in the nature of the human being to face challenges. It's by the nature of his deep inner soul... we're required to do these things just as salmon swim upstream."

– Neil Armstrong, American astronaut/combat pilot/educator; the first human to walk on the Moon; became a pilot prior to driving a car; more than a dozen schools are named in his honor

"Sometimes you just have to jump out the window and grow wings on the way down."

– Ray Bradbury, seminal American author; famed for science fiction, fantasy and social commentary; chose self-study in the library over college; wrote 'Fahrenheit 451' in one week

"I was poking fun at myself most of all."

– Marcel Duchamp, French-American artist/sculptor/writer/chess player; seminal figure in the development of 20th Century conceptual art; famed for "ready-made" common object pieces

"I always believe if you're stuck in a hole and maybe things aren't going well you will come out stronger. Everything in life is this way."

– Roger Federer, preeminent Swiss tennis champion/philanthropist; 20 men's Grand Slam titles is most in tennis history; ranked #1 in world for 237 weeks; major UNICEF supporter

"We all suffer. If a man's wise, he learns from it."

– Alex Haley, iconic American author; best known for 'Roots;' winner of a special Pulitzer Prize and NAACP honors; served in Coast Guard for two decades where he discovered love of writing

"I was in a taxi the other night, and we started talking about life and the taxi driver goes, 'Chaos and creativity go together. If you lose one per cent of your chaos, you lose your creativity.' I said that's the most brilliant thing I've heard. I needed to hear that years ago."

– Woody Harrelson, Emmy-winning American television and film actor; breakthrough role was Woody on 'Cheers;' known for role versatility; he is an ethical vegan and an environmentalist

"If you enjoy the fragrance of a rose, you must accept the thorns which it bears."

– Isaac Hayes, world-renowned American singer/songwriter/composer/actor; Oscar-winner for 'Theme from Shaft;' voiced Chef on 'South Park;' crusader for educational/humanitarian causes

"Just celebrate the life you had, not the life you could've had."

– Earvin "Magic" Johnson, all-time great pro basketball player; three time NBA MVP; retired from game after contracting AIDS virus; successful owner/executive in multiple industries

"I've learned you can make a mistake and the whole world doesn't end. I had to learn to allow myself to make a mistake without becoming defensive and unforgiving."

– Lisa Kudrow, Emmy-winning American actress/writer/producer; best known as Phoebe on 'Friends;' Vassar graduate; worked eight years in medical field before taking on acting

"The most terrifying fact about the universe is not that it is hostile but that it is indifferent; but if we can come to terms with this indifference, then our existence as a species can have genuine meaning. However vast the darkness, we must supply our own light."

– Stanley Kubrick, iconic American filmmaker; known for classics such as 'Spartacus,' '2001,' 'A Clockwork Orange,' and 'Dr. Strangelove;' loved classical music, cats and Woody Woodpecker

"Misery, anger, indignation, discomfort–those conditions produce literature. Contentment -never. So there you are."

– T. E. Lawrence, famed British military officer/author; staunch advocate of Arab independence; memoir titled 'The Seven Pillars of Wisdom' was inspiration for film 'Lawrence of Arabia'

"Sometimes you have to explore the darkness to get to the light and get back to who you are."

– Jennifer Lopez, award-winning American actress/singer/dancer/producer; breakthrough role was in 'Selena' biopic; at the forefront of the Latin pop explosion; generous philanthropist

Virgo 3

Nothing is more pleasing to the mind of a Virgo than orderliness... all the right things lined up in all the right places. Alas, in the third lunation phase this is hardly the operative character of perception. Third lunation phase reality promises less of a clear lens view and more of life as seen through a cracked kaleidoscope.

What is so fascinating about the Virgo 3 cadre is how many paths exist towards a reconciliation of this dilemma. Just about any Virgo 3 is willing to stipulate that the world is fundamentally a realm of contradictions. Where they differ is in how they manage perception so as take on the challenge of living a meaningful existence.

For some there is awareness that the circle of life will never actually be squared. Life turns wry for these Virgos and they become hilarious observers of the foibles of humankind. These are the Virgo 3's who are pressed into service as life's witty, if somewhat tragicomic, narrators.

Still others of the Virgo 3 tribe are willing to think their way out of the box into which a predilection for logic tends to put them. Here one encounters the Zen side of life, featuring a penchant for meditation. The best one can do, according to this Virgo 3 faction, is to get past the mind by encouraging it to quiet down and get out of the way.

In one way or another all Virgo 3's are wrestling with the chasm that can exist between real world perception and abstract philosophy. They aspire to the experience of a truth that may lurk beyond the insanity. In the fullness of their lives they realize that they may never get to that holy place...but no one can tell them they don't get the humor of the situation.

"It seems that every time I stick my neck out, I get my foot into something else."

– Patsy Cline, iconic American country singer; famous for 'Crazy' and 'I Fall to Pieces;' first female country singer to headline in Las Vegas and play Carnegie Hall; perished in plane crash at age 30

"Everything's funny for God's sake...everything."

– Gloria Estefan, Grammy-winning Cuban-American singer/songwriter/actress/businesswoman; sometimes called "the Latin Madonna;" recovered from broken back; Kennedy Center honoree

"There is a way of looking at an awful place from a certain angle that allows it to take on a beauty because it is what it is."

– Richard Gere, award-winning American actor/humanitarian; best known for sex symbol roles in romantic films; Tibetan Buddhist practitioner; strong supporter of indigenous population causes

"I'm happy to be here. I'm happy to be anywhere. I'm not kidding."

– Larry Hagman, iconic American actor/director; famous as J.R. on 'Dallas;' recovered from liver transplant; eccentric/eclectic collector; anti-smoking activist; observed a weekly 'silent day'

"You could be laughing one day about the same issues that you're crying about the next day, so that's life."

– Taraji P. Henson, Oscar-nominated American actress/singer/author; plays strong female roles; best known as Cookie on 'Empire,' studied engineering in college; animal rights activist

"What will I be doing in twenty years' time? I'll be dead, darling! Are you crazy?"

– Freddie Mercury, all-time great British pop singer/composer; flamboyant lead singer of 'Queen;' life featured in 'Bohemian Rhapsody,' most successful biopic of all time; AIDS casualty

"In basketball–as in life–true joy comes from being fully present in each and every moment, not just when things are going your way."

– Phil Jackson, American Hall of Fame basketball player/coach/executive; won 11 NBA championships as coach; best known as "The Zen Master" for his holistic coaching philosophy

"Just beat my record for most consecutive days without dying."

– Bill Murray, award-winning American comedy icon/actor; rose to fame on 'Saturday Night Live;' film roles include both comedy and drama; replaced his agents with an 800 number

"All men are the same age."

– Dorothy Parker, legendary American literary figure; best known for biting wit; founding member of the Algonquin Roundtable; hated 'Winnie the Pooh;' left entire estate to the NAACP

"I'm still alive, which is pretty cool."

– Charlie Sheen, Golden Globe-winning American film/television actor; has starred in action, comedy and dramatic vehicles; infamous for domestic violence/drug/sex issues

"If you want to know what you are here to do, how you can be more loving, or how to get through a difficult situation, my answer is always 'meditate.' The difference between prayer and meditation is that when we pray, we are asking for something, and when we meditate, we are listening to the answer."

– James Van Praagh, bestselling American author, television personality, producer, clairvoyant/psychic; renowned spiritual medium; best known work is 'Talking to the Dead'

"The sign of intelligence is that you are constantly wondering. Idiots are always dead sure about every damn thing they are doing in their life."

– Sadhguru Jaggi Vasudev, influential Indian yogi/mystic/author; founder of the non-profit Isha Foundation, dedicated to humanitarian works and heightening of self-awareness through yoga

Libra 3

There is a great deal of complexity in the life of a Libra forced to endure an incarnation in the third lunation phase. In all Libra lives there is a proclivity to find inner balance and to form a respectful reciprocal relationship with other beings. That's just a hard thing to do when the third lunation phase world has such a capricious predilection towards shaking things up.

Even in context of this crazy lunation phase many Libra 3's simply strive to be agents of peace. The traits of tolerance, empathy, and charity are especially welcome in the face of the storm. Most Libra 3's would concur with the notion that trying times makes trying more precious.

The complexity arises from the Libra 3 awareness that good intentions are often not enough. In a third lunation phase world the process of meaningful relating can be a product of chaos, but it can also be the cause. Most Libra 3's experience the human condition as a walk on a pretty funky plank, and they are capable of getting pretty freaked out when it comes to the shakiness of the situation.

Still, as it inevitably does with Libra, the concept of love rises to the surface of their worldview. Sadly, a Libra 3 often recognizes that even this best of motives is no guarantee of success. And yet love still seems worth the trouble—-if only for the reason that, when the shaking commences, one might have someone else on whom to hold on.

"If you can't help people, then what is the point of being successful?"

– Matt Damon, Oscar-winning American actor/screenwriter/producer; known for roles requiring intelligence; Harvard dropout; often dated co-stars; humanitarian who co-founded H2O Africa

"Relationships are like bubbles – they're fragile."

– Michael Douglas, Oscar-winning American actor/producer; often plays intense/flawed heroes; shares same birthday as wife; became anti-gun activist after friend John Lennon's death

"One cannot attend to oneself, take care of oneself, without a relationship to another person."

– Michel Foucault, influential and controversial French philosopher; concerned with nature of knowledge; explored power in relationships; critical of modern psychology; an AIDS casualty

"Watch out for each other. Love everyone and forgive everyone, including yourself. Forgive your anger. Forgive your guilt. Your shame. Your sadness. Embrace and open up your love, your joy, your truth, and most especially your heart."

– Jim Henson, world-renowned puppeteer/writer/producer; creator of the Muppets; wife Jane was collaborator; created 'Fraggle Rock' as an anti-war educational vehicle for children

"I always want to know what's wrong with you, why you ain't smiling. That's just my character; I just love people and want to see people having a good time."

– Wyclef Jean, Grammy-winning Haitian rapper/musician/actor; best known as co-founder of the Fugees; heavily involved in politics and Haitian charity efforts but attached to much controversy

"Everyone carries a piece of the puzzle. Nobody comes into your life by mere coincidence. Trust your instincts. Do the unexpected. Find the others."

– Timothy Leary, iconic counter-culture American writer/psychologist/educator; known for his advocacy of spiritual/therapeutic LSD use; first published academic work was on relationships

"A thing that you see in my pictures is that I was not afraid to fall in love with these people."

– Annie Leibovitz, award-winning American portrait photographer; known for work in 'Rolling Stone' & 'Vanity Fair' magazines; took famed photo of John & Yoko just prior to Lennon's death

"It matters not who you love, where you love, why you love, when you love or how you love, it matters only that you love."

– John Lennon, legendary English singer/songwriter/artist/actor/peace activist; co-founder of 'The Beatles;' proudly identified with the phrase "all you need is love;" assassinated by a fan

"Love is just a word, but you bring it definition."

– Marshall Mathers (Eminem), Grammy-winning American rapper/producer/actor; rose to prominence for brilliant but extremely violent lyrics; sued for slander by his own mother

"Be kind. It's worthwhile to make an effort to learn about other people and figure out what you might have in common with them."

– Viggo Mortensen, award-winning American actor; frequently plays warriors and hardened men; best known as Aragorn in the 'Lord of the Rings' trilogy; many creative interests

"For my part, I wish all guns with their belongings and everything could be sent to hell, which is the proper place for their exhibition and use."

– Alfred Nobel, world-renowned Swedish scientist/inventor/businessman/poet; founder of the Nobel Prize; inventor of dynamite; believed powerful weapons would discourage conflict

"When you start to develop your powers of empathy and imagination the whole world opens up to you."

– Susan Sarandon, Oscar-winning American actress; extraordinarily diverse in her role selection; outspoken politically; arrested multiple times for anti-war and civil rights activism

Scorpio 3

Scorpios get a bad rap a lot of the time. They can be so fiercely willful that their more admirable qualities, including acts of true moral courage and the manifestation of the fiercest sort of loyalty to those that are dear to them, can be overlooked. While it is alluring to describe their sexy ferocity, it's only fair to keep in mind that the potent Scorpio will may be consecrated to the general good.

Either way, whether they chose to attack or defend, most Scorpios are well-suited for the third lunation phase. The opportunity to pit oneself against a world of chaos is right up their alley. Whatever the specific circumstances and whatever the potential for grace or disaster, it is the rare Scorpio 3 who doesn't live for the opportunity of going a few rounds with fate.

Their survival mechanism is deeply ingrained but it is also fairly simple. One can be assaulted and beaten and deeply depressed, but giving up is never an option. A little self-destructive behavior might occasionally enter the picture, but the one true glory in the Scorpio 3 life is becoming strong enough to resist the dangerous intent of oppositional people, places and events, right up to bending back the fingers of the hand of God if that is what is required.

In all things the keyword for a Scorpio 3 is power. It is their lot in this incarnation to challenge things past the granular all the way to the sub-atomic...chewing up all the wild particles that blow their way and ejecting them back at the universe. Bottom line, you really do not want to kick sand in their faces, although you might want to share a beach blanket just for the thrill.

"Nobody picks on a strong man."

– Charles Atlas, iconic Italian-American bodybuilder/businessman; known for his mail order 'Dynamic-Tension' exercise program; once named "World's Most Perfectly Developed Man"

"The only way to deal with an unfree world is to become so absolutely free that your very existence is an act of rebellion."

– Albert Camus, Nobel-winning French-Algerian author; known for absurdist works 'The Stranger' and 'The Plague;' famous non-fiction work claimed human existence to be Sisyphean

"First principle: never to let one's self be beaten down by persons or by events."

– Marie Curie, eminent Polish scientist; won Nobel prizes in both physics and chemistry, the first woman recipient and two-time winner; famed for work with diagnostic/therapeutic radiation

"Always choose the hardest way, on it you will not find opponents."

– Charles de Gaulle, iconic French president; military hero; nationalistic; often judged "arrogant" by allies; championed France's nuclear arms development program to ward off U.S. influence

"The truth is I've been the Hulk my whole life."

– Lou Ferrigno, award-winning American bodybuilder/actor/fitness trainer; winner of Mr. America and Mr. Universe titles; best known for portrayal of 'The Incredible Hulk'

"I am Maradona, who makes goals, who makes mistakes. I can take it all. I have shoulders big enough to fight with everybody."

– Diego Maradona, legendary Argentine footballer; arguably the best player of all time; notorious for 1986 World Cup "hand of God" goal; suffered from cocaine/ephedrine addictions

"They're going to aim the hoses on you, show 'em you won't expire. Not till you burn up every passion, not even when you die."

– Joni Mitchell, iconic Grammy-winning Canadian singer/songwriter; breakthrough album was 'Clouds;' successful in many music genres; says surviving childhood polio made her "a warrior"

"Unless you give it all you've got, there isn't any sense in playing."

– Stan Musial, Hall of Fame American baseball player; known as "The Man" for his batting power; played 22 years and was NL MVP three times; Presidential Medal of Freedom recipient

"I was the first person Donald Trump threatened to sue on Twitter."

– Lawrence O'Donnell, Emmy-winning American television writer/producer/host/author; known for his work on "The West Wing' and 'The Last Word;' has a reputation for caustic candor

"There are times when you have to face your enemies...deal with it."

– Martin Scorsese, prolific Oscar-winning American director; known for gritty character-driven dramas like 'Taxi Driver,' 'Raging Bull, and 'Goodfellas;' directed Michael Jackson's 'Bad' video

"It's important to push yourself further than you think you can go each and every day as that is what separates the good from the great."

– Kerri Strug, iconic American gymnast; her final vault with a damaged foot to win the 1996 Atlanta Olympics is considered among the most valorous sports moments of all time

"I hold a beast, an angel and a madman within me."

– Dylan Thomas, seminal Welsh poet/essayist; best known for his poem 'Do not go gentle into that good night;' died young from alcoholism; major writing awards are given in his honor

Sagittarius 3

A third lunation phase life is generally about contending with full-blown universal chaos or, at the very least, successfully facilitating a response to life's unending twists and turns. In almost all cases the life objective in the third lunation phase is discovering a way to summon poise in the face of what is experienced as constant external metamorphosis. Personal patience and a versatile approach to complexity are essential to life success.

This is a fair description of what a Sagittarius 3 confronts, although the emphasis here is slightly different. Oh, they know that life is a series of surprise bumps and bruises and they often have the scars to bear this out. Yet the difference for a Sagittarius 3 is that they find it impossible to accept that a propensity towards random crash and bang is all there is to learn about the universe; rather, their Sagittarius nature forces them to search for an organizing principle in human affairs which they eventually come to discover exists within.

As the storm of existence rages a Sagittarius 3 lives a life in search of a single guiding ethic, creed or principle that will let them exist in the eye of the hurricane. For a Sagittarius 3, all reality ultimately swirls around a central source of serene understanding. The key epiphany in this Sagittarius incarnation is that any chaos in reality is inevitably a manifestation of chaos within.

When manifested with grace this unflagging Sagittarius 3 commitment towards finding a wisdom arrow and shooting it into the center of a moving philosophical target has a capacity for creating cultural heroes. Tossed by chance they seem most acutely aware in the midst of their greatest predicaments, and it's hard for the rest of the world not to notice and cheer the fortitude this takes. One would almost think that life has meaning.

"Thought is creative. Be mindful of where your attention is, because the universe doesn't know the difference. It only knows where your focus is. Life will surely manifest where you put that attention."

– Christina Applegate, Emmy-winning American film/television actress; best known for comedies 'Married...with Children' and 'Anchorman;' breast cancer survivor and animal rights activist

"I just want you to be yourself. Be a bigger yourself."

– Tyra Banks, American supermodel/actress/producer/philanthropist; first black woman to represent Cover Girl cosmetics and appear on the cover of 'Sports Illustrated' swimsuit issue

"When God has something for you, it doesn't matter who stands against it."

– Chadwick Boseman, award-winning American actor/director/writer; best known as the Black Panther; also has played historical black heroes such as Jackie Robinson and Thurgood Marshall

"Music isn't only a profession."

– Jose Carreras, world-renowned Spanish operatic tenor; famous for being one of the 'Three Tenors;' defeated leukemia and created a foundation to fight the disease

"As an artist, I feel that we must try many things–but above all we must dare to fail. Say what you are. Not what you would like to be. Not what you have to be. Just say what you are. And what you are is good enough."

– John Cassavetes, award-winning American actor/director/writer; best known as the innovative director of "fiercely independent" films such as 'Shadows' and 'A Woman Under the Influence'

"I played my best every day. You never know when someone may be seeing you play for the first time."

– Joe DiMaggio, legendary American HOF baseball player; star of Yankee team that won nine World Series; famed for 56-game hit streak; married to Marilyn Monroe; Mr. Coffee pitchman

"That is beautiful which is produced by the inner need, which springs from the soul."

– Wassily Kandinsky, famed Russian avant-garde artist; known as "the father of abstract art;" first to theoretically articulate colors and abstract forms as reflective of an artist's inner life

"I did what I felt, and I felt what I did, at all costs."

– Little Richard, seminal American musician/songwriter; self-proclaimed "architect of rock and roll;" among the first R&R HOF inductees; Grammy lifetime achievement award recipient

"Be yourself. No one can say you're doing it wrong."

– Charles M. Schulz, legendary American cartoonist; creator of 'Peanuts,' a 50-year long strip that ran in over 2,600 newspapers in 75 countries and became a global multi-media franchise

"I've made films that I've given all I had to, that no one has seen. The bottom line is I want to work and I want someone to enjoy it."

– Kiefer Sutherland, award-winning British-Canadian actor/producer/director; known best for coming of age roles and as agent Jack Bauer on '24;' released his own country music album

"Focus more on your desire than on your doubt, and the dream will take care of itself."

– Mark Twain (Samuel Clemens), famous American author/entrepreneur/adventurer/inventor; known best for the adventures of Tom Sawyer and Huckleberry Finn; invented the bra strap

"I want to be a joy to people through my work."

– Gianni Versace, world-renowned Italian fashion designer; known for his daring fashions and grand lifestyle; pioneered fashion's celebrity/supermodel culture; murdered by a serial killer

 Capricorn 3

The craziness of the third lunation phase can only be matched in intensity by the desire the average Capricorn 3 has to get on top of the dog pile. While there may be a whiff of some abstract artistic, spiritual or humanitarian urge here, it is the rare Capricorn 3 who will operate outside the realm of practical purpose and with a goal other than worldly success. Whatever passion may bloom in their spirit, the Capricorn 3 is almost always preoccupied with a life of achievement the real world, even a world as intensely unstable as one finds in the third lunation phase.

It's not just thriving in a difficult world that is a turn on to a Capricorn 3. More to the point is the process and satisfaction of becoming a captain on a stormy sea; in other words getting to the point where one can exercise some authority and maybe even be addressed as "your majesty" while the rest of the world bends a grateful supplicating knee. One thing that is sure is that you will hear no apology from these folks for their ambition.

In fact, there is often a fair amount of arrogance to the Capricorn 3 personality. They can have real self-awareness and a rich sense of humor about what they are, but this does not mitigate who they are. Capricorn 3's are souls in search of cultural primacy and their natural tendency is to look down on the world at the same time as they look towards the heavens.

In dealing with a Capricorn 3 one tends to take an impression of resourcefulness. What it pays to keep in mind is that all resources are fair game to them. Life may be ladder on shaky ground, in the Capricorn 3 view, but they are climbers and you can't help but look like a step to them.

"There's only one Elizabeth like me and that's the Queen."

– Elizabeth Arden, Canadian-born businesswoman; famous for building an upscale international cosmetics empire; owned thoroughbred horses including a Kentucky Derby winner

"People who think they know everything are a great annoyance to those of us who do."

– Isaac Asimov, distinguished Russian-American writer/biochemistry professor; lauded for both straight science and fiction; his 'Foundation' series won Hugo award for "best all-time SF series"

"Someone had to change the world. And obviously I was the one for the job."

– Joan Baez, iconic American folk singer/activist; the "Queen of Folk;" recipient of the Grammy Lifetime Achievement award; highly honored for her work in a broad array of social causes

"It's nice to see that look of alarm on the faces of the others."

– Graham Chapman, iconic English comedian/actor/author; known best for work as a member of 'Monty Python' in whose skits/movies he often played authority figures; gay rights activist

"I look at myself as a product of my choices, not a victim of my circumstances."

– Kellyanne Conway, successful American pollster/political consultant; best known as campaign manager/advisor to President Donald Trump; famed for creating term "alternative facts"

"Success ... seems to be connected with action. Successful men keep moving. They make mistakes, but they don't quit."

– Conrad Hilton, pioneering American businessman/humanitarian; founded a hotel empire; left 99% of his estate to the Hilton Foundation whose mission is to "alleviate human suffering"

"I'm going to use all my tools, my God-given ability, and make the best life I can with it."

– Lebron James, all-time great professional basketball player/entrepreneur; nicknamed "King James;" was an immediate pro star out of high school; established active charitable foundation

"When writing, I model all the heroes after myself. Of course, it's hard to make them quite as wonderful as I am, but I come as close as I can."

– Stan Lee, HOF American comic book writer; most famous for co-creating Marvel heroes like Spider-Man and Thor; contractually obligated to do cameos in Marvel movies

"Erica Kane is probably the best role ever written for a woman."

– Susan Lucci, Emmy-winning American actress/entrepreneur; dubbed the "Queen of Daytime;" nominated 19 times for an Emmy before winning; was highest salaried actor in daytime TV

"I'm sharp. What the street taught me how to do is how to hustle...how to make something out of nothing."

– Pitbull, Grammy-winning American rapper/songwriter/producer/entrepreneur; also known as 'Mr. Worldwide;' shrugs at "sellout" criticism of his many corporate endorsement deals

"You've got to be a little vicious. You've got to be narcissistic. You've got to be on fire about your career."

– Howard Stern, iconic award-winning American media personality/author/actor/producer; self-titled "King of All Media;" best known for his "shock jock" radio style; an OCD sufferer

"I look at what I have as a challenge and I could list a whole bunch of different challenges. And I choose not to be daunted by any of them."

– Justin Trudeau, 23rd prime minister of Canada; identified with "liberal" causes such as LGBTQ rights, addressing climate change, and accepting refugees; famously athletic and good-looking

Aquarius 3

Given their propensity for telling the whole truth, Aquarians can be experienced as very annoying human beings. Failing to notice that the rest of us may occasionally be fond of a little self-serving fact-bending, and that we cannot always keep up to their rapid computational frequency, an Aquarius can generate a pretty good headache in service to awareness. And in all truth, being surrounded by the chaotic circumstances of the third lunation phase does not make for a mellower passage of the Aquarius 3 among us.

From the Aquarius 3 perspective life is an enormous data dump and they are here to write the algorithms of successful living or at the very least a worthwhile survival. One might even argue that the crazier the world gets the more an Aquarius 3 is compelled to reveal behavioral truth...well, their truth anyway...to the rest of us. They do mean well, but their vaguely alien holistic thinking does tend to get a little trippy along the way.

To look at it another way, if every human being has a filter through which reality is viewed the Aquarius 3 has cornered the market on lens cleaner. Acting from a place remarkably devoid of prejudice and preconception, they give their forthright take on what is right, what is wrong, and what is possible. In this regard they are sometimes given gifts that border on the magical.

Are Aquarius 3's so sure of their clarity that they can become rude and pushy and self-righteous? Sometimes yes. Given the way that a third lunation phase life can so often take on the attributes of a demolition derby, however, they are also truly inspiring.

"How I hate those who are dedicated to producing conformity."

– William S. Burroughs, iconic American author/painter/narrator; identified with the Beat Generation; one-time junkie known best for 'Naked Lunch,' a dark exploration of drug culture

"No matter how chaotic it is, wildflowers will still spring up in the middle of nowhere."

– Sheryl Crow, Grammy-winning American singer/songwriter; her music contains elements of pop, rock, folk, country and blues; has sung backup for many famous singers; cancer survivor

"Human beings have an inalienable right to invent themselves."

– Germaine Greer, influential Australian writer/academician; a "second wave" feminist; known best for 'The Female Eunuch,' a study of female disempowerment in contemporary family life

"A lot of times, I can turn and pass without even looking."

– Wayne Gretzky, HOF Canadian hockey player/coach/businessman; "The Great One;" all-time NHL scoring leader; named by 'Sports Illustrated' as most dominant player ever in any sport

"I may have my faults, but being wrong ain't one of them."

– Jimmy Hoffa, infamous American labor leader; president of the International Brotherhood of Teamsters; imprisoned on various charges; pardoned by Nixon; vanished in presumed mob 'hit'

"Let's face it; God has a big ego problem. Why do we always have to worship him?"

– Bill Maher, Emmy-winning American talk show host/satirist/author/producer/political commentator; known for controversial wit and candor; animal rights activist

"You cannot be serious!"

– John McEnroe, American HOF tennis champion/commentator; was #1 men's player four years in a row; named "Superbrat" by English tabloids he was as famed for his tantrums as his tennis

"I never missed a putt in my mind."

– Jack Nicklaus, American HOF golfer/businessman; considered by many to be the best of all time; won 18 major championships; a major philanthropist, particularly in children's healthcare

"Happiness is where you start from rather than where you go. God, I sound like Yoda."

– Simon Pegg, award-winning English actor/screenwriter/director/producer; known best for his creative efforts in offbeat comedies like 'Shaun of the Dead' and 'Hot Fuzz;' a vocal feminist

"The secret of success is to be fully awake to everything about you."

– Jackson Pollock, iconic American artist; central figure of the abstract expressionist movement; became publically dismissive of other artists; controversy and alcoholism shadowed his life

"Who I am is the best I can be."

– Leontyne Price, internationally-acclaimed American operatic soprano; first black prima donna at New York's Metropolitan Opera; celebrated for televised performances; civil rights activist

"This is something I consider Enlightenment to be–and that is to give intellectual or spiritual understanding and to be free of ignorance, false beliefs or prejudice. Able to honor each person as they walk their own path and not infringe our own personal beliefs onto them but to accept whatever form that carries truth for them"

– Jane Seymour, award-winning English actress/writer/entrepreneur; known best for lead roles in TV dramas; was a 'Bond Girl;' created "social impact accelerator" Open Hearts foundation

Pisces 3

If a third lunation phase life is sort of a carnival fun house, it's not always particularly fun for a Pisces. It's not that a Pisces 3 can't lead a good life and accomplish great things. There's just an extraordinary sensitivity to these folks that can curdle a bit when everything in existence appears as if in a distorted mirror.

To be deeply honest, it's a little hard to anticipate who Pisces 3's are or what they might become. Avoiding linear paths and eschewing great chunks of what others might call reality, they tend to cast their lot into an oceanic consciousness freely roamed by saints and poets and monsters and everything in between. "Absolutely true," would be their reply if told that possessing consciousness and living in the material world...particularly a Pisces consciousness in a third lunation phase world...seldom makes sense.

And so one encounters a considerable variety of character twists and turns here, ranging from art to artifice and from great spirituality to suicidal thoughts. The truest expression of Pisces 3 character might be empathy, as they have a lot of room in their protean consciousness to try on the reality experienced by others. Just don't ask them to reveal too much of their worldview and the participation of their own inner selves...it's pretty strange to listen to and they don't particularly understand it or want to talk about it themselves.

"A person incapable of imaging another world than given to him by his senses would be subhuman and a person who identifies his imaginary world with the world of sensory fact has become insane."

– W. H. Auden, Pulitzer-winning English poet/author/playwright/teacher; obsessed with "unseen psychological effects" and the potential for social revolution vested in people's hearts

"I've always loved butterflies, because they remind us that it's never too late to transform ourselves."

– Drew Barrymore, award-winning American actress/director/screenwriter/ philanthropist; famous at age 7 for her role in 'E.T.;' drug/alcohol addicted in youth; romantic comedy star

"The more we mask ourselves, the freer we're able to be within ourselves."

– Emily Blunt, prolific award-winning British actress/humanitarian; known for role versatility; conquered an irrepressible stammer in youth; honored for her contributions to the Malala Fund

"No matter what you do or say, there's nothing that you can do to make people understand you."

– Kurt Cobain, iconic Grammy-winning American 'alternative' musician; co-founder of the band Nirvana and the Seattle grunge scene; wrote his suicide note to an imaginary childhood friend

"I don't see the world completely in black and white. Sometimes I do."

– Benicio Del Toro, Oscar-winning Puerto Rico-born actor/activist; known for intense/oddball characters; was a Bond villain at age 21; signature traits are mumbling and dark eyes

"Dreams become reality when we put our minds to it."

– Queen Latifah, Grammy/Golden Globe/Emmy-winning American actress/ musician/producer; Latifah means "delicate and sensitive" in Arabic; a Cover Girl spokesperson; private personal life

"I always wanted to play tennis. Otherwise, I always thought it would be fun to do something in mathematics or physics."

– Ivan Lendl, HOF Czech-American tennis player; ranked #1 in world for 270 weeks; winner of 8 Grand Slam titles; post-career life dedicated to playing golf and hanging out with his dog

"Reality is something you rise above."

– Liza Minnelli, Oscar/Tony/Grammy-winning American actress/singer/philanthropist; only Oscar-winner to have Oscar-winning parents; famous for 'Cabaret;' heavy addiction history

"Not every person is going to understand you and that's okay. They have a right to their opinion and you have every right to ignore it."

– Joel Osteen, charismatic American televangelist/author; pastor of Houston's 50,000-member Lakewood Church; preaches a "prosperity gospel," linking faith practice to material reward

"I do get cynical, but what can you do? It doesn't make any difference."

– Kurt Russell, award-winning American actor; known for rugged hero/anti-hero roles in films such as 'Escape from New York' and 'Tombstone;' he is a libertarian and an avid gun enthusiast

"The word philosophy simply means a pursuit of wisdom, the purpose of life, and a search for Truth. However, this quest, because it originates with man, can never find the answers. In fact, man cannot reach God or know God by intellectual pursuit."

– Jimmy Swaggart, influential American evangelist/media personality/gospel musician; endured devastating sex scandal in the 1990's, but engineered rebound via chain of cable/radio outlets

"Dreams come true; without that possibility nature would not incite us to have them."

– John Updike, Pulitzer-winning American novelist/poet/literary critic; best known for his 'Rabbit' novels; interested in the cultural breakdown of the everyman; stammered in childhood

4th Lunation Phase/Waxing Gibbous Moon

Moon is 136 to 180 degrees ahead of Sun

Keyword: Thought

At this stage in the reincarnation cycle the power of the mind to effectively filter reality begins to emerge. This is a lifetime of going to school, at least figuratively. The LP4 soul serves a thought-focused apprenticeship in how the individual's ability to perceive and think may serve the ways and needs of personal and cultural evolution.

To be sure this is a nascent phase of intelligence, and the work towards recognizing awareness and making a useful plan is often clumsy, slow, arduous, comical, and for much of one's life inconclusive. The LP4 soul is most often inclined to come up with something beneficial for self and useful for mankind, but the questions of what and why are especially tricky for the soul watching itself learn how to think. These individuals can be part of the most elegant and liberating and joyful efforts of their culture, but there is generally much navel gazing and more than a few cerebral pratfalls and delays on the road to personal epiphany.

The real obstacle in an LP4 life is the difficulty in reconciling mind and spirit. Mind is dominant in the LP4 phase, but it is always the underlying soul that is calling the shots. It is in understanding this truth, and in learning the mental gymnastics requisite of service to the soul, that the LP4 life comes to real fruition.

"I am, therefore I think," is a reasonable mantra.

Aries 4

An Aries will almost always have a bias towards action, regardless of the lunation phase. The quirk in an Aries 4 existence is that they will inevitably take at least a short moment to assemble facts and consider the playing field from a strategic vantage. Only then, when the capsule has been loaded with discernment, are they ready to do the Aries thing of firing off like a rocket hell-bent for Mars.

Lest that invocation of the nether world cause trouble, an Aries 4 is not inclined towards such evils as mean-spiritedness or confrontation for confrontation's sake. On the contrary, an Aries 4 is often genuinely concerned with discovering an action or active point of view that is to the greater benefit of one's fellow humans. Yet there is no mistaking that we are not dealing here with philosophy for philosophy's sake, but with a desire to launch the world into righteous action.

A good description for Aries 4 might be "information age warrior" (regardless of the historical era in which he/she resides). Blessed with that boundless Aries energy, the Aries 4 needs to dive right in and collect ALL the facts within range of one's perception and intelligence. These will be assembled, usually quickly, into a persuasive and potent cultural concept that depending on one's vantage point might prove to be constructive or destructive...you can be the judge.

Just be advised that there is often a lot of real learning and rarely much timidity to an Aries 4. They will press the boundaries of the status quo and fight for their truth when they see a good reason for it. And, of course, sometimes they will fight just for the hell of it because even a thinking Aries is an Aries.

"You don't need another person, place or thing to make you whole. God already did that. Your job is to know it."

– Maya Angelou, highly honored American author/poet/actress/civil rights activist; known best for her autobiographical work; inaugural poet for Bill Clinton; Medal of Freedom recipient

"There's less critical thinking going on in this country on a Main Street level–forget about the media–than ever before. We've never needed people to think more critically than now, and they've taken a big nap."

– Alec Baldwin, Oscar/Golden Globe/Emmy/Tony-winning American actor/writer/producer; specializes in morally challenged protagonists; famous for impersonating Donald Trump on SNL

"The number one benefit of information technology is that it empowers people to do what they want to do. It lets people be creative. It lets people be productive. It lets people learn things they didn't think they could learn before, and so in a sense it is all about potential."

– Steve Ballmer, iconic high-energy American businessman/investor/philanthropist; co-founder and CEO of Microsoft; owner of the L.A. Clippers; avid supporter of educational causes

"My rule of thumb is that if I am interested or intrigued by something, others will be as well."

– Wolf Blitzer, Emmy-winning American journalist/author/television anchor; best known for his work on CNN's 'The Situation Room;' passionate about objectively reporting all sides of a story

"You want to be interesting? Be interested."

– James Franco, award-winning American actor/director/writer; known for good looks and offbeat 'cultish' roles; devoted to higher education; as a youth fired twice for reading at work

"An artist, if he is truly an artist, is only interested in one thing and that is to wake up the minds of men, to have mankind and womankind realize that there is something greater than what we see on the surface."

– Marvin Gaye, iconic American R&B singer/songwriter/producer; nicknamed "The Prince of Soul;" earned Grammy Lifetime Achievement award; risked career over 'What's Going On'

"I have a hard time visualizing anything, which is why I'm not a director, and which is why I try to work with ones I know have a strong idea in mind."

– Catherine Keener, award-winning American actress; known for quirky cerebral characters in indie films; planned to be a nun until expulsion from Catholic school for "rebellious tendencies"

"Our society thrives increasingly on stupidity. It depends on people going along with whatever they are told."

– Anton Szandor LaVey, American author/musician/occultist; founder of the Church of Satan; author of 'The Satanic Bible;' was the devil in 'Rosemary's Baby;' philosophical and humanistic

"I became a journalist to come as close as possible to the heart of the world."

– Henry R. Luce, pioneering American magazine publisher; co-creator of the Time-Life media empire; arguably the most influential citizen of his day; passionate about educating the public

"Develop interest in life as you see it; in people, things, literature, music. The world is so rich, simply throbbing with rich treasures, beautiful souls and interesting people. Forget yourself."

– Henry Mancini, famed American music composer; won four Oscars and 20 Grammies; scored 81 movies including 'Breakfast at Tiffany's' and 'Pink Panther;' was a global concert attraction

"All objects, all phases of culture are alive. They have voices. They speak of their history and interrelatedness. And they are all talking at once!"

– Camille Paglia, prominent American academic/social critic/feminist; extremely outspoken and iconoclastic on the nature of sexuality; academically an interdisciplinary classicist

"I feel so free and open to ideas, and I get inspired by everything."

– Amy Sedaris, award-winning American actress/comedian/writer; best known as Jenny Blank on 'Strangers with Candy,' Princess Carolyn on 'Bojack Horseman;' writes comical self-help books

 Taurus 4

Rarely is there anything in the life of a Taurus 4 that can be described as entirely abstract or of facile purpose. These are folks who above all else make the effort to navigate with material purpose in the real world. Figurative beasts of burden, it is only when they have busted some sod and actually put some mileage under their hooves that they are prepared to make a communal effort towards insight and understanding.

Certainly a Taurus 4 will often have a truth, most often a deeply personal one tied to finding one's peace via passion. As the fourth lunation phase is about the mind's ability to conceptualize and communicate, the Taurus 4 is ultimately inclined to share an epiphany or two along these lines. It's just that these epiphanies will be carefully measured and hardly ever along the lines that life is essentially a thinker's game.

It is this very inclination away from the primacy of thought that makes a Taurus 4 so interesting, if also a little incarnation conflicted. If there is an active self-advocacy here it is the inner imprecation to move away from the head towards the heart and the joys of sensation. Their coding is to find a life of passion and purpose, to immerse themselves in their joys and sorrows and, afterwards perhaps, to let others know about it.

Ultimately, it is easy to recognize the Taurus 4 as one who takes the long view. Time is only made relevant by what the spirit masters and passion keeps alive. The fleeting thought engendered by today's events is simply punctuation.

"Feelings are much stronger than thoughts. We are all led by instinct, and our intellect catches up later."

– Bono, highly lauded Irish singer/songwriter/venture capitalist/humanitarian; known best as lead singer/lyricist of HOF rock band U2; has been nominated for a Nobel Peace Prize

"It is true that I have had heartache and tragedy in my life. These are things none of us avoids. Suffering is the price of being alive."

– Judy Collins, Grammy-winning American folk &pop artist/writer/activist; memorable records include 'Both Sides Now' and 'Send in the Clowns;' contributor to many social welfare causes

"You've got to experience failure to understand that you can survive it."

– Tina Fey, award-winning American comedian/actress/writer/producer/philanthropist; known best for work on 'SNL' and '30 Rock;' funds a scholarship in father's name to support veterans

"My definition of success is doing what you love. I feel many people do things because they feel they have to and are hesitant to risk following their passion."

– Tony Hawk, iconic American athlete/entrepreneur; the world's most significant skateboarder; winner of over 70 competitions including two X-Games; owns successful skateboard company

"If you are not doing what you love, you are wasting your time."

– Billy Joel, Grammy Legend HOF American singer/songwriter; has had 33 Top 40 hits; named a music "franchise" at New York's Madison Square Garden; active musical education advocate

"Your goal is not to battle with the mind, but to witness the mind."

– Swami Muktananda, esteemed Indian spiritualist; sometimes referred to as "the guru's guru;" identified with ritual meditation; popular in America; dogged by ethical/sexual controversy

"There are teachers and students with square minds who are by nature meant to undergo the fascination of categories. For them, 'schools' and 'movements' are everything; by painting a group symbol on the brow of mediocrity, they condone their own incomprehension of true genius."

– Vladimir Nabokov, renowned Russian-American novelist/chess expert; famous for 'Lolita' and 'Pale Fire;' literary style characterized as "ecstatic;" an inventor of "poetic" chess problems

"People who speak in metaphors should shampoo my crotch."

– Jack Nicholson, iconic three-time Oscar-winning American actor/writer/director; famous for his wicked smile and rich screen portrayal of eccentrics; complicated history; avoids TV talk shows

"For me, punk is about real feelings. It's not about, 'Yeah, I am a punk and I'm angry.' That's a lot of crap. It's about loving the things that really matter: passion, heart and soul."

– Joey Ramone, Grammy HOF American punk rocker; known best as the lead singer of the hugely influential Ramones; suffered from severe OCD; rumored to have died listening to U2

"The only things worth learning are the things you learn after you know it all."

– Harry S. Truman, 33rd president of the USA; plain spoken; succeeded FDR just 82 days into his VP term; authorized the atom bombing of Hiroshima/Nagasaki to end WWII; anti-Communist

"Nothing is worthy of man as man unless he can pursue it with passionate devotion."

– Max Weber, eminent German sociologist/political economist; famed for theory praising the link between ascetic Protestantism and capitalism; pioneered bureaucratic management theory

"I'm here to build something for the long-term. Anything else is a distraction."

– Mark Zuckerberg, prominent American internet entrepreneur/ philanthropist; co-founder/CEO of Facebook; youngest ever Fortune 500 CEO; 50% of lifetime wealth is pledged to charity

 Gemini 4

The 4th lunation phase is a lifetime in which the power of thought dominates. How resonant this is for a Gemini, a sign identified with a sharp mind and a facility for personal expression. Talk about being in one's element!

As with other Gemini's, the Gemini 4 has an inherent bias towards understanding reality as painted in shades of grey. Perceive deeply enough and every fact has its counter-fact. Ultimate truths, particularly as grounded in subjective moral codes or passionate emotional compulsions, are rarely if ever pure and inviolable.

For a Gemini, whose power is at an apotheosis in the fourth lunation phase, there is frequently an impulse to outmaneuver the world with one's mind. If facts are personal and somewhat arbitrary and if therefore nothing is ultimately true, reasons the Gemini 4, the one who wins the prize is the one who can most cogently frame the argument. Their own talk, whether they actually are committed to the truth what they are saying, is never cheap to a Gemini 4.

Alas, working from the thesis that everyone else can be manipulated does sometimes cause a Gemini 4 to wander down a culturally abrasive path. Nobody likes to be taken for stupid, and that is a charge that a Gemini 4 can dish out with total alacrity. In the worst cases Gemini 4 can come across as insufferably self-superior.

What one might keep in mind is that, as with all 4th lunation phase lives, the Gemini 4 life is preparation for an incarnation in which the soul just absolutely shoves the mind off its pedestal. That's an extraordinary impending change here. Life can be so interesting.

"Don't play what's there, play what's not there."

– Miles Davis, essential American jazz trumpeter/composer/bandleader; earned Grammy HOF and Lifetime Achievement recognitions; known for acerbic takes on just about everything

"The two most common elements in the universe are hydrogen and stupidity."

– Harlan Ellison, award-winning American author/television writer; leading voice in 'New Wave' science fiction; only three-time winner of the Nebula Award; known for his abrasive personality

"It doesn't matter what I do. People need to hear what I have to say. There's no one else who can say what I can say. It doesn't matter what I live."

– Newt Gingrich, iconic American politician/author/media analyst/entrepreneur; served as House Speaker; led conservative "Contract with America" movement; history of ethics charges

"I'm lucky that people believe me when I'm in character."

– Neil Patrick Harris, Emmy and Tony-winning American actor/writer/producer/singer/magician; key role was Doogie Howser M.D.; popular awards show host; openly gay and a father of twins

"Regrets are ridiculous, so I don't regret, no."

– Nicole Kidman, Oscar-winning Australian actress/producer/humanitarian; recognized for work in a variety of genres; named a U.N. Citizen of the World; adventurous but afraid of butterflies

"It is not a matter of what is true that counts, but a matter of what is perceived to be true."

– Henry Kissinger, Nobel laureate American statesman/educator/political consultant; Secretary of State under Nixon and Ford; described as "brilliant," "complicated," "abrasive," "self-serving"

"In a perfect world, there would be no censorship, because there would be no judgment."

– Alanis Morissette, Grammy-winning Canadian singer/songwriter/musician/ actress; known best for album 'Jagged Little Pill;' was God in the film 'Dogma;' started writing at age 10

"For all of nature's wonder and beauty, it is also hostile and unpredictable."

– Liam Neeson, charismatic North Ireland actor; known for roles as either an avenging hero or an arch villain; was a boxer and a forklift operator; his first film role was Jesus Christ

"I would rather be without a state than without a voice."

– Edward Snowden, infamous American computer programmer/political fugitive; former CIA employee; leaked classified NSA info regarding surveillance practices; granted Russian asylum

"I have an attention span that's as long as it has to be."

– Donald Trump, famed American real estate developer/entrepreneur/ politician/television personality; 45th American president, his first government job; outspoken and divisive

"I never lie. I believe everything I say, so it's not a lie."

– Mark Wahlberg, award-winning American actor/producer/singer/model/ writer/businessman; known for raucous/sexy public persona; troubled past includes prison and charges of bigotry

"Life is hard; it's harder if you're stupid."

– John "Duke" Wayne, legendary Oscar-winning American actor; famed for heroic/stoic roles, particularly in Westerns and war films; Stalin put out a hit on him for his anti-Communist views

 Cancer 4

Cancer 4 lives a life that is a bit of a conundrum. Emotional/ instinctive by nature, Cancers in the fourth lunation phase are presented with a strong directive to think about life. In their efforts to conceptualize and articulate 'truth' they are driven to some pretty passionate explanations regarding what it's all about.

Considered collectively, it's hard to avoid the description "tough minded." This is because a Cancer 4 is not ultimately concerned with life as a series of facts. A Cancer judges truth to be something other than knowing what is irrefutably true, unless by knowing one is referring to an honest reckoning of character and manifesting the will to express it.

Cancer 4 thoughts, in other words, rise from somewhere deep down around the gut. The decision one makes is to express one's will, in spite of anything and everything that might put up intellectual resistance. The goal for most Cancer 4's is not riches or popularity, although these may accrue in the wake of fierce revelation and effort, but rather the satisfaction one obtains from knowing one has made a decision to fearlessly give their all.

Alas, when one's mind is so consciously assigned a lesser role, mistakes can be made and dangerous boundaries crossed. Cancer 4 lives may circle the periphery of tragedy and sometimes dive right in. In all though, the Cancer 4 lives a life that establishes the difference between words and action.

No apologies will be made.

"Darkness feeds on apathy."

– Dan Brown, prolific American author; known for intricately plotted thrillers such as the 'Da Vinci Code;' fascinated by the interplay of science and religion; reputedly never takes a day off

"What use is my mind? Granted it enables me to hail a bus and to pay my fare. But once I am inside my studio, what use is my mind? I have my model, my pencil, my paints. My mind doesn't interest me."

– Edgar Degas, world-renowned French artist; famous for depicting dancers and movement; a founder of Impressionism; reputation has suffered from charges of misogyny and anti-Semitism

"Nothing comes easy when I'm in character, because everything I do in character, I take seriously."

– Vin Diesel, iconic American actor/screenwriter/director/producer; known for tough-guy hero roles in movies such 'The Fast and the Furious' and 'Chronicles of Riddick;' mom is an astrologer

"Throughout my career I've played a lot of parts that might've been played by a man. They're human roles rather than specifically men or women. I've never been as hooked into that as a lot of women are, you know, like, 'There aren't enough roles for women.' There aren't necessarily a lot of good roles for anybody."

– Edie Falco, Emmy-winning American actress; known best for TV series 'The Sopranos' and 'Nurse Jackie;' Buddhist; describes her work as "intrinsic" as opposed to "intellectual"

"I've seen John Wayne's 'True Grit' about 10 times."

– John Glenn, American hero Marine aviator/astronaut/businessman/ politician;1st American to orbit the earth; at age 77 the oldest person to walk in space; U.S. Senator; married for 73 years

"Appreciate hard work and the process of hard work. Because after that's over and you get the rewards of success, you look back on these moments and you respect those moments the best."

– Kevin Hart, award-winning American actor/comedian/producer/humanitarian; breakout was his 'Laugh at My Pain' comedy tour/album/television special; marathon running enthusiast

"There is nothing to writing. All you do is sit down at a typewriter and bleed."

– Ernest Hemingway, Nobel and Pulitzer winning American author/journalist/sportsman; known for his austere style ("the iceberg theory"); WW II Bronze Star recipient; life ended by suicide

"If you want to be the best you have to do things that other people aren't willing to do."

– Michael Phelps, distinguished American athlete; competed as Olympic swimmer at age 15; holder of all-time Olympic gold medal record; major celebrity endorser; suffers from ADHD

"Only you can judge your life. You have to live up to your own expectations."

– Wolfgang Puck, legendary Austrian-American restaurateur/chef/author/television personality/humanitarian; introduced 'nouvelle cuisine' at L.A.'s Ma Maison and Spago

"I'm not just the young girl everybody thinks I am. I'm actually a woman."

– Ashley Tisdale, award-winning American actress/singer/producer; achieved fame on Disney Channel, particularly in 'High School Musical;' her first music album was titled 'Headstrong'

"Fighting is not physical, fighting is spiritual. It's the determination and the will in the guy."

– Mike Tyson, iconic American boxer; nicknamed "Iron Mike;" known for ferociousness; became youngest ever world heavyweight champion; marked by notorious behavior inside/outside ring

"I have a desperate longing to have a desperate longing."

– Joss Whedon, iconic American screenwriter/director/producer; work includes 'The Avengers,' 'Buffy the Vampire Slayer' and 'Firefly;' known for witty dialogue and strong female characters

 Leo 4

A Leo 4 lives by a principle that can seem downright magical. If one has an incandescent spirit then one can think themselves to wherever they need to go. It may not be a straight shot, and there always might be aspects of fate that blow out a tire or two, but a satisfactory arrival is somehow inevitable.

To be sure, for any Leo to accept that life is essentially a dark place would be tantamount to the Sun deciding not to shine. Even though forthright thinking is the hallmark of the fourth lunation phase, a Leo 4 is disinclined to formulate an outcome that is ultimately bleak. Whatever their origination circumstances, the Leo 4 thought process is inclined to a steadfast, one might even say a "mighty," optimism.

Whether their lives start off in poverty or are subject to various other forms of want and limitation, the charm of a Leo 4 is that they feel that somewhere along the way they deserve to be happy. They get that this can seem a joke from those on the outside looking in, but in no way are they merely whistling in the dark. They really intend a life in which extraordinary accomplishments, and occasionally a refreshing immersion in outright comedy, are available to the spirit bright enough to think happy thoughts.

A Leo 4 would prefer others to think the way they think, but they will not be stopped by those who don't. They will even go to great lengths to put smiles on grim faces. If you can't beat them, says the Leo 4, get real clever and make them smile.

"It's a helluva start, being able to recognize what makes you happy."

– Lucille Ball, beloved red-headed American comedian/actress/singer/model/businesswoman; known best as the star of "I Love Lucy;' first female head of a Hollywood production company

"I just know that something good is going to happen. I don't know when–but just saying it could even make it happen."

– Kate Bush, award-winning British singer/songwriter; known for imaginative and artistic "art rock;" debut 'Wuthering Heights' was the 1st British #1 song written and sung by a female artist

"Dreams are so important. You need to have big goals and expect a lot of yourself but you have to enjoy the ride too."

– Sidney Crosby, eminent Canadian hockey player; winner of multiple Olympic gold medals, NHL championships and top individual awards; youngest team captain in NHL history

"I just look at women sometimes and I just want to ask them, 'Do you know how fabulous you are?' I look back at pictures of myself and I remember thinking, 'I was so fat when I was growing up. I was 165 pounds when I graduated from high school. I was a mess.' And then I look back at pictures of myself, and I'm like, 'You were fabulous.' I wish I would have known that then."

– Viola Davis, iconic American actress; first black actor to win Oscar/Tony/Emmy trifecta; was raised in abject poverty; 'Time' named her one of the world's 100 most influential people

"A poor man is not the one without a cent. A poor man is the one without a dream."

– Henry Ford, world-famous American industrialist/philanthropist; founder of Ford Motors; credited with the creation of the assembly line and fair working wage; breast cancer crusader

"I make music because of the love and joy of it and I try to make music to take you to a feel-good place and remind you that maybe there's a brighter day."

– Joe Jonas, award-winning American singer/songwriter/actor; found fame as a Disney-featured Jonas Brother; lead singer of band DNCE; key supporter of 'Movember' men's health charity

"You dance love, and you dance joy, and you dance dreams. And I know if I can make you smile by jumping over a couple of couches or running through a rainstorm then I'll be very glad to be a song and dance man."

– Gene Kelly, legendary American actor/dancer/choreographer/director; known for athletic style; oft cited as "king of the musicals;" starred in 'Singin' in the Rain;' Grammy HOF honoree

"I can zero in on a vision of where I want to be in the future. I can see it so clearly in front of me, when I daydream, it's almost a reality. Then I get this easy feeling, and I don't have to be uptight to get there because I already feel like I'm there, that it's just a matter of time."

– Arnold Schwarzenegger, world-renowned Austrian-American actor/ filmmaker/businessman/ author/philanthropist/activist/politician/ professional bodybuilder; known as "The Governator"

"I have seen competent leaders who stood in front of a platoon and all they saw was a platoon. But great leaders stand in front of a platoon and see it as 44 individuals, each of whom has aspirations, each of who wants to live, each of whom wants to do good."

– Norman Schwarzkopf, esteemed American general; led coalition forces in Gulf War

"You can either look at things in a brutal, truthful way that's depressing, or you can screw around and have fun."

– David Spade, award-winning American actor/comedian/writer; rose to fame playing snarky characters on SNL and TV sitcoms; known best for 'Tommy Boy' partnership with Chris Farley

"As long as we dare to dream and don't get in the way of ourselves, anything is possible–there's truly no end to where our dreams can take us."

– Hilary Swank, Oscar-winning American film actress/entrepreneur; famed for heroic roles in 'Boys Don't Cry' and 'Million Dollar Baby;' founded Hilaroo charity to unite animals and children

"At first, I only laughed at myself. Then I noticed that life itself is amusing. I've been in a generally good mood ever since."

– Marilyn vos Savant, celebrity American smart-person/author/columnist/media personality; her 228 IQ is one of the highest ever recorded; admired for fun-loving lack of pretentiousness

 Virgo 4

Virgo is a sign known for its mostly rational processing of real world data, so the fourth lunation phase is for them a pretty good fit. On the plus side there is a high tolerance level for vast amounts of input. On the downside, people with aware minds are inevitably in danger of drowning in a truly bottomless sea of possibilities and peculiarities.

Most Virgo 4's cope with life by accepting that life is a life-long process. They recognize that minds must change and grow and adapt to odd pathways. Mistakes will be made and false conclusions reached, and triumph and despair are embroiled in the way one approaches the dynamics of growth and recovery.

So it is that many a Virgo 4 has an orientation towards fixing things that life can't help but breaking sometimes. Practice and tireless work are strongly identified here. Success is related to a focused passion, intelligent management and a willingness to take on the down and dirty work of situational triage.

Where Virgo 4's are particularly unique among their Sun sign brethren is in sometimes having a poetic/spiritual streak (astrological note: it is common for a Virgo 4 have a Moon in Pisces). This is obviously of some aid in trying to make peace with their logical selves, allowing for a healthy acceptance of the truly inexplicable to enter the equation. And yet one will ultimately know these Virgo 4 souls through the sincere practicality of their efforts, even as they hint at the emergent prophecies of a greater Soul.

"One person's craziness is another person's reality."

– Tim Burton, award-winning American director/producer/screenwriter/animator; known for dark fantasies like 'Beetlejuice' and Edward Scissorhands;' he celebrates the triumph of misfits

"The cutting of the gem has to be finished before you can see whether it shines."

– Leonard Cohen, Canadian poet/singer/songwriter; composed 'Hallelujah;' recipient of Grammy HOF/Lifetime Achievement awards; called "the poet of brokenness;" was a Buddhist monk

"The minute you think you know everything about tennis is the minute your game starts going down the tubes."

– Jimmy Connors, HOF American pro tennis player/coach; ranked #1 men's player for 160 weeks; won 8 grand slam events; known for his rude intensity; autobiography is titled 'The Outsider'

"Usually, about two years of work go into each illusion, whether it's big or small. Two years of work on each five-minute piece."

– David Copperfield, Emmy-winning American magician; considered the most commercially successful illusionist in history; famed for live presentation of Statue of Liberty's disappearance

"Even though I am extremely blessed to have accomplished many of my goals at such a young age, I am still reaching, still striving."

– Jennifer Hudson, Oscar and Grammy winning American singer/actress; known best for a shocking loss on 'American Idol' and her role in 'Dreamgirls;' a Weight Watchers ambassador

"It's a mistake to think that once you're done with school you need never learn anything new."

– Sophia Loren, Oscar-winning Italian actress; considered one of the world's most beautiful women; acted in over 100 films during a 60-year career; a Dolce & Gabbana brand icon

"Parents are not the all-knowing, ideal people we would like you to think we are. We've made wrong choices before, and will again, like everyone else. But our mistakes are not the measure of our love for you. You are that measure, and how well you are prepared to make better choices than we have made."

– John McCain, decorated American politician/naval aviator; a Viet Nam-era prisoner of war; long-term U.S. Senator and presidential candidate; one of the best-liked politicians of his era

"No one runs fast without an extreme amount of training. Like today, you see kids walking around dribbling a basketball. I had a bag with track shoes in it, and I used to go to the track every day."

– Edwin Moses, American gold-medal Olympic hurdler/physicist/sports diplomat; won 122 consecutive 400-meter races with four world records; prominent in drug testing science/policy

"You've got to learn your instrument. Then, you practice, practice, practice. And then, when you finally get up there on the bandstand, forget all that and just wail."

– Charlie "Bird" Parker, legendary Grammy-winning American jazz saxophonist/composer; a hugely influential creator of the bebop style; tragic substance abuse history led to early death

"I had my years of struggling. Some of my shows failed miserably, and I was upset by it and it dented my confidence. But I never stopped. I kept going for it."

– Regis Philbin, Emmy-winning American television personality; best known for his long-running talk show co-hosted with Kathy Lee Gifford; holds record for most television on-air hours

"Do your homework all of your life."

– Muriel Siebert, pioneering American investor/financial entrepreneur/philanthropist; first woman member of the New York Stock Exchange; devoted to the cause of financial literacy

"What a player does best, he should practice least. Practice is for problems."

– Duke Snider, HOF American baseball player/announcer/avocado farmer; famed as star center fielder of the Brooklyn Dodgers "Boys of Summer" team; beloved as "The Duke of Flatbush"

Libra 4

The path of a Libra 4 is most often perplexing. Like any of its Sun sign family, the Libra 4 is concerned with relating to others and, in a sincere manner, experiencing love. Where it all goes a little awry here, though, is that a Libra 4 generally processes the act of relating through a busy head rather than a peaceful heart.

This is not to absolutely decry such a situation. Libra 4's can be enormously smart when it comes to articulating the nature of relationships. There are also many instances when they can express the many varieties of grace (aesthetic, athletic, philosophical) so often associated with the incomparably balanced sign of The Scales.

Yet the Libra 4 exits in an incarnation before the emergence of the pure soul power that takes place in the fifth lunation phase. Theirs is the love garden that is a bit over tended by the capriciousness of observation and possibility and sometimes, alas, a fascination with perversion. The desire to be constant in affection, challenged by a mind hungry for experience, is not always matched by a heart strong enough to stick the landing.

As can be seen in the list of Libra 4 icons below, there is a tendency for these interesting souls to become objectified by the rest of society. There is a disproportionate lot of physical beauty and youthful sexuality that hovers around these souls. Their facility in messing up relationships may just be a comfort to those of us who are primarily involved with the magazines at the checkout counter.

"Everything I wrote about wasn't about me, but about the people listening."

– Chuck Berry, legendary HOF American rock & roller; famed for lead guitar and stylized stage moves; won Grammy HOF/Lifetime Achievement awards; numerous sexual depravity charges

"Confounding people's expectations was a way to maintain integrity."

– Lindsey Buckingham, Grammy-winning American musician/singer/songwriter; best known as lead guitarist/vocalist of Fleetwood Mac; life marked by complicated relationship issues

"What surprises me in life are not the marriages that fail, but the marriages that succeed."

– Rita Hayworth, iconic American actress/dancer/sex symbol; press nicknamed her "The Love Goddess;" fame came via a seductive WWII pinup photo; married five times; surprisingly shy

"I love when people underestimate me and then become pleasantly surprised."

– Kim Kardashian, iconic American celebrity/socialite/reality TV star; fame traced to Paris Hilton friendship and a viral sex tape; oft cited as famous for being famous; odd relationship history

"Like they say, you can learn more from a guide in one day than you can in three months fishing alone."

– Mario Lopez, Emmy-winning American actor/television personality/dancer/author; achieved teen fame on 'Saved by the Bell;' a 'People' hottest bachelor; often works with Kim Kardashian

"I came to live in a country I love; some people label me a defector. I have loved men and women in my life; I've been labeled the bisexual defector. Want to know another secret? I'm even ambidextrous. I don't like labels. Just call me Martina."

– Martina Navratilova, world-renowned HOF Czech tennis player/author/gay rights activist; considered by many to be the greatest tennis player of all time; won 59 'Slam' titles (18 singles)

"Some singers want the audience to love them. I love the audience."

– Luciano Pavarotti, world-famous Italian tenor; only opera star to win Grammy Legend award; renowned as "King of the High C's;" fond of popular music; known as a notorious philanderer

"Whatever will happen will happen, but choose your companions with care. Choose them because you like to look at them and you like the sound of their voices, and they have profound secrets in them that you wish to know. In other words, choose them because you love them. Otherwise you will not be able to bear their company for very long."

– Anne Rice, award-winning American author; best known for her series 'The Vampire Chronicles;' has sold over 100 million books in genres ranging from gothic to Christian to erotica

"It's not who wants to sleep with you; It's who wants to sleep with you again."

– David Lee Roth, iconic American rock vocalist/songwriter/author; best known as flamboyant lead singer of Van Halen; sex obsessed; called his penis "Little Elvis" and insured it for $1 million

"I think people want love in their lives."

– Alicia Silverstone, award-winning American actress; achieved teen idol status in Aerosmith rock videos; achieved fame as Cher in 'Clueless;' named PETA's "sexiest female vegetarian"

"Learn from the mistakes of others. You can't make them all yourself."

– Usher, Grammy-winning American singer/songwriter/actor; released first album at age 15; known for rap and R&B hits; founder of New Look youth-oriented charity; a prominent vegan

"If my revelation of having bipolar II has encouraged one person to seek help, then it is worth it. There is no need to suffer silently and there is no shame in seeking help."

– Catherine Zeta-Jones, Oscar-winning Welsh actress/singer/dancer; known for roles in films 'The Mask of Zorro' and 'Chicago;' she and husband Michael Douglas staged a $1.5M wedding

 Scorpio 4

A Scorpio life is far more about passion than thought, so the 4th lunation phase becomes a little tricky for them. They are simply not inclined by the solar force within them to bottom line anything because of the way it presents to their mind. The notion that "talk is cheap" has never found a more willing adherent than a Scorpio 4.

Still, this is an incarnation in which the mind and the communication of awareness must be dealt with. Scorpio 4's will marshal their thoughts to support causes about which they feel strongly. And they are more than up for a fight when they encounter concepts that they experience as hostile.

Actually, a Scorpio 4 is sort of infatuated with the things that present themselves as antagonistic. If we're talking about things that excite the mind, nothing is more interesting to a Scorpio 4 than an impediment to their will. Few things deliver more intellectual satisfaction than developing the means by which a foe is dispatched.

Ultimately, the pattern one often encounters in a Scorpio 4 life has to do with the encountering and engagement of dark experiences for the purpose of developing will. In this context the Scorpio 4 is steadfast in creating a message that the righteous will is not subject to outside influence and is in fact strengthened by adversity. They strive to be unbreakable.

Insofar as they are thinkers, they are the intellect's commandos. Scorpio 4's know their mind. They will not refrain from attempting to influence yours.

"Failure at some point in your life is inevitable, but giving up is unforgivable."

– Joe Biden, popular American lawyer/politician; U.S. vice president; Delaware's longest serving senator; Presidential Medal of Freedom recipient; personal life marred by multiple tragedies

"There's nothing like a jolly good disaster to get people to start doing something."

– Charles, Prince of Wales, environmentalist/philanthropist/screenwriter/artist; oldest and longest-serving heir-apparent in British history; served in both the RAF and Royal Navy

"It's only on the brink that people find the will to change. Only at the precipice do we evolve."

– John Cleese, Emmy and BAFTA award-winning British comedian/actor/screenwriter/producer; known for 'Monty Python' and 'Fawlty Towers;' corporate trainer; holds Cambridge law degree

"Always aim high, work hard, and care deeply about what you believe in. And, when you stumble, keep faith. And, when you're knocked down, get right back up and never listen to anyone who says you can't or shouldn't go on."

– Hillary Clinton, distinguished American attorney/politician/diplomat/author; First Lady of the U.S.; Sec'y of State; presidential candidate; won a Grammy for recording of 'It Takes a Village'

"No matter what you do next, the world needs your energy, your passion, your impatience for progress. Don't shrink from risk. And tune out those critics and cynics. History rarely yields to one person, but think, and never forget, what happens when it does. That can be you. That should be you. That must be you."

– Tim Cook, American business executive/industrial engineer; CEO of Apple; self-proclaimed workaholic with a "no mercy" personal style; first CEO of major company to come out as gay

"Yeah, September 11 happened and all my friends were like, 'Let's join the military!' and I was the only one who actually did."

– Adam Driver, award-winning American actor; rose to prominence in TV series 'Girls;' played a 'Star Wars' villain; served in the Marines; won't watch himself on screen; avoids social media

"Fear is where the information is."

– Sally Field, Oscar/Emmy/Golden Globe/SAG -winning American actress/director/activist; known for TV roles 'Gidget' and 'The Flying Nun;' movie roles feature strength of character

"Life is not fair; get used to it."

– Bill Gates, eminent American programmer/entrepreneur/executive/philanthropist; co-founder of Microsoft; one of the world's wealthiest people; named "most generous" U.S. philanthropist

"Almost every week, someone's mad at me."

– Jimmy Kimmel, Emmy-winning American television personality/producer; host of ABC's longest running late night talk show; once named "biggest badass on television;" known for candor

"Some of my lowest points were the most exciting opportunities to push through to be a better person."

– Demi Moore, award-winning American actress/producer; breakthrough role was in 'St. Elmo's Fire;' known for roles emphasizing body image/sexuality; her charity fights child sex trafficking

"Any idiot can be brave, but courage is about knowing what's at stake, and moving forward anyway."

– Meg Ryan, iconic American actress/producer; dubbed "America's Sweetheart" for work in romantic comedies; graphic sex scenes hurt career; passed on 'Ghost' and 'Pretty Woman'

"Everyone should be sacked at least once in their career because perfection doesn't exist. It's important to have setbacks, because that is the reality of life."

– Anna Wintour, British-American global fashion icon; editor of 'Vogue;' inspiration for the film 'The Devil Wears Prada;' frosty and fastidious; a Dame Commander of the British Empire

Sagittarius 4

Few souls of any Sun sign in any incarnation would entirely deny that the world can be a crazy place. Confronting this apparent universal truth drives many behaviors, each earnestly reflecting some coloration of embrace, confrontation and/or avoidance. Yet to the somewhat sanguine Sagittarius 4, perhaps more than to any other soul, the squirrely nature of human affairs is just the amusing way things go for the nuts in the consciousness forest.

This is not to say that a Sagittarius 4 is a silly person. On the contrary, these souls are particularly attuned to the shortcomings of the human mind in apprehending a spectacularly large universe. They are wide open to the inevitability of paradox and downright strangeness, and simply make a conscious decision to go with, rather than against, the flow.

While this Zen-like attitude certainly does not guarantee a life filled with success and happiness, it seems to have a salutary effect. It's noteworthy how many fourth lunation Sagittarians stumble across luck because they are not disposed to blocking energy with expectations regarding outcomes. Conversely, it's remarkable how many of them find their soul's true path, and a fair amount of success, early in their lives.

In fact the great epiphany of the Sagittarius 4 is that we are probably at our best, when it comes to the workings of the mind and spirit, as children. Even when fate bestows a fourth lunation phase life, a Sagittarius 4 recognizes that some things just don't need to be overthought or ponderously developed. Small wonder that many a Sagittarius 4 is devoted to child-centric philanthropic causes, for these are souls happy to advocate wherever innocent clarity and honest wonder need advocacy and protection.

"I think it would be great to play a nice, romantic-comedy type role, the sort with real dialogue. That's something I haven't really gotten to do, so far. It's probably not as fun as getting to kill people and being able to chase monsters and all of that, though."

– Amy Acker, award-winning American actress/model; best known for her offbeat characters in television series; trained as a dancer but hurt her knee; found immediate success as an actress

"People expect me to cry, but I always laugh when things go wrong."

– Christina Aguilera, Grammy-winning American singer/songwriter/actress/philanthropist; child star on 'The Mickey Mouse Club;' has a diva/control freak reputation; sexually emancipated

"If some crazy idea stays in my head for long enough, then there's no fighting it. I just say, 'Okay, let's go'."

– Jeff Bridges, iconic Oscar-winning American actor; best known as The Dude in 'The Big Lebowski;' famed for his "naturalness;" acting since he was a baby; founded 'No Kid Hungry'

"A perfect martini should be made by filling a glass with gin then waving it in the general direction of Italy."

– Noel Coward, award-winning English playwright/actor/composer/raconteur; known for his sophistication and acerbic wit; child actor/teen playwright; knighted By Queen Elizabeth II

"I think I do find humor in disorder, and reality is disorder."

– Julie Delpy, award-winning French-American actress/screenwriter/director/singer-songwriter; known for romantic trilogy 'Before Sunrise/Sunset/Midnight;' discovered by Godard at age 14

"I play a slave. How black is that? I have to wear chains. How whack is that? But don't worry. I get free. I save my wife and I kill all the white people in the movie. How great is that?"

– Jamie Foxx, Grammy/Oscar-winning American actor/comedian/musician; fame came via sketch comedy on 'In Living Color;' was Ray Charles in 'Ray;' created foundation for child aid

"I like both slapstick and contradiction. Like philosophers."

– Jean-Luc Godard, internationally-acclaimed French-Swiss movie director/ screenwriter/critic; a pioneer of the 1960's New Wave film movement; sometimes called an anti-film filmmaker

"Crazy people don't sit around wondering if they're nuts."

– Jake Gyllenhaal, award-winning American actor; breakthrough role came in cult hit 'Donnie Darko;' partial to complex character roles; an actor since childhood; a practicing Buddhist

"I started super young, but when I think about myself at that age–what I thought I knew, and how priggish I was, how certain of things–now I realize that nothing is certain."

– Milla Jovovich, award-winning American actress/model/musician; known for kick-butt roles in sci fi/action films; Leeloo in 'The Fifth Element;' was once the highest paid model in the world

"I've always believed in experiencing everything in life. When you walk out with blinders on, you cut yourself off from the angels and the fairies."

– Alyssa Milano, award-winning American actress/philanthropist; known best for role as witch in TV's 'Charmed;' at age 8 acted in national tour of 'Annie;' spokesperson for UNICEF and PETA

"This is the strangest life I've ever known."

– Jim Morrison, legendary Grammy-winning American rock singer/composer; leader of 'The Doors;' self-styled as the shamanistic 'Lizard King;' lived/died with few perceptual restraints

"If you don't have a sense of humor, you'll hurt yourself arguing with me."

– Ted Nugent, iconic American singer/songwriter/guitarist/political activist; achieved fame with the Amboy Dukes before launching solo career; intensely right wing; spokesperson for D.A.R.E.

Capricorn 4

In any lunation phase one can count on the worldly ambition of a Capricorn. Their ethos is defined by a mixture of earthy pragmatism and an unbridled desire to attain a place at the crown of creation. All Capricorns, including the Capricorn 4, are rightly recognized for the indefatigability that keeps them rolling the stone until it perches on the mountain peak.

As with other 4th lunation phase lives, one encounters in Capricorn 4 a bias towards apprehending reality through the workings of the mind. The notion of making careful observations and having a well thought out plan is very real to these souls, and one often encounters a highly orchestrated blueprint when dealing with the Capricorn 4 as a careerist. Their stories far more often deal with conscious choices and measured progressions than with radical personality breakthroughs and sudden new directions.

Their key, if they are prone to volunteer one, is to point to their own mental tenacity. Even though there are considerable examples of sheer brilliance in the tribe of Capricorn 4's, they are far more likely to extol their willingness to keep on keeping on as the source of their success. They can be open-minded to a fault when gathering data, but they are extremely disciplined practitioners and straight as a ruler when it comes to establishing a bottom line.

Perhaps counter-intuitively, these fundamentally practical souls often reference the subject of God and spirituality in their worldviews. To whatever task they consecrate themselves there must be a defining hierarchical Absolute, a one and only Power they consider above themselves. To a Capricorn 4, real world virtue (not always easily attained) is accomplishing something noteworthy on high.

"I never thought I was finished when people said I was finished, or any of that stuff. I always had this undying belief that even if I was in a wheelchair and I could only move my finger, somehow I would become the guy who does this amazing thing with his finger."

– Jim Carrey, Golden Globe-winning Canadian-American comedian/actor/writer/producer/artist; known best for his wild slapstick performances; first film actor to earn $20M for a single role

"Of course, I continue to play and to practice. I think I would do so if I lived for another hundred years."

– Pablo Casals, world-renowned Spanish cellist/composer/conductor; recipient of Grammy HOF/Lifetime Achievement honors; acclaimed as the most influential cellist of the 20th Century

"All I've done all my life is just tried to better the game for our players and for those people watching."

– Bobby Hull, HOF Canadian pro hockey star; known as "The Golden Jet" for his blonde hair and fast/aggressive skating; two-time MVP; played for 23 years; brother and son also hockey stars

"Stay focused, go after your dreams and keep moving toward your goals."

– LL Cool J, Grammy-winning American hip hop artist/actor; associated with the famed Def Jam records; many featured movie/TV roles; has hosted Grammys four times; tithes to the Church

"You are what you settle for."

– Janis Joplin, iconic American rock/blues singer/songwriter; winner of Grammy HOF/Lifetime Achievement honors; the "Queen of Rock & Roll;" a Karate black belt; died of a drug overdose

"If there is anything that can bind the heavenly mind of man to this dreary exile of our earthly home and can reconcile us with our fate so that one can enjoy living, then it is verily the enjoyment of the mathematical sciences and astronomy."

– Johannes Kepler, eminent German astronomer/mathematician/astrologer; discovered the elliptical orbits of planets; coined the term "satellite;" optical pioneer; wrote horoscopes

"The individual has always had to struggle to keep from being overwhelmed by the tribe. If you try it, you will be lonely often, and sometimes frightened. But no price is too high to pay for the privilege of owning yourself."

– Rudyard Kipling, Nobel-laureate English journalist/poet/novelist/short story writer; first English writer to win the Nobel Prize; best known for stories set in India during the British Imperial era

"I have to keep testing myself."

– Eartha Kitt, acclaimed Emmy-winning American singer/dancer/actress/author/activist; first achieved popularity in Paris nightclubs; TV's first 'Catwoman;' known for song 'Santa Baby'

"If others would think as hard as I did, then they would get similar results."

– Isaac Newton, historically renowned English scientist/mathematician; father of modern physics; discoverer of calculus; revealer of the principle of gravity; described as "obsessive"

"I'm at my best when I'm exhausted and under pressure."

– Jimmy Page, iconic Grammy-winning English rock guitarist/songwriter/producer; inducted into R&R HOF with both the Yardbirds and Led Zeppelin; occultist; U.N. Peace Award recipient

"Let me tell you the secret that has led me to my goal. My strength lies solely in my tenacity."

– Louis Pasteur, distinguished French chemist/microbiologist; invented "pasteurization" and rabies/anthrax vaccine; continued research for 27 years after major stroke and paralysis

"Just being a mediocre driver has never been my ambition. That's not my style."

– Michael Schumacher, iconic German racecar driver; seven times Formula One world champion; 10-year chairman of the Grand Prix Drivers Ass'n; known for competitiveness and wet track skill

 Aquarius 4

If you really pressed them about it, most Aquarius 4's would cop to an uncomfortable aspect of their nature. Namely, they tend not to have a very high opinion of other people. Yes this sounds awful, but the extraordinarily capable and forthright mind of an Aquarius 4 just won't let them deny the fact that many (most?) of their fellow humans are willing to run at a mental capacity far below species potential.

Happily, for most Aquarius 4's this is not where the story ends. The leading lights of this soul station are devoted to conscientiously instructing the rest of humanity on the ways life should be engineered for the good of all. This is not ordinarily some ego grab, but rather a true commitment to honesty and sincere desire to have the present morph into a future in which the human race might collectively be able to make a fortunate go of it

Certainly the Aquarius 4 can be among the most frustrating of souls when they are in full critic mode, or when their hard charging sense of righteousness has all the subtlety of a an aerial bombardment. And yet many of these folks are quite popular, having an aura of heroism or at the very least a strong charismatic vibe about them. They are imbued with a fierce interest in the condition of humanity, and they function as goads to mankind's potential, may any prevailing lesser truths be damned.

Just don't expect them to not be disappointed in you personally. An Aquarius 4 will always be present to the truth that what you could be thinking is better than what you are thinking now. Perhaps it is simply best to consider that this is their curse as well as yours.

"A celebrity is one who is known to many persons he is glad he doesn't know."

– Lord Byron, key British poet/politician; a leading figure of 19th Century Romanticism; led a scandalous personal life that led to his expatriation; fought as a revolutionary in Greece

"The reason the all-American boy prefers beauty over brains is that the all-American boy can see better than he can think."

– Farrah Fawcett, iconic American model/actress; known best for the world's most popular swimsuit poster and her role on 'Charlie's Angels;' praised as dramatic actress in later career

"The only reason they come to see me is that I know that life is great–and they know I know it."

– Clark Gable, legendary Oscar-winning American actor; dubbed "The King of Hollywood;" famed as Rhett Butler in 'Gone with the Wind;' married five times; decorated military veteran

"I'm the last person to tell my friends to go see something I'm in. I could care less if friends of mine never saw anything I'm in."

– Joseph Gordon-Levitt, acclaimed American actor/filmmaker/musician/entrepreneur; rose to prominence on '3rd Rock from the Sun;' created 'HitRecord' artist collaboration community

"If I have one technology tip of the day, it's this: No matter how good the video on YouTube is, don't read the comments, just don't, because it will make you hate all humans."

– Matt Groening, Reuben/Emmy-winning American cartoonist/writer/producer/actor; creator of 'Life in Hell'/co-creator of 'The Simpsons;' history's most financially successful cartoonist

"If someone ever asks you to do something for them, do it really bad so you never have to do it again."

– Paris Hilton, notorious American heiress/socialite/actor/author/entrepreneur; leak of sex tape led to reality television stardom and considerable business success; always in on the joke

"As human beings, why does it take somebody to feel like they're close to us for us to see their humanity? Why can't we see the humanity in people that are distant from us?"

– Michael B. Jordan, award-winning American actor/producer; breakthrough role was a teenage drug dealer on 'The Wire;' known for 'Black Panther' and 'Creed;' major supporter of diversity

"Every jackass going the roads thinks he has ideas."

– James Joyce, internationally acclaimed Irish author/poet; perfected many modern/avant-garde literary techniques in works such as 'Ulysses;' one of the 20th Century's most influential voices

"Rules are mostly made to be broken and are too often for the lazy to hide behind."

– Douglas MacArthur, iconic 5-star American General; a West Point legend; commanded in WWII and Korea; AOC president; helped build the CCC; fired by Truman for insubordination

"Do something. If it works, do more of it. If it doesn't, do something else."

– Franklin D. Roosevelt, renowned 32nd president of the U.S.; famous for leadership during WWII and the New Deal; only four-term president; polio victim; instituted the March of Dimes

"I didn't mean to hit the umpire with the dirt, but I did mean to hit that bastard in the stands."

– Babe Ruth, legendary HOF American baseball player; prodigious slugger known as 'The Sultan of Swat;' one of history's most popular athletes; celebrated for large appetites and candor

"I prefer an ugly truth to a pretty lie. If someone is telling me the truth, that is when I will give my heart."

– Shakira, globally-acclaimed Colombian singer/songwriter/dancer/entrepreneur/philanthropist; most awarded Latin female artist of all time; extensively honored for humanitarian work

 Pisces 4

A Pisces 4 lives a life in which the mind often becomes an object of mockery or, at the very least, some sort of inside joke. This is not to imply that the Pisces 4 is part of some sort of comical crowd. It's just that when it comes to making deep decisions about life and its meaning a Pisces soul in the fourth lunation phase finds a rigidly logical approach rather like trying to unlock a bank vault with a tuna salad sandwich.

To be sure, all Pisces have a fairly vague relationship with consensual reality. For some this is a freeing truth that enables considerable spiritual and creative depth, a life in which there are no obstacles at all to the ability to fashion the impossible into the genuine. On the other hand some Pisces, even some of the ones with a gift for imagined existence, just go mad.

For a Pisces 4 the stakes are augmented by having to form a coherent mental perception of the real world. A fourth lunation phase life tends to hinge upon this. A fourth lunation phase soul sees what is in front of them and studiously considers the implications; unless one is assigned to a Pisces 4 life in which one is generally inclined to see the brain as a cheap camera giving one a distorted picture of an unfathomable universe.

Ultimately a Pisces 4 succeeds insofar as he or she can make peace with the mystifying nature of the all, by finding an inner vision that simultaneously embraces and transcends the mundane. Sometimes it helps a Pisces 4 to adapt a profound bias towards the virtues of peace and love and beauty, which at least help in the matter of remaining calm. And heck, when all else fails it is remarkable what one may be able to accomplish with an unshackled imagination and a tuna salad sandwich.

"There are worlds of experience beyond the world of the aggressive man, beyond history, and beyond science. The moods and qualities of nature and the revelations of great art are equally difficult to define; we can grasp them only in the depths of our perceptive spirit."

– Ansel Adams, landmark American photographer/environmentalist; known for B&W photos of American West; pursued sharp focus multi-tonal photography; Medal of Freedom recipient

"Reality is hopelessly inaccurate."

– Douglas Adams, award-winning English writer/dramatist/musician/technophile; famed for 'The Hitchhiker's Guide to the Galaxy;' a "radical atheist;" claimed "42" as the answer to life

"I've always said I don't believe in God, I believe in Al Pacino."

– Javier Bardem, Oscar-winning Spanish actor; has played an extraordinary variety of intense characters; prior to acting pursued careers in painting and rugby; non-violent; afraid of cars

"All you have to tell me is that something's not normal and I'll go for it!!"

– Karen Carpenter, Grammy-winning American singer/drummer/bassist; best known for work with brother as 'The Carpenters;' disliked spotlight; died from anorexia complications at age 32

"We are the masters of our reality."

– Kat Von D, notorious American tattoo artist/cosmetics mogul/reality TV star; a magnet for controversy; has launched products named "Underage Red" and "Celebutard;" unapologetic

"I'm not prepared for a zombie apocalypse. I need more bottled water, a shotgun, and stronger abs. I have plenty of canned food."

– Jenna Fischer, award-winning American actress; best known as Pam on "The Office;' once worked as a telephone psychic; animal advocate; easily terrified by scary surprises

"The last Martian report station on Earth was established in the Pyrenees."

– L. Ron Hubbard, controversial award-winning American science fiction author/philosopher; best known for his self-help book 'Dianetics' and his creation of the Church of Scientology

"The more clearly one sees this world; the more one is obliged to pretend it does not exist."

– John Irving, Oscar and National Book Award winning American author; best known for 'The World According to Garp' and 'A Prayer for Owen Meany;' writes the end of his novels first

"My whole wretched life swam before my weary eyes, and I realized no matter what you do it's bound to be a waste of time in the end so you might as well go mad."

– Jack Kerouac, iconic American author; a seminal figure of the Beat Generation; known best for 'On the Road;' college scholarship athlete; discharged from Marines for "strong schizoid trends"

"I pretty much operate on adrenaline and ignorance."

– Johnny Knoxville, idiosyncratic American actor/screenwriter/producer/comedian; best known as co-creator/star of reality show 'Jackass;' frequently injured performing bizarre stunts

"Life is like Sanskrit read to a pony."

– Lou Reed, "out there" Grammy HOF American songwriter/singer/guitarist; co-founder of the Velvet Underground; famous for song 'Walk on the Wild Side;' ambisexual; manic depressive

"I like writing because you can make things happen and turn out the way they never do in real life."

– Rob Reiner, award-winning American actor/director/producer/activist; debuted as 'Meathead' on 'Archie Bunker;' directed 'Spinal Tap,' 'The Princess Bride,' 'When Harry Met Sally'

5th Lunation Phase/Full Moon

Moon is 181 to 225 degrees ahead of the Sun

Keyword: Depth

It is during the full Moon phase that individuals consciously experience the transition from a reliance on mind and biology to the promptings of soul. The peak brightness of the Moon during LP5 births is symbolically manifest in the incomparably deep feelings of its natives, who experience lifetimes in which spirit (the Moon) and ego (the Sun) are both equal combatants and co-collaborators. But how is one to talk in general about the experience of myriad emergent souls; and how does this rich subjectivity result in some sort of collectivized understanding?

Well, one can't and one doesn't. All one can do is to recognize the power of any individual soul to manifest its own subjective version of cognitive/spiritual integrity. Rather than just expressing ego qualities and considered reactions to external stimuli, LP5's bring to their existence a depth of feeling that transcends mere objectivity and identity...here there are uncharted depths.

As with any lunation phase the difficulty here is in the process of growth, an extraordinary qualification in this incarnation. In the LP5 lifetime one is effectively birthing into the world one's own soul. It's an awesome accomplishment of being, but the exhausting labor can seem to last forever and so much can go wrong.

Perhaps that is why LP5 individuals are most extraordinarily concerned with relationships and the emotional protection they can afford. LP5's need connectivity to others to lend definition to who/what they are, to chase away the incipient madness of the often lonely road upon which they are embarked, to validate a reality bathed in Moonlight.

The mantra with multi-dimensional possibilities that constantly plays in their head, whether looking in the mirror or through the window, is “who are you?”

 Aries 5

The fifth lunation phase, for all Sun signs, is characterized by potency and conflict. As has already been indicated this is a crucial lifetime in which the developed ego wrestles with the ambiguous promptings of an emerged soul. Traditions that express the full Moon station as an instant of the ‘normal’ being overrun by emotional imperatives, sometimes verging on the lunatic, are applicable here.

Consider the plight of such a soul tethered to the inclinations of an Aries Sun. Aries is the archetype of the personal will in a fight for predominance. It is not an energy that is naturally oriented toward any sort of soul puppetry, even that which may lead to peaceful co-existence or willing equilibrium with the rest of creation.

For the most part an Aries 5 tends to live a life of urgent self-definition that manifests as defensiveness against a shadow enemy. Ambition, domination and abundant procreation are part of an arsenal employed in a battle against what is experienced, certainly early in life and often throughout, as an external threatening force that can’t quite be perceived much less corralled. For an Aries 5 the soul task is learning how to admit the necessity of spiritual surrender in a lifetime in which capitulation of the will feels less like a type of grace than a form of public self-immolation.

If there is an upside to the Aries 5 life it is that these souls are not entirely put off by figuratively and literally smashing into things. They are Rams after all, and one must be true to one’s nature. One might suggest that what an Aries 5 truly needs is to accept the self-sacrifice that attaches to universal purpose, but in the meanwhile it's a lot of fun to knock other people into the next world.

"Even when I was in the orphanage, when I was roaming the street trying to find enough to eat, even then I thought of myself as the greatest actor in the world. I had to feel the exuberance that comes from utter confidence in yourself. Without it, you go down to defeat."

– Charlie Chaplin, all-time great Oscar-winning British actor/filmmaker/composer; rose to fame in the silent movie era as "The Little Tramp;" wed teenagers three times; fathered 11 children

"My talent is that I just try and try and try and try again and little by little it comes to something."

– Francis Ford Coppola, seminal Oscar-winning American director/producer/screenwriter; famed for 'The Godfather' and films such as 'Patton' and "Apocalypse Now;' a childhood polio survivor

"I love scars on people. Scars to me are so attractive."

– Shannen Doherty, American actress/director/producer/animal activist; child star on 'Little House on the Prairie;' known for TV series '90210' and 'Charmed;' identified with anger issues

"There are ugly aspects to every single person's character. In being truthful, actors do have to show the ugly side of someone's character. We all behave like dicks sometimes."

– Claire Foy, award-winning British actress; best known as the young Queen Elizabeth on 'The Crown;' generally plays strong women testing their limits; survived serious childhood ailments

"My definition of courage is never letting anyone define you."

– Jenna Jameson, award-winning American "adult-entertainment" actress/entrepreneur/author; world's most famous porn star, a.k.a. "The Queen of Porn;" survived violent/traumatic youth

"If I don't die in a plane crash or something, this country has a rare opportunity to watch a great talent grow."

– Eddie Murphy, award-winning American stand-up comic/actor/writer/director/singer; famed for his "ethnic" SNL characters; hugely successful film actor; has nine children by five mothers

"I act irrationally, I defy the odds, I engage when others would run. I look for trouble, I seek chaos. It is a burden."

– Rosie O'Donnell, award-winning American comedian/actress/author/activist; outspoken co-host of 'The View;' committed to child welfare and LGBTQ causes; has five adopted children

"Anybody who's ever dealt with me knows not to mess with me."

– Nancy Pelosi, American politician; first ever female Speaker of the House; was a 47 year-old housewife with five children when she first ran for Congress; iron-willed; legendary work ethic

"Don't you ever let a soul in the world tell you that you can't be exactly who you are."

– Lady Gaga, Oscar-winning American singer-songwriter/actress/philanthropist; personified by edgy flamboyance; first person ever to win a Grammy and a BAFTA on the same day

"Somebody's gotta win and somebody's gotta lose and I believe in letting the other guy lose."

– Pete Rose, all-time great American professional baseball player; nicknamed "Charlie Hustle;" retired as MLB all-time hits leader; amazingly competitive; denied HOF status due to gambling

"I got in trouble my whole life for having a big mouth."

– Steven Tyler, American rock singer/songwriter/actor/musician/actor/TV personality; best known as the lead singer of Aerosmith; a great showman nicknamed "The Demon of Screamin'"

"Swim upstream. Go the other way. Ignore the conventional wisdom. If everybody else is doing it one way, there's a good chance you can find your niche by going in exactly the opposite direction."

– Sam Walton, American business pioneer; creator of Wal-Mart; ran his stores until the day he died at age 74; at one time he was the richest American; his favorite diversion was hunting

 Taurus 5

There is something scary about a Taurus 5 life. It's a little hard to put a finger on it because the prospect of formulating an idea about it will never quite capture the reality of this incarnation. And maybe this is the thing...what is scary about the Taurus 5 life is that cows (bulls!) need one hell of a boost to actually jump over the Moon.

Consider that any Taurus, even those inclined to creative expression, will rarely function in an abstract mode. Here in the fifth lunation phase, when ego identity squares off against the promptings of soul, there is simply no apparatus in the Taurus arsenal for effortless spiritual intercourse. If one expects the uber-materialistic Taurus ego to separate from the promptings of an earthy reality and move towards a transcendent soul discovery, one had better be carrying a big dish of ambrosia and a very large stick of spiritual dynamite.

It shakes out to a Taurus 5 life story being a difficult and strange tale of the mountain attempting to move to Muhammad. It's a serious, sometimes violent, enterprise in which fortitude is way past tested and nothing less than the foundation of the world is at stake. This is not the playing field of a faint humility or a hands-off God.

Indeed, God does fill an important role in many a Taurus 5 life. Presumably well aware that these denizens of the material plane are capable of great feats of strength, God shouts in an ear and demands they accomplish His will. Alas, while such convocations can yield the most potent and poignant expressions of consciousness, not all consecrations so ordained are free from tragedy.

Perhaps humankind is blessed in the fact that most people do not see themselves as instruments of delivery for the divine will. It would be hard to live in a world populated solely by angels and assassins. But if you do need either of those roles filled, you should probably get in touch with a Taurus 5...it's their thing.

"I'm ballsy. I have guts. I'm not afraid of anyone. I think that's what makes me feel powerful."

– Adele, Grammy-winning British singer/songwriter; co-holder of record number of Grammies (6) won on a single night; won Oscar for '007' song 'Skyfall;' known for songs of love and loss

"I'm not playing a role. I'm being myself, whatever the hell that is."

– Bea Arthur, Emmy/Grammy/Tony-winning American actress/singer; best known for role on TV sitcoms 'Maude' and 'Golden Girls;' was a sergeant in the Marines; a staunch rights activist

"Men die in despair, while spirits die in ecstasy."

– Honore de Balzac, French novelist/playwright/critic; best known for 90-novel series 'The Human Comedy;' the originator of social realism; richly profiled 2000+ personalities in his work

"Straightaway the ideas flow in upon me, directly from God."

– Johannes Brahms, revered German composer/conductor/musician; attained fame with 'The German Requiem' and four symphonies; willed his estate to the Gesellschaft der Musikfreunde

"My films must let every man, woman, and child know that God loves them, that I love them, and that peace and salvation will become a reality only when they all learn to love each other."

– Frank Capra, Oscar-winning Italian-American director/producer/ screenwriter; famed for classic films like 'It's A Wonderful Life' and 'It Happened One Night;' work salutes the brave underdog

"My prayer, my sacrifice, my life and my death is all for Allah, The Lord of The Worlds."

– Louis Farrakhan, polarizing American cleric; leader of the religious group Nation of Islam; historically anti-Semitic, anti-white, and anti-homosexual; organizer of the Million Man March

"Don't be attracted to easy paths because the paths that make your feet bleed are the only way to get ahead in life."

– Saddam Hussein, dictatorial Arab socialist president of Iraq; nicknamed 'The Butcher of Baghdad;' brutal rule marked by armed conflicts and human rights atrocities; executed

"If I'm too strong for some people, that's their problem."

– Glenda Jackson, Oscar-winning British actress/politician; noted for tense portrayals of complex women; served in British House of Commons; has played both Queen Elizabeth and 'King Lear'

"Sometimes I underestimate the magnitude of me."

– Reggie Jackson, HOF American baseball player; a powerful slugger who won two World Series MVP awards, earning the nickname "Mr. October;" larger-than-life personality caused conflicts

"Happy are those who have departed through martyrdom. Unhappy am I that I still survive."

– Ayatollah Ruhollah Khomeini, Iranian religious and political leader; made Iran the world's first Islamic republic; equated political loyalty with obedience to God; violent 'fatwa' history

"Any writer worth his salt writes to please himself."

– Harper Lee, Pulitzer-winning American novelist; famed for 'To Kill a Mockingbird,' widely hailed as "best novel of the century;" a tomboy known for protecting childhood friend Truman Capote

"You can have either the Resurrection or you can have Liberace. But you can't have both."

– Liberace, beloved American pianist; famed for a flamboyant/ostentatious personality and an ever-present piano candelabra; in his prime he was the highest paid entertainer in the world

 Gemini 5

The Gemini Sun is associated with extraordinary mental flexibility. A Gemini notices and reports the littlest truths in the smallest occurrences while maintaining an honest reticence about any truth that wants to present itself with a capital 'T.' Their open mindedness counts fickle chance and subjective circumstance to be the lenses through which reality must be negotiated.

In the Gemini 5 incarnation, this mental agility comes up against everything the conflict of will and spirit has to offer. The result is somewhat akin to a gallon of fruit being processed in a half-gallon blender. One may end up with a whole lot of juice, but there is also definitely going to be a need for a mop.

Plainly speaking, a Gemini 5 tends to discover that they are living a life in which their mental powers are tested by the most extreme polarities of awareness. Dealing with a reality greater than anyone can process, they often find misperception on their path and they attain results that can best be characterized as round and round and up and down. It is illustrative that while many a Gemini 5 avoids mind altering substances like the plague, there are also many examples of a Gemini

5 forming an intimate relationship with agents that they hope can kick their perception into a higher functioning.

Ultimately, the beauty of the successful Gemini 5 life is its resiliency. If one is knocked down, then hopefully one learns something; if one gets something wrong then hopefully one discovers what is right. A Gemini 5 is at their best when they get back on the road after having taken a foolish turn.

From the outsider's perspective, a Gemini 5 may seem to be straddling the line between authenticity and eccentricity. Perhaps it is best to just pour a little tequila in that blender and stand out of the way.

"When people expect me to go right, I'll go left. I'm unpredictable."

– Paula Abdul, Canadian-American singer/dancer/choreographer/TV personality; career began as L.A. Lakers cheerleader; had six #1 pop hits; Grammy winner; judge on 'American Idol'

"Everybody has their own way of tapping into their realness."

– Sandra Bernhard, American comedian/actress/singer/author; known for acerbic critique of celebrity culture and political figures; played groundbreaking openly lesbian role on 'Roseanne'

"You affect the world by what you browse."

– Tim Berners-Lee, British engineer/computer scientist; inventor of the World Wide Web; knighted by Queen Elizabeth; one of Time Magazine's most important people of the 20th C

"I try to stay in a constant state of confusion just because of the expression it leaves on my face."

– Johnny Depp, award-winning American actor/musician/producer; sex symbol known for his richly eccentric characters; often dons Jack Sparrow costume to visit children's hospitals

"I've always taken 'The Wizard of Oz' very seriously, you know. I believe in the idea of the rainbow. And I've spent my entire life trying to get over it."

– Judy Garland, Grammy HOF American singer/actress/dancer/vaudevillian; legendary career in multiple genres spanned 45 years; battled with addiction; known for setbacks/comebacks

"You can't become a decent horseman until you fall off and get up again, a good number of times. There's life in a nutshell."

– Bear Grylls, British adventurer/television personality/author/businessman; known best for the TV series 'Man vs. Wild;' former military survival instructor; climbed Mt. Everest at age 23

"My emancipation don't fit your equation."

– Lauryn Hill, American singer/songwriter/rapper; co-founder of the 'Fugees;' her eponymous solo album was the first ever hip-hop Grammy Album of the Year; difficult legal/personal issues

"My life has always been high-low. The middle does nothing for me."

– Lenny Kravitz, American musician/singer/songwriter/actor; of mixed race he was told his music "wasn't black enough;" set Grammy record for consecutive best vocal wins (4); addiction issues

"I know there is no straight road, no straight road in this world; only a giant labyrinth of intersecting crossroads."

– Federico Garcia Lorca, Spanish poet/playwright/director; famed for surrealist works inspired by gypsy culture; his writings advocated for the rights of women/minorities; executed by fascists

"I'm not a witch, I just like Halloween, and I thought that blondes look skinnier in black."

– Stevie Nicks, iconic American singer/songwriter; sold over 140M albums; best known for work with Fleetwood Mac; famous for changing outfits and partners; struggled with addiction

"You wanna hear it straight, buy the album."

– Dean Martin, American singer/actor/entertainer; known for film partnership with Jerry Lewis; member of the legendary Rat Pack; affected a cool/tipsy stage persona; privately complex

"I thought the script was very good, but something was missing. I wanted to come out with a cane, come down slowly, have it stick into one of the bricks, get up, fall over, roll around, and they all laugh and applaud. The director asked, 'what do you want to do that for?' I said from that time on, no one will know if I'm lying or telling the truth."

– Gene Wilder, American actor/director/writer/producer; best known for zany collaborations with Mel Brooks and as the original 'Willie Wonka;' cancer education/support activist

 Cancer 5

In any Cancer lifetime the Moon is deeply linked to personality. All solar egos inhabiting this Sun sign must negotiate and express a consciousness predicated on the waxing and waning of feelings. The Cancer 5 individual, born during the full Moon, is particularly challenged by the immersion of identity in an emotional reality cresting at full flood.

In a Cancer 5 lifetime we encounter individuals whose feelings are not merely near the surface. That level is breached early in the game. What one most often finds in the Cancer 5 life is an extraordinary deluge of poignancy, nostalgia, hope, courage, clown laughter, loyalty, visionary purpose, and true love... in other words, just about any strong feeling that may possibly saturate the personality with a fierce sense of emotional identity.

Alas, the emotional rip currents are rarely simple here; rather they are complex and commanding and not always kind to a Cancer 5. Theirs are hearts prone to breaking, and they suffer abandonment terribly in the search for safe harbor. Sometimes it gets "all too much" to a degree that goes way past the figurative, all the way to the tragic headlines.

Still there is much loveliness to the Cancer 5 spirit, even when the journey is in peril. Through art, through laughter, through devotion, through strength of will, it's sort of magnificent to see these souls fight for a felicitous survival as avatars of feeling. Believing that even the most terrifying realms can be crossed in the proper mood, they are the truly luminescent guides in a dark night.

Or maybe it's just that they are honestly fatalistic about the power of the soul. A Cancer 5 feels life as something so much more than can be defined by the ego. Their grace is recognition of an oceanic reality that ultimately takes them, and eventually takes us all.

"It's been an adventure. We took some casualties over the years. Things got broken. Things got lost. But I wouldn't have missed it for the world."

– Anthony Bourdain, Emmy-winning American chef/author/media personality; known for TV shows 'No Reservations' and 'Parts Unknown;' passionate and forthright; died by suicide

"Humor is just another defense against the universe."

– Mel Brooks, Oscar/Tony/Emmy/Grammy winning American comedian/actor/writer/director; films included 'Blazing Saddles' and 'Young Frankenstein;' married 41 years to Anne Bancroft

"Will God or someone give me the power to breathe my sigh into my canvases, the sigh of prayer and sadness, the prayer of salvation, of rebirth?"

– Marc Chagall, proto-Surrealist Russian-French artist/designer; known for fantastical paintings with strong poetic-emotional content; Picasso described him as having "an angel in his head"

"Be positive, be positive. It's rough out there, but don't succumb. Don't succumb to the cynicism in the world."

– Cameron Crowe, Oscar-winning American journalist/screenwriter/director; teen writing stint at 'Rolling Stone' was foundation for films; made 'Jerry Maguire' as a paean to loyalty

"I had insecurities and fears like everybody does, and I got over it. But I was interested in the parts of me that struggled with those things."

– Philip Seymour Hoffman, Oscar-winning American actor/director/producer; known for dark/eccentric/melancholic roles; breakthrough was 'Capote;' died from drug intoxication

"I found the emotion that as an athlete you block out, and it really helped me to understand myself as a person. I'm a really emotional person and it helped make me a better person."

– Carl Lewis, American track & field athlete/actor/entrepreneur; winner of 9 Olympic gold medals; named 'Sportsman of the Century' by the IOC; difficult post-career personality issues

"We will cope."

– Angela Merkel, German politician; first woman Chancellor of Germany; described as the de facto leader of Europe and the most powerful woman in the world; holds degree in physics

"The thing you have to be prepared for is that other people don't always dream your dream."

– Linda Ronstadt, Grammy-winning American singer; "The First Lady of Rock;" multi-genre; sold over 100M records; breakout work was 'Heart Like A Wheel;' retired due to Parkinson's Disease

"If by chance someday you're not feeling well and you should remember some silly thing I've said or done and it brings back a smile to your face or a chuckle to your heart, then my purpose as your clown has been fulfilled."

– Red Skelton, American radio and TV host/comedian/actor/artist/humanitarian; "America's Clown Prince;" son of a circus clown he never knew; famed for funny/sentimental characters

"I just–I love my job. I love doing it. It's a passionate endeavor. And sometimes you can get close to something that you believe is the truth... the truth of something. Not all the time, but sometimes."

– Donald Sutherland, Canadian film actor; has appeared in over 200 films including 'The Dirty Dozen,' 'Mash,' and 'The Hunger Games;' received honorary lifetime achievement Oscar

"Armageddon was not an acting experience. That's why I was depressed. It was about the effects and not about the performances. I had the really rough part of being the emotional person who's like, you know, upset all the time."

– Liv Tyler, American model/actress/humanitarian; best known for her work in 'Lord of the Rings;' never took an acting lesson; suffers from ADHD; is a goodwill ambassador for UNICEF

"I used to think the worst thing in life was to end up all alone. It's not. The worst thing in life is to end up with people who make you feel all alone."

– Robin Williams, Oscar-winning comedian/actor/humanitarian; known for manic energy and rapid wit; lauded for roles in movie dramas; pioneered celebrity voice acting; took his own life

Leo 5

The Leo born during a full Moon is really something to behold. There's just no limit to their natal glow. They are bonfires of personality fed by an inexhaustible supply of extravagant feelings.

Often this works out great for the Leo 5, especially those who are inclined to creative pursuits or anything that places them before the cultural collective. They may not produce the greatest art or the most timeless innovations, but you can't take your eyes off of them. They display a kind of human potential that simply must be acknowledged for its brilliant manifestation of personality.

Of course, the downside for a Leo 5 is that they have the potential to be human torches. As they inhabit a phase in which the ego is just learning to co-exist with the soul, things can get incendiary rather quickly. Weird and out-of-control and confrontational stuff often happens around Leo 5's, and they have the relationships (or lack thereof) to prove it.

Their vitality can sometimes be rightfully read as arrogance, but a Leo 5 is probably more fairly charged with an abundance of self-esteem. Yes, this can result in an Ozymandian fate (and yes, of course, the poet Percy Shelley who wrote 'Ozymandias' was a Leo 5). They can also be extraordinary philanthropists who truly function as lights to the world.

On one level it is not unfair to think of Leo 5's as experiencing life as both progenitor and progeny. They may not be all the way actualized, but they are amply endowed with the potential to bring forth the worthy fruits of their creative identity. And if no one else cares to love them they are amply capable of digging themselves.

"I wouldn't say I'm normal. But I'm relatively stable. When I think of normal, I think of mediocrity, and mediocrity scares the f—- out of me."

– Gillian Anderson, Emmy-winning American actress/writer/humanitarian; best known as Agent Scully on the 'The X-Files;' voted "most bizarre" in high school; an active supporter of PETA

"A lot of legends, a lot of people, have come before me. But this is my time."

– Usain Bolt, legendary Jamaican sprinter/philanthropist; world's fastest man; first athlete to win Olympics 100m and 200m races in world record times; committed to his charitable foundation

"I'm not afraid to be lonely at the top."

– Barry Bonds, American HOF baseball player; three-time MVP; set all-time career record for home runs; only player to have 500+ home runs/steals; career tarnished by steroid allegations

"Savor what you are and not what everyone else wants you to be."

– Sandra Bullock, Oscar-winning American actress/producer/philanthropist; 'Speed' launched her to global fame; one of history's highest paid actresses; a major supporter of the Red Cross

"Condemn me, it does not matter; history will absolve me."

– Fidel Castro, Cuban revolutionary/politician; a dictator who championed egalitarianism; led the first communist regime in the western hemisphere for 47 years; complex character/legacy

"Always wake up with a smile knowing that today you are going to have fun accomplishing what others are too afraid to do."

– Mark Cuban, billionaire American businessman/investor; owner of the Dallas Mavericks; a 'shark' on the reality TV show 'Shark Tank;' candid/eccentric; fined over $2M by the NBA

"I've run into certain geniuses of individualism–they are very few and far between–who live their lives completely on their own terms; they are very powerful and have a great amount of happiness. We all should aspire to that."

– David Duchovny, American actor/writer/producer/director/novelist/singer-songwriter; played Agent Mulder on the 'The X-Files;' Princeton and Yale graduate; treated for sex addiction

"Women have got to stop being polite. If I ever had children, which I don't, the first thing I'd teach a girl of mine is the words 'f–off.' "

– Helen Mirren, eminent British actor; winner of Oscar, BAFTA, Tony, Emmy and SAG awards; has memorably played a queen six times; known for sexually charged roles in her early career

"Thank goodness I was never sent to school; it would have rubbed off some of the originality."

– Beatrix Potter, English writer/illustrator/natural scientist/conservationist; best known for children's 'talking animals' books such as 'The Tale of Peter Rabbit;' sold over 100M books

"If this is your God, he's not very impressive. He has so many psychological problems; he's so insecure. He demands worship every seven days. He goes out and creates faulty humans and then blames them for his own mistakes. He's a pretty poor excuse for a Supreme Being."

– Gene Roddenberry, American writer/producer; creator of 'Star Trek;' was a decorated WWII pilot and an LAPD cop; first person to have ashes 'buried' in space; marked by marital infidelity

"There is no point in being confident and having a small position."

– George Soros, billionaire Hungarian-American investor/philanthropist/activist; famed for a one day $1B trading gain; has donated $32B+ to global charities; a prominent political progressive

"I figured I would have to tell someone to kiss my ass before it was all over, and I have — twice."

– Billy Bob Thornton, Oscar-winning American actor/writer/director/musician; known as versatile/eccentric; married six times; fronts a successful "psychobilly" band; OCD sufferer

Virgo 5

If one intends to identify the Sun sign most clearly aligned with pragmatism and linear thinking, Virgo is the likeliest candidate. Normal is normal for most Virgos, and real is real. And then we get to the Virgo who is born during a full Moon.

Certainly, a Virgo 5 never stops being a Virgo. The compulsion to address life in a rational fashion remains, and like other Virgos the Virgo 5 can structure a pretty tight argument. They tend to observe their lives closely and well, and they have an excellent facility for telling it like it is.

The twist is that the fifth lunation phase finds Virgo 5's rigorous intellect and observational skills are dropped into an ocean of emotional 'Moonstuff.' The precision gears that are engaged in a typical Virgo life become submerged in a medium that is absolutely antithetical to mechanical processes. The result is kind of a "what the hell!?" existence.

So it is that success for a Virgo 5 entails a great tolerance for, or at least an accepting recognition of, life's instability. Virgo artisans, who are generally so oriented to building the functional supports of great human truths, here find themselves in a dreamscape. Truth is elusive here, and grounded reality is kind of an inside joke.

Many a Virgo 5 works things out by paying attention to that other great quality of the Virgo persona, namely giving service. The ranks of Virgo 5 are full of philanthropists, humanitarians, and activists. There is particular gravitation towards the welfare of children and animals, beings that are seen as manifesting something natural, basic, pure, and agreeably in need of protection.

Still, when one looks closely at a Virgo 5 it's hard not to see the cracks. Reason is damaged here. That seems to be the point.

"Life is amazing, life is odd. Life is not what you expected it to be. Things happen."

– Lauren Bacall, American model/actress; breakthrough was 'To Have and Have Not' with future husband Humphrey Bogart; known for a smoldering look linked to control of a nervous tremor

"I'd rather be the king of kids than the prince of fools."

– Jack Black, Grammy-winning American actor/comedian/musician/songwriter/humanitarian; 'School of Rock' inspired by Black's actual life; committed to environmental/anti-poverty efforts

"Michael Jackson and I talk all the time. I think we understand each other in a way that most people can't understand either of us."

– Macaulay Culkin, American actor/musician; a child star best known as Kevin McAlister in the 'Home Alone' films; emancipated from parents at age 16; he is Paris Jackson's godfather

"If I were a headmaster I would get rid of the history teacher and get a chocolate teacher instead and my pupils would study a subject that affected all of them."

– Roald Dahl, beloved British author; wrote 19 classic children's books; was a child chocolate tester; flew as a combat pilot in the RAF; spied alongside Ian Fleming; invented a medical shunt

"Even as a very small child I used to talk to God."

– Gloria Gaynor, Grammy HOF American singer/songwriter/actress/author/motivational speaker; best known for disco hit 'I Will Survive;' has recorded in multiple genres for 5 decades

"We do not have to visit a madhouse to find disordered minds; our planet is the mental institution of the universe."

– Johann Wolfgang von Goethe, German poet/playwright/novelist/scientist/statesman/theatre director/critic; one of the most influential thinkers of the 18th/19th centuries

"Escapism, that's what I like. I'm not so crazy about the reality of everything."

– Michael Jackson, Grammy HOF American singer/songwriter/Moonwalker; won 197 major awards during his life; nicknamed the "King of Pop;" led child-centric life at "Neverland Ranch"

"Whether the Virgin Mary existed, I don't know. But the human need for her to appear in tortilla, that's what inspires my interest."

– Moby, American singer/songwriter/disc jockey/photographer/humanitarian; his album 'Play' is history's best selling electronic album; known as a committed vegan and animal rights activist

"Have nothing to do with coaches. In fact, if you should see one coming, go and hide behind the pavilion until he goes away."

– Bill O'Reilly, Emmy-winning American journalist/author/television host; known best as the biggest star in FOX news history; dogged by domestic violence and sexual abuse allegations

"When you feel like an oddball, it never really leaves you. Even now, I'm better around people who are uncomfortable with themselves–the misfits."

– Chris Pine, American actor/humanitarian; known for playing Capt. James T. Kirk in 'Star Trek' movie franchise reboot; afraid of the dark and a shoe fetishist; his fans are called "Pine Nuts"

"My mom has always wished me a daughter just like me."

– Pink, Grammy-winning American pop singer/songwriter/activist; known for candor; breakout album was 'MisSundaztood;' acrobatic in performance; labeled a "bad influence" in childhood

"I can handle reality in small doses, but as a lifestyle it's much too confining."

– Lily Tomlin, award-winning American actress/comedian/writer/singer/producer; hailed as a multi-media comedy legend; author of 'The Search for Signs of Intelligent Life in the Universe'

Libra 5

It can seem a bit of a paradox, but the signature of the Libra ego is an awareness of outside forces. To those born under the Libra Sun the art of living is a matter of mastering relativity. It is in the response to exogenous energy that one builds one's purpose and experiences one's identity.

The predicament of a Libra 5 lifetime is the considerable weight brought to this dualistic state of affairs. Employing the classic image of the Libra scale, the Libra 5 lives a life in which figurative elephants (Sun/ full Moon) are dancing on opposite ends of the beam trying to reach stasis. It is a challenging task that is simultaneously elegant and absurd.

As befits the duality of the Libra archetype, some Libra 5's succeed at mastering this intense range of social/psychological spectra, and others fail. Some become great Universalists who champion the ideal of a world at peace in which all are included and respected. Others live a life in which a complex reality defies equilibrium at every turn.

What most Libra 5's eventually discover is that there are few absolutes in this lifetime. One manifestation of this awareness is an ardent resistance to systems that proscribe reality in terms of hierarchical value. Another is adherence to the traits of courage and optimism that it takes to survive the times when life presents as a hell hole.

And of course, as with every other Libra incarnation, the Libra 5 finds the greatest consolation in primary relationships. As has been mentioned elsewhere, all beings in the fifth lunation phase are overwhelmed by the nascent emergence of soul and seek others to essentially buffer the birth of an overwhelming transition into universal consciousness. Through it all, and especially to the Libra 5, the only unqualified good remains love.

"I start in the middle of a sentence and move both directions at once."

– John Coltrane, Grammy HOF American saxophonist/composer; best known work is 'A Love Supreme;' canonized by the African Orthodox Church; posthumously awarded the Pulitzer Prize

"The hardest challenge is to be yourself in a world where everyone is trying to make you be somebody else."

– e. e. cummings, award-winning American poet/painter/essayist/author/ playwright; known for stylistic innovation/non-conformity; his best known poem is titled 'I Carry Your Heart With Me'

"I get lots of awards for being mentally ill. Apparently, I am better at being mentally ill than almost anything else I've ever done. Seriously–I have a shelf of awards for being bipolar."

– Carrie Fisher, award-winning American actress/writer/ philanthropist; best known as Princess Leia in 'Star Wars;' took pride in writing female characters/ love scenes; HIV and AIDS activist

"...the test of a first-rate intelligence is the ability to hold two opposed ideas in the mind at the same time, and still retain the ability to function."

– F. Scott Fitzgerald, American writer; famed for 'The Great Gatsby;' he and wife Zelda are regarded as seminal figures of the Jazz Age; great appreciation of his work came post-mortem

"People want economy, and they'll pay any price to get it."

– Lee Iacocca, American industrialist/author; father of the Ford Mustang/ Chrysler Minivan; revived Chrysler Corporation in the 1980's; established diabetes foundation after wife's passing

"When everyone is included, everyone wins."

– Jesse Jackson, iconic American civil rights activist/minister/politician; founder/president of the Rainbow PUSH Coalition; presidential candidate; Medal of Freedom recipient

"Tragedy is a close-up; comedy, a long shot."

– Buster Keaton, iconic American actor/comedian/director/producer/screenwriter/stuntman; improvised clever physical comedy; dubbed "The Great Stone Face;" battled personal demons

"I think one of the most beautiful things about YouTube is that it makes the world a smaller place. You realize that we're all different, but we're all the same."

– Lilly Singh, Indian-Canadian comedian/actress/author; rose to fame via her 'Superwoman' YouTube channel; the first woman named to host a daily latenight show for a major network

"We must all learn to adjust with our surroundings."

– T-Pain, Grammy-winning American rapper/singer/songwriter/producer; identified with the creative use of Auto-Tune; has sold over 5 million ringtones, mostly 'I'm N Luv (Wit a Stripper)'

"Since no one can ever know for certain whether or not his own view of life is the correct one, it is absolutely impossible for him to know if someone else's is the wrong one."

– Gore Vidal, award-winning American writer/intellectual; known for his cool and witty patrician manner; anti-academic, anti-patriarchy; often considered "the godfather of gay literature"

"I feel self-doubt whether I'm doing something hard or easy."

– Sigourney Weaver, award-winning American actress; dubbed the "Sci-Fi Queen;" stardom came as Ripley in 'Alien;' named for a 'Gatsby' character; holds degrees from Stanford and Yale

"All collective judgments are wrong. Only racists make them. No human race is superior; no religious faith is inferior."

– Elie Weisel, Nobel-Prize winning Romanian-American writer/teacher/activist; famed for 'Night,' a personal account of the Holocaust; with wife created a humanitarian foundation

Scorpio 5

One of the signature qualities of any fifth lunation phase life is a sense of vulnerability. Deep feelings test the dam of personality and it is hard to shore up one's fixed sense of self. There is a war between the ego and the soul.

How mightily this state of affairs is exacerbated in a Scorpio 5 lifetime! For it is a prime tenant of the Scorpio character that the self will neither be marginalized nor defeated. The rub in the fifth lunation phase is that the Scorpio ego picks a fight with a cosmic tide that is every bit as fierce as is the Scorpio ego.

Thus, the Scorpio 5 is charitably characterized as living on the edge. It is their nature to look anyone and anything directly in the eye and express exactly what they feel without qualification or apology. It gets truly interesting for them living in a lifetime in which the universe pretty much looks unflinchingly back.

Oddly, one hears a lot of talk about God and Love and Joy along the Scorpio 5 path. It is only in the search for and reconciliation with such Big Truths that a Scorpio 5 feels like there is any headway to be had in existence. Of course, any such search and reconciliation takes place in a dangerously active mine field that tends to blur the differences between a search for profundity and surrender to cynicism.

Working under such powerful conditions of consciousness, the well-focused Scorpio 5 often leaves a work legacy worthy of consideration. Existence may be tearing them apart, but they are profound observers of the essence of the human condition. And, if they are bent in a particular way, their gallows humor is second to none.

"I'm not upset about my divorce. I'm only upset that I'm not a widow."

– Roseanne Barr, Emmy-winning American actress/comedian/writer/producer; known for title role on TV sitcom 'Roseanne;' popularized "domestic goddess" persona; difficult childhood

"Living systems are never in equilibrium. They are inherently unstable. They may seem stable, but they're not. Everything is moving and changing. In a sense, everything is on the edge of collapse."

– Michael Crichton, award-winning American author/screenwriter/director/producer; worked in many "thriller" genres; wrote 'Jurassic Park;' twelve of his books have been made into films

"Pain and suffering are always inevitable for a large intelligence and a deep heart. The really great men must, I think, have great sadness on earth."

– Fyodor Dostoevsky, eminent Russian philosopher/author; best known for novel 'Crime and Punishment;' his work dealt with suffering, doubt and God; spent years in a forced labor camp

"When I die I hope I'll have a chance to hit God in the face."

– Richard Dreyfuss, Oscar-winning American actor; appeared in several of the top all-time movies including 'American Graffiti' and 'Jaws;' was a CO during Viet Nam; battled drug abuse

"So I wonder if anything should ever be off limits."

– Kathy Griffin, Emmy and Grammy winning American comedian/actress; known for sharp criticism of celebrity culture; infamous for 'joke' involving fake severed Donald Trump head

"I don't have expectations. Expectations in your life just lead to giant disappointments."

– Michael Landon, award-winning American actor/writer/director/producer; known for work on 'Bonanza,' 'Little House on the Prairie,' and 'Highway to Heaven;' pancreatic cancer victim

"There is no such thing as inner peace. There is only nervousness or death. Any attempt to prove otherwise constitutes unacceptable behavior."

– Fran Lebowitz, American author/public speaker/actor; known for sardonic social commentary; called "the last of the funny public intellectuals;" subject of documentary 'Public Speaking'

"We want to be the band to dance to when the bomb drops."

– Simon Le Bon, Grammy-winning English musician/singer/songwriter; best known as the sexy lead singer and lyricist of Duran Duran; his audacious life as a yachtsman is chronicled in 'Drum'

"If I hurt someone, if I were to accidentally poke someone's eye out, I would laugh. And then I'd say, 'I'm sorry, I really do feel bad,' but then I'm on the floor rolling."

– Rachel McAdams, award-winning Canadian actress/activist; breakout role was "Queen Bee" in 'Mean Girls;' identified with romantic parts but successful in many genres; an environmentalist

"I think any good actor is an anarchist. They have to be."

– Sam Rockwell, Oscar-winning American actor; known best for playing psychologically dark and eccentric characters; a child of divorce largely raised by father; does not want children

"There should be no argument in regard to morality in art. There is no morality in nature."

– Auguste Rodin, transformative French sculptor; creator of many iconic post-classical works including 'The Age of Bronze,' The Thinker,' and 'The Kiss;' a Legion of Honor designate

"I remembered when I was four or five, I tried to kill my own brother. He was newly born and I was disappointed, because he was the third baby. That was enough as far as I was concerned."

– Tilda Swinton, Oscar-winning British actress/model; known for mystique in both art house and blockbuster roles; detached from fame/the Hollywood scene; raised entirely around men

Sagittarius 5

The Sagittarian quality of expansiveness is well-suited to the fifth lunation phase, a lifetime that tends to put few limitations around the possibilities of personal evolution. How does any individual introduced to spirit manage to get safely and sanely acclimated to the emergent revelation of one's greater place in the universe? Well, if anyone can handle the challenge it's a Sagittarius 5.

To be sure a Sagittarius 5 is no less human than any other member of the species. They encounter pain, fear and failure at about the same rate as the rest of us. Additionally, it is the nature of every Sagittarius to sometimes leap before they look, and they can sometimes make their greatest impression by landing awkwardly.

Still, the Sagittarius 5 has been dealt a great gift, a hand that contains a virtual trump card. They simply do not believe that what manifests at any moment in the real world, however dire, is the end of the story. They possess a philosophical disposition that enables them to gain a constructive perspective on just about anything and a perennial willingness to take one more step towards a felicitous understanding.

It's probably important to stress that this is not inherently a lifetime about finding a personal truth via a contemplative faith epiphany. The Sagittarius 5 is much more persuaded to investiture in real world experience. As they roll along they may be making much of the map up as they go along, but it's hard not to give a respectful nod to their conceptual embrace of finding a worthy destination at the end of a real life road.

In a difficult world it's not always easy to find God, knows the Sagittarius 5, but surely there are less helpful things than possessing optimism about getting a look at something truly grand. On the way, it's also a lot of fun to sing in the car.

"If the doors of perception were cleansed everything would appear to man as it is, infinite."

– William Blake, seminal English poet/artist/visionary; experienced visions from an early age; famed for poem 'Tyger' and painting 'The Ancient of Days;' largely unrecognized in his lifetime

"I think age is terribly overrated. You're okay as long as you don't grow up. By all means grow old, but don't mature. Remain childlike; retain wonder, the ability to be flabbergasted by something."

– Billy Connolly, award-winning Scottish comedian/actor/musician/ philanthropist; known for combining a folksy style with biting social commentary; suffered years of childhood abuse

"Follow your bliss. Find where it is and don't be afraid to follow it."

– Joseph Conrad, acclaimed Polish-British author; wrote of the enigma of existence in books such as 'Heart of Darkness' and 'Lord Jim;' a master prose stylist not fluent in English until his 20's

"I always say YCDA: you can do anything."

– Michael Clarke Duncan, American actor; started out as a bouncer/ bodyguard; breakthrough film role was in 'Armageddon;' hailed as a gentle giant in the prison drama 'The Green Mile'

"I believe that if one always looked at the skies, one would end up with wings."

– Gustave Flaubert, seminal French author; important figure in the history of literary realism; wrote his first book, the masterpiece 'Madame Bovary,' in his mid-30's taking 5 years to finish

"The fact that our heart yearns for something Earth can't supply is proof that Heaven must be our home."

– C. S. Lewis, award-winning Irish author/scholar; best known for fantasy series 'The Chronicles of Narnia;' also wrote influential Christian apologetics; donated most of his income to charity

"We are imprisoned in the realm of life, like a sailor on his tiny boat, on an infinite ocean."

– Anna Freud, Austrian-British psychoanalyst; a founder of psychoanalytic child psychology; youngest daughter of Sigmund Freud, she suffered through his prejudice against lesbianism

"I'd like to be a giant enabler."

– Daryl Hannah, award-winning American actress/environmental activist; featured in a wide range of modern film genres; hailed as an environmental hero; an ASD sufferer since childhood

"If your world doesn't allow you to dream, move to one where you can."

– Billy Idol, award-winning English musician/singer/songwriter/actor; was a legendary punk/glam rocker; early user of modern music tech; was the original choice to be T-1000 in 'Terminator 2'

"Be yourself, chase your dreams, and just never say 'never.' That's the best advice I could ever give someone."

– Taylor Swift, Grammy-winning American singer/songwriter/actress/humanitarian; huge success in country and pop genres; songs feature her personal life; first song titled 'Lucky You'

"I believe that if you'll just stand up and go, life will open up for you."

– Tina Turner, Grammy HOF American singer/songwriter/actress; biggest hit was 'What's Love Got to Do with It?'; holds all-time record for career concert tickets sold; a devoted Buddhist

"Everything is explained now. We live in an age when you say casually to somebody 'What's the story on that?' and they can run to the computer and tell you within five seconds. That's fine, but sometimes I'd just as soon continue wondering. We have a deficit of wonder right now."

– Tom Waits, Grammy-winning R&R HOF American singer/songwriter/actor; an "American mythologist;" gravelly singing voice; his music has played in 50+ films; a loner; partial to silence

 Capricorn 5

Of all the Sun signs, the one that may be the most constant from phase to phase is Capricorn. No matter the incarnation, a Capricorn almost invariably manifests the traits of ambition, conscientious effort, and practicality. In any lifetime, the heights of personal fulfillment are scaled by assiduous effort one step at a time.

In the fifth lunation phase it is the spiritual terrain that changes rather than the Capricorn essence. In a lifetime marked by full Sun (ego) and full Moon (spirit) the Capricorn 5 is often shaped into someone awesomely resolute. Resisting the fey lunar qualities in their personal equation, the Capricorn 5 tends to clench pragmatism in a psychological death grip.

Of course, the fifth lunation phase is hardly a primer in sobriety and linear manifestation, so there is much the Capricorn 5 has to contend with. What the successful member of this cohort learns is a practical and conscientious relationship with adaptability. As the vagaries of spirit manifest, the Capricorn 5 strives to master outlooks and techniques that successfully manage the inevitability of changing circumstances.

What one ultimately gets in a Capricorn 5 is an individual who will work though change and crisis with a bias towards tough-mindedness and, as necessary, a practical penchant for moving with the tide. If life inflicts change, so be it. The Capricorn 5 will simply not surrender to the principle of inconstancy.

It is noteworthy, as the names attached below will suggest, that meditation is a quality often encountered in the clan of Capricorn 5. One senses that in the fulsome reality of the fifth lunation phase one must make space for visualizing a purposeful outcome. Apparently, these inwardly directed techniques sometimes elicit personal reinvention, but a goal in the manifest world will inevitably be the lodestar.

Ultimately though, as with all Capricorns, the main principles of Capricorn 5 survival appear to be a sense of duty and a relentless work ethic. Take that, Mr. Moon!

"Keep working hard and you can get anything that you want."

– Aaliyah, award-winning American singer/actress/model; all three of her albums certified multi-platinum; sometimes referred to as the "R&B Princess;" perished in plane crash at age 22

"I am trying to show the world that we are all human beings and that color is not important. What is important is the quality of our work."

– Alvin Ailey, American choreographer; credited with popularizing modern dance and fostering African-American concert dance participation; Presidential Medal of Freedom recipient

"The minute you know you're on safe ground, you're dead."

– David Bowie, iconic English singer-songwriter/actor; one of the most influential artists of the 20th C; famed for musical personality evolution; Grammy Lifetime Achievement honoree

"It's not enough to have good thoughts for the world. You must get out there!"

– Ted Danson, Emmy-winning American actor/producer/author/activist; breakout role was Sam Malone in 'Cheers;' anxiety-sufferer; workaholic tendencies; a marine ecology crusader

"Duties are what make life most worth living. Lacking them, you are not necessary to anyone."

– Marlene Dietrich, German-American actress/singer; known for intense personal style during a career that spanned seven decades; Medal of Freedom recipient for WWII anti-Nazi efforts

"Champions aren't made in the ring, they are merely recognized there. What you cheat on in the early light of morning will show up in the ring under the bright lights."

– Joe Frazier, champion American boxer/entertainer/businessman; Olympic gold medalist; heavyweight champ for 4 years; a hard trainer who inspired the beef punching scene in 'Rocky'

"The dream is free, but the hustle is sold separately."

– Steve Harvey, Emmy-winning American comedian/TV host/producer/actor/author; gained his work ethic farming; believes in goal visualization; four-time winner of the NAACP Image Award

"You can't wait for inspiration. You have to go after it with a club."

– Jack London, iconic American writer/social activist; known for 'The Call of the Wild;' worked a variety of hard jobs in youth; pioneered magazine adventure fiction; father was an astrologer

"Meditation is not a selfish thing. Even though you're diving in and experiencing the Self, you're not closing yourself off from the world. You're strengthening yourself, so that you can be more effective when you go back into the world."

– David Lynch, award-winning American filmmaker/painter/musician/actor/photographer; style is described as disturbing, violent and surreal; built foundation to teach meditation in schools

"Every seven years, I sit down and make a whole new plan."

– Dolly Parton, Grammy HOF American singer-songwriter/actress/entrepreneur/philanthropist; "The Queen of Country;" had #1 hits in four consecutive decades; has written over 5,000 songs

"The secret of success is conviction and persistence."

– Maharishi Mahesh Yogi, iconic Indian guru; introduced Transcendental Meditation to the West; built a meditation-practice global empire; famed as The Beatles spiritual advisor

"Don't wait until problems pile up and cause a lot of trouble before trying to solve them. Leaders must march ahead of the movement, not lag behind it."

– Mao Zedong, Chinese political leader; Communist revolutionary; served as Chairman of the Chinese Communist Party for 27 years; fought to rid China of traditional and capitalist elements

Aquarius 5

The key to the Aquarius 5 personality is their willingness to champion personal authenticity, no matter what crazy situations the universe decides to thrust upon them. Innately open-minded and tolerant of situational vagaries, like most Aquarius Suns, they are pretty much undaunted in the face of full Moon madness, rather enjoying the prospect of playing hub to a rolling wheel. More than most other souls the Aquarius 5 simply accepts and embraces the evolution as part of the human condition and as a great test of worthiness.

Having stipulated the vibe of broadmindedness that surrounds most of these souls, it is not surprising that the battle that the Aquarius 5 does wage is in the establishment of personal space. The fifth lunation phase emergence of soul is an extraordinarily individualistic proposition to Aquarius 5. The biggest trouble they have is enduring the influence of beings who refuse to accept that free-ranging consciousness is as worthy as the confines of any vested outlook or code...in other words, their radars are easily jammed

When they are left to manage their own paths, Aquarius 5's are capable of dazzling feats of creativity and cultural contribution. The process of knowing themselves fosters the liberation of human potential. They may aptly be described as avatars of awareness, veritably dancing into tomorrow.

It's little surprise that these folks are often among the most popular of humans, bringing an attractive mix of self-awareness and open-mindedness into the human space. They are firm of purpose but open to surprise. Most of all, the Aquarius 5 life speaks credibly to the human desire to be, at least within the confines of one's own consciousness, free.

"I cannot stand authority."

– Mikhail Baryshnikov, Emmy-winning Russian-American dancer/choreographer/actor; Soviet defector; considered one of ballet's all-time greats; recipient of Kennedy Center Honors

"Children, listen, I'm trying to tell you something good, don't get caught up in the hood."

– Dr. Dre, Grammy-winning American rapper/producer/entrepreneur; was an original member of the Compton-based rap group N.W.A.; sold his Beats headphone company to Apple for $3B

"Attitude is more important than the past, than education, than money, than circumstances, than what people do or say. It is more important than appearance, giftedness, or skill."

– W. C. Fields, iconic American comedian/actor/juggler/writer; famed for his perpetually drunk misanthropic comic persona and his distaste for children and Philadelphia, the place of his birth

"I am a huge believer in giving back and helping out in the community and the world. Think globally, act locally I suppose. I believe that the measure of a person's life is the affect they have on others."

– Steve Nash, HOF Canadian pro basketball player/sports executive/filmmaker/philanthropist; two-time NBA MVP; politically outspoken; created foundation for children living in poverty

"I had a lot of resentment for a while toward Kim Novak. But I don't mind her anymore. She's okay. We've become friends."

– Kim Novak, award-wining American actress/painter; best known for her dual role in 'Vertigo;' extremely successful at the box office but conflicted by the Hollywood system; bullying victim

"I am for an art that takes its form from the lines of life itself; that twists and extends and accumulates and spits and drips, and is heavy and coarse and blunt and sweet and stupid as life itself."

– Claes Oldenburg, award-winning Swedish American sculptor; associated with the "pop art" movement; best known for public art installations featuring large replicas of everyday objects

"Love life and life will love you back. Love people and they will love you back."

– Arthur Rubinstein, Grammy HOF Polish-American pianist; extroverted; famed for Chopin interpretations; prestigious int'l piano competition bears his name; Kennedy Honors recipient

"I've learned by hanging out in Hollywood, where I disagree politically with most people, that most people's hearts are in the right place, and the only thing we have to argue about is the way to solve the problems"

– Tom Selleck, Emmy-winning American actor/producer/writer; best known for lead roles in TV action dramas 'Magnum P.I' and 'Bluebloods;' attended USC on a basketball scholarship

"If each one of us could make just one other happy, the whole world would know happiness."

– Georges Simenon, award-winning Belgian author; wrote hundreds of books with sales in the hundreds of millions; best known for detective Jules Maigret; wrote conflicting autobiographies

"The one thing that everybody wants is to be free not to be managed."

– Gertrude Stein, iconic American novelist/poet/playwright/art collector; immersed in the consideration of human awareness; a founder of 20thC modernism; famed for her Paris salon

"It's easier to be responsible for the decisions that you've made yourself than for the ones that other people have made for you."

– John Travolta, award-winning American actor/producer/dancer/singer; breakthrough was as Vinnie Barbarino on 'Welcome Back, Kotter;' best known for hit movie musicals; a Scientologist

"I simply find that as a songwriter, my goal is to try to move people. And I feel that before I can move other people, I have to genuinely be able to move myself."

– Travis Tritt, Grammy-winning American country singer/songwriter/actor; incorporates rock and R&B into country music; big hit is post-divorce 'Here's A Quarter (Call Someone Who Cares)'

 Pisces 5

The oceanic potential of the fifth lunation phase is certainly not wasted on Pisces. Inclined to experience life emotionally/intuitively in any incarnation, the vastness of feeling that floods into the full Moon phase creates an extraordinary opportunity for Pisces 5. The conditions of this phase ultimately invite them to go anywhere and manifest anything.

As even the limited list of note worthies below suggests, it's hard to round up this crew into a neat little goldfish bowl of consistent sense. Here there is immersion in, and surrender to, the All. Establishing a firm behavioral bottom line is both a fool's errand and rather beside the point.

How the Pisces 5's may be somewhat collectivized is via an appreciation of the intensity of their immersion in life. Rather than abstracted observation, their métier is feeling on the cellular level. Only somewhat inclined to establish the sense of things, they are far more keen to dwell amidst life's subtlest rhythmic intensities and to plumb the depths of sensation.

Assuredly, this orientation can lead to intoxication and a general strangeness as part of the story. Yet with the Pisces 5 one also tends to encounter inspiration and empathy that are second to none. When they report that they feel something or someone, they are not just being metaphorical.

Inevitably both Love and God enter the Pisces 5 picture. What else besides the touching of hearts by grace could possibly explain the place of humanity in this boundless and basically incomprehensible universe? With Pisces 5 one is not likely to get more, or less, of an explanation than that.

"God has strewn our paths with wonders and we certainly should not go through life with our eyes shut."

– Alexander Graham Bell, famed Scottish-American scientist/engineer/inventor/businessman; invented/patented the first telephone; co-founded AT&T; spent life aiding the hearing impaired

"The success I've achieved comes to me from God"

– Justin Bieber, Grammy-winning Canadian singer/songwriter/musician; discovered at age 13 as a YouTube performer; personal motto is "never say never;" claustrophobic; fans are "Beliebers"

"When I stand before God at the end of my life, I would hope that I would not have a single bit of talent left, and could say, 'I used everything you gave me'."

– Erma Bombeck, popular American humorist/author; famed for a syndicated column describing suburban home life; typed all of her work, claiming she could not be funny on a word processor

"You're something between a dream and a miracle."

– Elizabeth Barrett Browning, celebrated English romantic poet; famed for her poem 'How Do I Love Thee?'; not formally educated; lifelong neurological disorders led to opium dependence

"Do I believe in God? Yes I do. When you've had a life like mine, you have to."

– Michael Caine, Oscar-winning English actor; known for a prolific career including roles in 130+ movies; says near-death experience in Korean War defined his life; at times a notorious drinker

"The greatest thing you'll ever learn is just to love and be loved in return."

– Nat King Cole, Grammy HOF American jazz pianist/singer/actor; first African-American to host a TV variety show; 'Unforgettable' and 'The Christmas Song' are iconic among his 100+ hits

"Well, you know, it's really been, you know, quite a trip for me."

– Patty Hearst, American; granddaughter of William Randolph Hearst; famously kidnapped and radicalized by left-wing terrorists; received 35-year sentence for bank robbery (pardoned)

"Where I live if someone gives you a hug it's from the heart."

– Steve Irwin, iconic Australian zookeeper/conservationist/television personality; grew up in a reptile park; his show, 'The Crocodile Hunter,' aired in 130 countries; died from stingray wound

"Let's not get too full of ourselves. Let's leave space for God to come into the room."

– Quincy Jones, Grammy Legend Award-winning American producer/composer/musician; a key music influencer for 60 years; holds record 80 Grammy nominations; a global humanitarian

"You have to allow for the impossible to be possible."

– Lupita Nyong'o, Oscar-winning Kenyan-Mexican actress/producer/spokesperson; earned a Masters degree in drama from Yale; won an Oscar for '12 Years A Slave,' her first film

"Technique is what you fall back on when you run out of inspiration."

– Rudolf Nureyev, preeminent Russian ballet dancer/choreographer; nicknamed "Lord of the Dance;" first Soviet artist to defect during Cold War; non-conformist; died of AIDS complications

"To call the world God is not to explain it; it is only to enrich our language with a superfluous synonym."

– Arthur Schopenhauer, esteemed German philosopher; known as "The Artist's Philosopher;" incorporated Eastern thought into his work; sometimes called "the first European Buddhist"

6th Lunation Phase/Disseminating Gibbous Moon

Moon is 226 to 270 degrees ahead of the Sun

Keyword: Realization

Much has been written through the ages about man's search for identity. This is not so much of an issue for people living a 6th lunation phase life; for these are the individuals who, with souls fully manifest, damn well can't help but being who they are.

The ego influence of the Sun sign will clarify the nature and modulate the strength of the LP6 personality, but the common thread is living out loud with purpose. There is an extraordinary lack of doubt regarding one's mission. These are lives in which the immortal soul is fully developed and ready to give marching orders.

Now to be clear, there are some really terrible human beings who fall into the LP6 category. Adolph Hitler and Machiavelli, for example, lived in LP6 incarnations. Sadly, in the range of lifetimes consecrated to living out one's idealized self, there are not only altruistic possibilities.

Mostly, though, one has to stand in awe of the individuals who reflect the glorious possibilities of an LP6 incarnation. Mother Teresa and Joan of Arc come to mind. So do Albert Einstein, Thomas Jefferson, Winston Churchill; or to be less historically sophisticated, Yogi Berra and Marilyn Monroe. In general, the LP6 individual simply brands themselves on humanity because they are incapable of being anything but totally authentic and true to their stars.

There's not much more to say than that. As for a mantra, these words of LP6 Vincent Van Gogh should suffice: "One must never let the fire go out in one's soul."

 Aries 6

In the sixth lunation phase, the natural boldness and exuberance that exists in almost all Aries Sun individuals is uniquely enhanced by a capacity for constancy. Not merely content to punch and run, the Aries 6 is imbued with a unique sort of steadiness that emanates from soul knowledge. These are Aries who live not only to be passionate in the moment, but to fiercely build a life (and institutions) full of worthy purpose.

As with any other iteration of their Sun sign, an Aries 6 appreciates the primacy of the individual in worldly affairs. Yet the Aries 6 also appreciates the need for strong individuals to form a compact regarding social purpose. They may be classicists or capitalists or conservationists or comedians, anything really, but their defining collectivism resides in the notion that life is a challenge for everyone and cannot be conquered without the exercise of a consortium of righteous wills.

In this vein, one of the more arresting features of an Aries 6 is their philosophical orientation towards humanism. It's not that they lack a belief in a cosmological spirit; it's simply that they ARE the Spirit. Worldly troubles, according to an Aries 6, are created by man and therefore must be addressed by man.

At times the willful outlook of an Aries 6 seems to push the envelope of sanity. They are quite capable of making others uncomfortable via their unique combination of energy and lack of doubt. Yet these are true warriors of the valid purpose, and their contributions to the cause of humanity are not for those who value a shrug over a shared capacity for individuals to grow.

In all the Aries 6 tends to be an exemplar of a dedicated spirit in an existence that beckons for far more than just a passing through.

"Man's main task in life is to give birth to himself, to become what he potentially is. The most important product of his effort is his own personality."

– Erich Fromm, eminent German-American psychoanalyst/social philosopher; contemplated interaction between psychology and society; major humanism award given annually in his name

"Above all we must realize that each of us makes a difference with our life. Each of us impacts the world around us every single day. We have a choice to use the gift of our life to make the world a better place–or not to bother."

– Jane Goodall, award-winning English primatologist/anthropologist/author; known for seminal field work with chimpanzees; tireless wildlife/conservation/environmental/peace activist

"We can believe in the future and work to achieve it and preserve it, or we can whirl blindly on, behaving as if one day there will be no children to inherit our legacy. The choice is ours; the earth is in balance."

– Al Gore, Nobel-laureate American politician/environmentalist; served eight years as V.P. of the U.S; his fierce global warming concerns are chronicled in Oscar-winning 'An Inconvenient Truth'

"We will be soldiers, so our sons may be farmers, so their sons may be artists."

– Thomas Jefferson, legendary American statesman/diplomat/lawyer/architect; a U.S. Founding Father and the nation's third president; author of the Declaration of Independence

"Anything worth doing is worth overdoing."

– David Letterman, Emmy-winning American television host/comedian/writer/producer; hosted a late night show for record 33 years; recipient of Mark Twain Prize and Kennedy Center Honors

"I have great energy and I have great tasks ahead of me."

– Garry Kasparov, famed Russian chess grandmaster/writer/political activist; arguably the greatest chess player of all time, ranked world #1 for 20 years; a strident democracy advocate

"Optimism is important. You have to be a little silly about the goals you are going to set. There is a phrase I learned in college called, 'having a healthy disregard for the impossible.' That is a really good phrase. You should try to do things that most people would not do."

– Larry Page, award-winning American computer scientist/Internet entrepreneur; co-founder of Google; CEO of Alphabet, Inc. for which he earns $1/yr; great supporter of alternative energy

"We never thought we'd get this far, but we're here."

– Selena Quintanilla, Grammy-winning American singer/songwriter/spokesperson/model/ actress/fashion designer; the "Queen of Tejano" music; murdered at age 23 by an associate

"I'm the person who writes most of my movies so every role is exactly what I want to be doing."

– Seth Rogen, award-winning Canadian-American actor/comedian/writer/producer/director; twice selected as 'High Times' Stoner of the Year; a crusader for an Alzheimer's Disease cure

"One must never let the fire go out in one's soul, but keep it burning."

– Vincent Van Gogh, seminal Dutch post-Impressionist painter; one of the most renowned artists of the 20th C; many of his best known works were created while he was in an asylum

"Don't let anyone tell you what you can and can't do or achieve. Do what you want to do and be who you want to be."

– Emma Watson, award-winning British actress/model; famed as the young witch Hermione in the Harry Potter films; she's a certified yoga teacher and an active advocate for gender equality

"There is a garbage culture out there, where we pour garbage on people. Then the pollsters run around and take a poll and say, do you smell anything?"

– Bob Woodward, Pulitzer-winning American journalist/author; best known for investigative reporting on the Watergate scandal; has written twelve #1 non-fiction bestsellers

Taurus 6

The Taurus imbued with the strength of a fully realized soul is a being arguably as resolute as the phenomenon of incarnation can manage. Born with a figurative hammer in their hand and placed in front of a metaphorical mountain, the Taurus 6 life tends to end up as an exquisite monument to talent and perseverance, or as crushing testimony to the process of making boulders.

At their best, and even at their worst for that matter, the Taurus 6 launches a balled fist at the collective concept of struggle. The 'get up after you have been knocked down' wisdom that proliferates through much of human effort is a head scratcher to Taurus 6. Why, they are prone to wonder, would anyone let themselves get knocked down?

Whatever fate decides to hand a Taurus 6 in terms of personal qualities, be they good or evil, there are invariably markers of amplified strength and endurance. Whatever they do or become in the realms of thought or art or commerce or physical accomplishment it is hard to label them as mere flash in the pans. The Taurus 6 is far more inclined to profound traction, lengthy investment and, ultimately, historical dominance.

It might seem to others that these Taurus 6's are over-ponderous and that they often take themselves too seriously. There's probably no upside in making fun of them, though...at least not to their face.

"People react to criticism in different ways, and my way is definitely to come out fighting."

– David Beckham, iconic English pro footballer/international celebrity/ businessman; one of the great players of his generation; highly paid endorser; suffers from OCD; a tattoo "fanatic"

"If you are going to wait for someone to encourage you to do something, you just better give up."

– Cher, Oscar/Grammy/Emmy-winning American singer/actress/producer/ philanthropist; the "Goddess of Pop;" beloved for her style, her projection of strength and her independence

"Life does not forgive weakness."

– Adolf Hitler, German statesman/dictator; Chancellor/Fuhrer of Germany; leader of the Nazi Party; initiated WWII by ordering the invasion of Poland

"Be the person that when your feet touch the floor in the morning the devil says, 'awe s***... they're up'."

– Dwayne Johnson, award-winning American actor/producer/pro wrestler/ philanthropist; known as "The Rock;" plays powerful tough guys with a heart; aspires to be a Bond villain

"I can show you how to box. I can teach you every technique and trick I know, but I can never make you a fighter. That comes from inside, and it's something no one else can ever give you."

– Joe Louis, champion American boxer; the "Brown Bomber;" held the world heavyweight crown for 13 years through 25 defenses; known for honesty and hard work; a true American hero

"You have to find something that you love enough to be able to take risks, jump over the hurdles and break through the brick walls that are always going to be placed in front of you. If you don't have that kind of feeling for what it is you're doing, you'll stop at the first giant hurdle."

– George Lucas, iconic American movie writer/director/producer/philanthropist; created 'Star Wars' and 'Indiana Jones;' founded Industrial Light & Magic; a signer of The Giving Pledge

"In order to excel, you must be completely dedicated."

– Willie Mays, all-time great HOF American baseball player; "The Say Hey Kid;" known for his great all-around skills; two-time MVP; selected as an all-star in 19 consecutive seasons

"A battle that you win cancels all your mistakes."

– Niccolo Machiavelli, famed Italian Renaissance diplomat/philosopher/writer; the father of modern political theory; best known for 'The Prince,' a cynical tract about political power

"Life is not a finished product, it is only what we make of it, and if we make nothing of it, someone else will, and we will be his slave."

– Yehudi Menuhin, Grammy HOF American violinist/conductor/humanitarian; one of the great violin virtuosos of the 20th C; his career spanned eight decades; introduced yoga to the West

"I don't want people leaving the theater depressed after my movies. I want them angry."

– Michael Moore, Oscar-winning American filmmaker/author/activist; known best for controversial documentaries attacking capitalism and right wing politics; uninhibited muckraker

"There is no happiness. There is only concentration."

– Al Pacino, Oscar/Tony/Emmy-winning American actor; renowned for his dramatic intensity; signature films include 'Serpico' and 'The Godfather;' legendary career has spanned 5+ decades

"I believe you have to live the songs."

– Tammy Wynette, Grammy HOF American country singer/songwriter; known as "The First Lady of Country Music" and "The Heroine of Heartbreak;" suffered from addiction to pain-killers

Gemini 6

Mental dexterity is a quality that is deeply vested in the Gemini nature. In the Gemini sixth lunation phase, a lifetime in which personality is brought into its fullest expression via fullness of soul, one not does suddenly encounter a celebration of absolutes. Rather, the Gemini 6 life tends to be a willing testament to the fullest possibilities of the vague, the puzzling and the flat-out contradictory.

Living a life in which no truth can be classified as evident might seem burdensome to most. Yet for the Gemini 6 the condition of their perception serves more as a goad than an obstacle. A mystery may be sweetest at the point of its solution, but flexible participation in the collection of clues also has its charms.

If there is a capital-T Truth in a Gemini 6 life, it's mostly that everyone else in the world is suffering from a failure to perceive that life rarely presents itself in anything but shades of grey. Ask most Gemini 6's what they want out of life and the answer is simple. They want other people, who they inevitably regard as compromised sources, to refrain from telling them about propriety, communal wisdom and conformity.

In most cases, when a Gemini 6 is directed towards a consideration of absolutes, they are happy to admit that a God surely exists. The existence of this Supreme Being though, the Gemini 6 argues not unreasonably, is entirely predicated on a perfection that must be apprehended through a mind whose central perceptive condition is ambiguity. This is the kind of conundrum that a Gemini 6 just loves.

Mostly it gets down to the fact that a Gemini 6 loves thinking but has little use for certainty. They need to go their own ways intellectually, without taking themselves or anyone else as too much of an authority. They are compelling speakers, often identifiable by their distinctive voices, and in any situation they tend to have something really interesting to say.

"There is nothing more deceptive than an obvious fact."

– Sir Arthur Conan Doyle, award-winning British writer; best known as the creator of Sherlock Holmes; originally a physician; eclectic interests included sports, architecture and spiritualism

"The odds are lousy that I actually said something attributed to me."

– Morgan Freeman, Oscar-winning American actor/director/humanitarian; claims he knew he would be offered a role as God; co-owns a blues club; keeps bees; has written a cookbook

"I don't think there is any truth. There are only points of view."

– Allen Ginsberg, award-winning American poet/philosopher; a leading figure of the Beat Generation; famous for the epic poem 'Howl;' led a liberated globally-expansive life

"How can you be a vegetarian atheist and own a gun? Well, that's who I am."

– Bobcat Goldthwait, award-winning American comedian/director/actor/screenwriter; known for acerbic observations and crazed stage persona; stridently non-conformist

"Who is going to believe a con artist? Everyone, if she is good."

– Andy Griffith, Grammy-winning American Gospel singer/actor/comedian/producer; famed as Sheriff Andy of Mayberry and as 'Matlock;' often played sociopaths/alcoholics in TV movies

"The best way to describe myself would be...unpredictable."

– Kendrick Lamar, Grammy and Pulitzer-award winning American rapper/songwriter/producer; gangster roots; a straight-A student; an ardent born-again Christian, was Jesus for Halloween

"It's all make-believe, isn't it?"

– Marilyn Monroe, award-winning American actress/model/singer; "The Blonde Bombshell;"one of history's great sex symbols; very bright and well-read; spoke of "Marilyn" in the 3rd person

"As long as I do not take myself too seriously I should not be too badly off."

– Prince, Grammy/R&R HOF/Oscar-winning American singer/songwriter/musician/record producer/dancer/actor/filmmaker; played 27 instruments; a vegan and a Jehovah's Witness

"The individual's duty is to do what he wants to do, to think whatever he likes, to be accountable to no one but himself, to challenge every idea and every person."

– Jean-Paul Sartre, iconic French philosopher/playwright/novelist/political activist/biographer/literary critic; an eminent existentialist; famously declined the Nobel Prize

"I hate to tell people what they should think 'cause I really have an aversion when people tell me what to think."

– Octavia Spencer, Oscar-winning American actress/author/producer; played dozens of small parts before career breakthrough in 'The Help;' celebrated for her intelligence and versatility

"I don't expect to be understood at all."

– Kanye West, iconic American rapper/singer/songwriter/producer/entrepreneur/designer; music distinguished by diverse cultural influences; winner of 21 Grammy Awards (so far)

"People who lean on logic and philosophy and rational exposition end by starving the best part of the mind."

– William Butler Yeats, Nobel-laureate Irish poet/politician; considered one of the greatest literary figures of 20th C; poignantly wrote of Irish lore; devoted to occultism/spiritualism[1]

 Cancer 6

In most of the Cancer Sun descriptions to this point, the emphasis has been on the nature of defining oneself in an emotions-based reality. When passion is the predominant lens through which life is experienced, there is often a danger of drowning in feeling. A useful image is the Moon's tidal effects and the rather high unlikelihood of successfully surfing every wave.

In this light, what makes the Cancer 6 lunation phase so compelling is that there is ample evidence of the development of life skill that manifests as self-control. Granted fullness of soul, the Cancer 6 is an individual who uniquely knows, if not how to entirely manage the emotions, at least where to usefully place the surfeit of feelings that tends to envelop every Cancer Sun native.

The magic, if it may be so called, is a constructive transference of one's emotional core to the welfare of others. Clannish by nature, the Cancer 6 lives a life that most often manifests in an extraordinary devotion to loved ones, particularly family. Truly though, the prime directive of this incarnation may be applied to any group in which the Cancer 6 native feels a strong membership...up to and including all of humanity.

---

1 It was no small surprise for me to find out that Yeats had himself written about the lunation phases and personality in his book 'A Vision,' published in 1925. His observation is that every individual symbolically passes through all the lunation phases in the course of a lifetime, but he also concluded that one phase provides an overall characterization of the individual's entire life. Imagine that.

Ultimately, the successful Cancer 6 lives a life that exalts the principal of responsibility in the context of human relatedness. One may experience the rewards of being loved in such a life, but the emphasis... the emotional ballast as it were...comes from an appreciation of love's outward directedness. One's life is ultimately defined by participation rather than introspection.

To fully appreciate the Cancer 6 is to recognize that they are not constructing an intellectual justification of their lives. Theirs is a gut choice made by the animating soul spirit. They are, especially among Cancers, remarkably and counter-intuitively adept at letting the waves help them keep their balance.

"You have to have something in your life that's more important than the work. People don't really like to admit that. I think that you have to find something else. I don't know what it is. Is it yoga or God or politics? For me it's just family."

– Kevin Bacon, award-winning American actor/musician; breakthrough film was 'Footloose;' wryly known as the actor to whom all actors are ultimately related; his wife is a distant cousin

"Family is the most important thing in the world."

– Princess Diana, England's premier celebrity royal; beloved for her warmth and her devotion to charitable causes; personal life marred by intrigue and tragedy, including her own death

"You do not belong to you. You belong to the universe. The significance of you will remain forever obscure to you, but you may assume you are fulfilling your significance if you apply yourself to converting all you experience to highest advantage to others."

– R. Buckminster Fuller, renowned American architect/inventor/futurist/author; dedicated life to search for human purpose; identified with the geodesic dome and the term "Spaceship Earth"

"Success is nothing if you don't have the right people to share it with; you're just gonna' end up lonely."

– Selena Gomez, award-winning American singer/songwriter/actress/ entrepreneur; famed as a star on the Disney Channel; youngest-ever UNICEF ambassador; "Selena" is Greek for "Moon"

"A home isn't just a roof over our heads. A home is a place where we feel loved and where we love others. It's a place we belong. Love is what makes a home, not the contents inside the house or the number on the door. It's the people waiting for us across the threshold, the people who will take us in their arms after a bad day and kiss us good night and good morning everyday for the rest of our lives."

– Herman Hesse, Nobel-laureate German-Swiss poet/novelist/painter; famed for works such as 'Siddhartha' and 'The Glass Bead' that explore self-knowledge, spirituality and responsibility

"My most important projects have been the building and maintaining of schools and medical clinics for my dear friends in the Himalaya and helping restore their beautiful monasteries, too."

– Edmund Hillary, iconic New Zealand mountaineer/explorer/philanthropist; first summiter of Mt. Everest; Nepalese medal awarded annually in his name for mountain culture conservation

"We are never really happy until we try to brighten the lives of others."

– Helen Keller, award-winning American author/philanthropist; famed for great accomplishment despite being deaf and blind; famous autobiography made into 'The Miracle Worker'

"I'm happy to be stuck with you."

– Huey Lewis, Grammy-winning American musician/songwriter/actor; known best for his work as the lead singer with the rock/pop group The News; left Cornell's engineering program for music

"God can only be comprehended as Love."

– Gustav Mahler, award-winning Austrian composer/conductor; wrote ten late Romantic-period symphonies; considered a great conductor, his own music was recognized mostly posthumously

"On the one hand, the businessman in me understands it. But the lover of movies in me wants desperately to hang on to the movie house as a collective experience with the audience."

– Sydney Pollack, Oscar-winning American film director/producer/actor; very prolific, his most lauded directorial efforts were 'Out of Africa' and 'Tootsie;' emphasized rapport with his actors

"The world is a wonderfully weird place, consensual reality is significantly flawed, no institution can be trusted, certainty is a mirage, security a delusion, and the tyranny of the dull mind forever threatens — but our lives are not as limited as we think they are, all things are possible, laughter is holier than piety, freedom is sweeter than fame, and in the end it's love and love alone that really matters."

– Tom Robbins, award-winning American author; books include 'Even Cowgirls Get the Blues' & 'Jitterbug Perfume;' called "one of the wildest and most entertaining novelists in the world"

"When two people love each other, they don't look at each other; they look in the same direction."

– Ginger Rogers, Oscar-winning American actress/dancer/singer/director/ artist; celebrated for film pairing with Fred Astaire; only child of a driven mother; married/divorced five times

"Story writers say that love is concerned only with young people, and the excitement and glamour of romance end at the altar. How blind they are. The best romance is inside marriage; the finest love stories come after the wedding, not before."

– Irving Stone, award-winning American biographical novelist; wrote 'The Agony and the Ecstasy' (Michelangelo) and 'Lust for Life' (Van Gogh); founded literary societies; married his editor

Leo 6

With any Leo Sun individual, one is dealing with a being whose life is an exaltation of an illuminated ego. Boorishly crafted or pressed too demonstratively, the Leo personality can cause considerable disturbance in the cultural environment. To those inclined to a little detachment in their lives, the effect of Leo glow can be negatively experienced as a noisy party in a quiet neighborhood.

What makes the situation so much more comfortable, inside and out, with a Leo 6 has to do with a talent for projecting genuine and compelling feelings. Living a life in which the ego has comfortably bonded with the vagaries and inhibitions related to one's emotional life, the typical Leo 6 finds himself/herself to be uniquely liberated to indulge and express their truest passion without the collateral damage of an aggrieved society. The Leo 6 is the lion who unashamedly roars its central truth with every fiber of its majestically self-conscious being, often engendering plenty of fans to appreciate the show.

Unsurprisingly, the reward and challenge of a Leo 6 life are two sides of the same coin. The Leo 6 is an individual who knows how to get high on their own illumination, and they rarely shrink or apologize from indulging in a little incandescence. Of course, despite their tendency to not ground themselves in the thoughts of others, being constantly high is not always an easy route to peace.

Still, you have to give a Leo 6 a lot of credit for knowing what they love and running towards it with the fullness of their being. Their stories are often made more wondrous by the fact that many of these souls start out from nowhere and end up as iconic champions of whatever enterprise to which they are called. Despite the pain and detours suffered in any life, these are the souls who truly believe that once can attain anything to which one sets their heart.

Ultimately, the Leo 6 is simply gifted in knowing what the heart desires. It's not the worst of soul draws.

"My whole life, my whole soul, my whole spirit is to blow that horn."

– Louis Armstrong, Grammy HOF American trumpeter/composer/vocalist/actor; a legendary jazz figure; known for 'What a Wonderful World;' oldest musician with #1 hit ('Hello, Dolly'/age 62)

"Football is unconditional love."

– Tom Brady, champion pro American football player; three-time NFL MVP, four-time Super Bowl MVP; was the third-string QB on a winless high school team; was a 199th NFL draft pick

"There's no life like the life I've lived. You're free like a cloud floating up in the sky."

– Doyle Brunson, champion American pro poker player/author; a rare multiple winner of WSOP Main Events; played for 50 years; key figure in making pro gambling respectable

"I like the job. That's what I'll miss the most... I'm not sure anybody ever liked this as much as I've liked it."

– William J. Clinton, Arkansas-born 42nd President of the United States; first Baby Boomer president; oversaw the longest period of peacetime economic expansion in American history

"I just wanted to perform. I just wanted to perform in whatever capacity, whether it was acting, singing, dancing, comedy–whatever it was, I just loved it and felt at my absolute happiest when I was performing for people."

– James Corden, Emmy and Tony-winning English actor/singer/comedian/TV host; known for 'The Late Late Show' and the Tony Awards; created worldwide phenomenon 'Carpool Karaoke'

“For me, I think the only danger is being too much in love with guitar playing.”

– Jerry Garcia, R&R HOF American singer/songwriter/guitarist; “Captain Trips;” best known as a founding member of The Grateful Dead; played despite a finger lost in a childhood accident

“I was aware of people staring at me. No one moved. They seemed almost in trance. I just stared at the clock in the center of the church. When I finished, everyone clapped and started crying.”

– Whitney Houston, Grammy HOF American singer/actress/model; cited as the most awarded female artist of all time by Guinness World Records; only artist to chart eight straight #1 hits

“You have to be doing something you enjoy. That is the definition of happiness.”

– Jackie Kennedy Onassis, distinguished American; First Lady of the United States during the presidency of John F. Kennedy; goodwill ambassador; an international style and culture icon

“I used to be self conscious about my height, but then I thought, f*** that, I’m Harry Potter.”

– Daniel Radcliffe, award-winning British actor/producer; star of the Harry Potter film series; took only two days off in 10 years of HP filming; self-described as an “addictive personality”

“I love the challenge of the game. I love the work. My goal right now is to have a season next year that will make people forget about this one. I’ll use things like this for motivation. I’m pumped. I’m hungry.”

– Alex Rodriguez, all-time great American pro baseball player; three-time MVP; played 22 years, earned over $300M in 12 seasons with the Yankees; late career marred by doping allegations

"I was a sportsman for years. I've always had a physical background. I've always had an interest in boxing and fighting. To get physical in films is a dream. I love it."

– Jason Statham, iconic British actor/producer; an action star, most often an antihero; does his own film combat and stunts; was a competitive diver; discovered while street-corner grifting

"I just do art because I'm ugly and there's nothing else for me to do."

– Andy Warhol, bellwether American artist/director/producer/author; a leader of the American pop art movement; a champion of Bohemian/celebrity culture; uniquely humorous & irreverent

Virgo 6

There is something in the Virgo character that gravitates towards earnestness. Most feel thoroughly complimented to be known as pragmatists and realists. They are at their best, and seem to be at their happiest, when called to give constructive and generally humble service to a conception or cause greater than themselves.

In the sixth lunation phase, the incarnation stage in which people are most inclined to be at peace in their own skins, the Virgo Sun fully radiates its nature in and via a universe of particularities. The typical Virgo 6 is unique in mining the delight and purpose of just about anything at all that they encounter. While Virgos in any lunation phase are rarely identified by surrender to the abstract, the Virgo 6 sees a higher purpose or the true depth in just about everything they come across.

So it is that while celebrity is not a stranger to the ranks of Virgo 6, there is little in this incarnation to suggest a desire for fame for its own sake. A concept that rings much truer here is *authenticity*. Getting close to life and to one's fellow humans is primarily an act of willing engagement with circumstances as they present themselves, not of blind ambition for a greater state of affairs.

Lest this sound somehow too saintly (and there *are* saints in the Virgo 6 lineup), it must be stressed that the Virgo 6 primarily has an endless capacity for being normal. Like others, they love and they hate; they succeed and they fail; they are here and then they are gone. Their uniqueness lies in an ability to bring everything down to a manageable scale, to let the value of even the smallest moments dictate the terms of time well spent.

There is wisdom in the Virgo 6 incarnation, although most of them would be too humble to make a fuss over it. It might be encapsulated as an admonishment to do whatever has value to one's spirit. It might be anything.

"Give me an hour and I'll make a lifetime out of it."

– Ingrid Bergman, Oscar/Emmy/Tony/Golden Globe-winning Swedish actress; nominated for 7 Oscars; 'Casablanca' made her a star; acted in 5 languages; saintly image tarnished by scandal

"If I don't become Brahms or Tchaikovsky or Stravinsky when I'm conducting their works, then it won't be a great performance."

– Leonard Bernstein, Grammy HOF American composer/conductor/author/educator/pianist; the first American conductor to achieve worldwide acclaim; best known for 'West Side Story' score

"If you do it right, your game will live on in others."

– Kobe Bryant, champion American pro basketball player/philanthropist; "Black Mamba;" NBA MVP; two-time NBA Finals MVP; entered NBA at 18 and played for LA Lakers for 20 years

"I would rather five people knew my work and thought it was good work than five million knew me and were indifferent."

– Colin Firth, Oscar-winning English actor/humanitarian; famed for "The King's Speech;' active in Survival International; author of a scientific paper on brain function and political affiliation

"There's a lot of times that both myself and my brother wish, obviously, that we were just completely normal."

– Prince Harry, Duke of Sussex, son of Charles and Diana; he's a decorated military pilot and has trekked to the South Pole; created the Invictus Games; active in many humanitarian causes

"Life happens. Adapt. Embrace change, and make the most of everything that comes your way."

– Nick Jonas, award-winning American singer/songwriter/actor; a Disney star as a member of the Jonas Brothers band; diabetic, he created a charitable foundation to assist kids with the illness

"I don't need much of a character in my life. I've already got one; my family knows who I am, and I don't have a reason to make an impression on the world around me unless it's in a professional context. Acting is not a personal experience; it's a job."

– Tommy Lee Jones, Oscar/Emmy/SAG-winning American actor/filmmaker; a Texan best known for playing smart/gritty lawmen; a *cum laude* Harvard graduate, starred on the football team

"The trouble with super heroes is what to do between phone booths."

– Ken Kesey, award-winning American novelist/essayist; was a key literary figure of the 1960's counterculture; wrote 'One Flew Over the Cuckoo's Nest;' did time for narcotics possession

"Be your authentic self. Your authentic self is who you are when you have no fear of judgment or before the world starts pushing you around and telling you who you're supposed to be. Your fictional self is who you are when you have a social mask on to please everyone else. Give yourself permission to be your authentic self."

– Dr. Phil McGraw, Emmy-winning American TV personality/author/psychologist/humanitarian; known for 'tough love' counseling on his popular TV show; prone to legal/ethical controversy

"Put your heart, mind, and soul into even your smallest acts. This is the secret of success."

– Sivananda Siraswata, Indian-born Hindu spiritual teacher/author/physician; founded the Divine Life Society; venerated in the world of classical yoga; was a medical minister to the poor

"I don't do great things. I do small things with great love."

– Mother Teresa, Albanian-Indian nun/missionary; honored in the Roman Catholic Church as a Saint; founded the Calcutta-based Missionaries of Charity; devoted life to serving those in need

"I like to unplug and enjoy being a human."

– Zendaya, award-winning American actress/singer/dancer/entrepreneur/humanitarian; a Disney star; known for 'Spiderman' and "The Greatest Showman;' Zendaya is "to give thanks"

 Libra 6

In considering the Libra 6 incarnation, it might be enough to report that these people are thoughtful and tend to have a highly developed sense of humor. It's not, definitely not, that these folks view life as a joke. They simply get a chuckle out of humankind's penchant for living and dying in a quest for absolute truth.

Certainly, any Libra Sun is inclined to seek a balance of life's oppositional forces. The Libra 6 gift, however, is to pursue this balance without a whole lot of upsetting emotional baggage. Tirelessly striving for understanding may well be a worthy goal, knows the Libra 6, but so is allowing oneself the spiritual/emotional/physical freedom to be at peace with whatever life presents and to appreciate the keen ameliorative possibilities of a good nap.

As with other members of the Libra tribe, the Libra 6 does have one particular orientation that keeps them tethered to a functioning existence in the earth plane. When all other reconciliations of reality fail, one can always open oneself up to the possibility of grace. They may sometimes not understand the question, but a Libra 6 knows a good answer, always, is love.

The real charm of the Libra 6 is that they are rarely inclined to shove love or anything else into the face of their earthly co-inhabitants. Their métiers are humor, companionability and a flexible appreciation for existence that represents anything but weakness. Disinclined to drown in complexity, they prefer an honest simple truth with plenty of balance and a side of really crispy fries.

In all, the Libra 6 incarnation is one that acknowledges life is an experience for contemplating rather than for reaching verdicts. It may not run smooth. But how hard is it to crack a smile?

"Do you have to have a reason for loving?"

– Brigitte Bardot, award-winning French actress/singer/animal rights activist; globally renowned sex symbol of the 1950's/60's; popularized the bikini and inspired the term "sex kitten"

"To do the useful thing, to say the courageous thing, to contemplate the beautiful thing: that is enough for one man's life."

– T.S. Eliot, Nobel laureate American poet/essayist/publisher/playwright/critic; wrote his poetry in his spare time; wrote famous nihilistic/philosophical works and the lyrics for 'Cats'

"I would start a revolution, but I just bought a hammock."

– Zach Galifianakis, Emmy-winning American actor/comedian/writer/humanitarian; major fame came via 'The Hangover;' known for 'Baskets' and 'Between Two Ferns;' raises horses and bees

"The word philosophy sounds high-minded, but it simply means the love of wisdom. If you love something, you don't just read about it; you hug it, you mess with it, you play with it, you argue with it."

– Hugh Jackman, Tony-winning Australian actor/singer/producer/philanthropist; iconic as Marvel's Wolverine; musicals include 'Les Misérables' and 'The Greatest Showman;' yoga buff

"Those are my principles, and if you don't like them... well, I have others."

– Groucho Marx, award-wining American actor/comedian/writer/TV host; a master of wit; best known for his 13 Marx Brothers films; received an honorary lifetime achievement Oscar

"I live my life in gratitude."

– Olivia Newton-John, Grammy-winning Australian singer/songwriter/actress/entrepreneur/ dancer; famed as Sandy in the film 'Grease;' had 5 #1 pop hits; breast cancer survivor/activist

"I love being. There's so much wisdom in it. You wake up in the morning and you think, Hey, isn't it great just being?"

– Gwyneth Paltrow, Oscar/Emmy-winning American actress/singer/author/entrepreneur; known for roles in 'Shakespeare in Love' and 'Iron Man; founder of the Goop wellness lifestyle brand

"Love is more important than what we can take...Please say with me three times–Love! Love! Love!"

– Pele, HOF Brazilian soccer player/goodwill ambassador; widely regarded as one of the greatest footballers of all time; only player to have won three World Cups; IOC Athlete of the Century

"All God requires from us is to enjoy life and love. That's the whole point."

– Paul Simon, R&R/Grammy HOF American singer/songwriter/musician/actor; 3-time winner of Album of the Year; helmed Simon & Garfunkel; first inspired by Chuck Berry's "effortless lyrics"

"You don't have to tell a child to explore the backyard."

– Neil deGrasse Tyson, award-winning American astrophysicist/author/communicator; Hayden Planetarium director; embroiled in Pluto's demotion; once named "sexiest astrophysicist alive"

"A good laugh makes any interview, or any conversation, so much better."

– Barbara Walters, Emmy-winning American broadcast journalist/author; has hosted numerous TV news shows; was the first female network news co-anchor; famed for establishing rapport

"It was difficult to get into my friends' rock bands when I was a teenager. They somehow didn't see the need for an accordion player. That's when I realized that I had to find my own path in life."

– "Weird Al" Yankovic, Grammy-winning American singer/songwriter/actor/author/director; best known for song parodies; breakthrough hit was 'My Bologna' recorded in a tiled bathroom

 Scorpio 6

Nobody embraces concepts such as "victimless crime," "profiting from one's mistakes," and "when life hands you lemons, make lemonade" better than a Scorpio 6. For sure, life hands out chaotic, disastrous and wholly unprompted assaults on the integrity of one's existence. And yet, asks the Scorpio 6, are the only sensible reactions to place blame and cry?

In the case of the Scorpio 6, living in the lunation phase in which one's emotions are especially manageable, one comes very close to turning the universe's propensity for meanness into an odd sort of gift. Nobody better appreciates that there is a kind of human magic at the extreme limits of the human will. It mostly boils down to the classic proposition that what doesn't kill you makes you stronger.

To be sure, the demands on one's body and spirit tend to be strong in most Scorpio lifetimes. They all tend to breathe complexity and confrontation as readily as oxygen. A testing of will in the face of adversity is what this Sun sign is all about.

For a Scorpio 6 the difference, though, may simply be one of enthusiasm in a harder they come the harder they fall kind of way. Battle scars are not simply to be endured. They are gifts to be pronounced beautiful and cherished as the key to self-actualization.

Thus, the Scorpio 6 lives a warrior/survivalist life of willing engagement and shrewd adaptation. Frankness, fearlessness and ferocity are the choice of weapons. Life is not sweet, growth is not for the weak, and the only thing one can count on is the unexpected.

Just be sure, when it is said and done, to give as good as you get.

"Tables turn, bridges burn, you live and learn."

– Drake, Grammy-winning Canadian rapper/singer/songwriter/producer/ actor/entrepreneur; bullied in youth as a black Jew; associated with the phrase YOLO; has his own record label

"I've given up asking questions. I merely float on a tsunami of acceptance of anything life throws at me ... and marvel stupidly."

– Terry Gilliam, award-winning British screenwriter/director/animator/ actor/comedian; only American-born member of Monty Python; work touts imagination and anti-authoritarianism

"We have to be able to grow up. Our wrinkles are our medals of the passage of life. They are what we have been through and who we want to be."

– Lauren Hutton, famed American model/actress/entrepreneur; was a 'Vogue' cover girl a record 26 times; first million-dollar model; a free spirit; signed at age 73 to rep Calvin Klein underwear

"I've always been happy to take a gamble on myself. "

– Peter Jackson, Oscar-winning New Zealand film director/screenwriter/film producer; best known for the 'Lord of the Rings' trilogy; third highest-grossing box-office director of all time

"Today we are engaged in a final, all-out battle between communistic atheism and Christianity. The modern champions of communism have selected this as the time, and ladies and gentlemen, the chips are down–they are truly down."

– Joseph McCarthy, influential American politician; a U.S. Senator; as the political face of the 1950's "Red Scare" known for his belligerent crusade to rid American society of communism

"If all difficulties were known at the outset of a long journey, most of us would never start out at all."

– Dan Rather, Emmy-winning American journalist; best known as a TV correspondent/anchor; came to prominence reporting the JFK assassination; distinguished career has lasted 60+ years

"Life is full of surprises and serendipity. Being open to unexpected turns in the road is an important part of success. If you try to plan every step, you may miss those wonderful twists and turns. Just find your next adventure-do it well, enjoy it-and then, not now, think about what comes next."

– Condoleezza Rice, iconic American educator/diplomat; first African-American woman to serve as U.S. Secretary of State; Stanford University provost/professor; aspired to be a concert pianist

"Good judgment comes from experience, and a lot of that comes from bad judgment."

– Will Rogers, Cherokee-American actor/cowboy/humorist/writer; earned legendary status as a cowboy philosopher; annual awards are given in his name for Western Americana contributions

"Nothing in the world is worth having or worth doing unless it means effort, pain, difficulty... I have never in my life envied a human being who led an easy life. I have envied a great many people who led difficult lives and led them well."

– Theodore Roosevelt, American statesman/politician/conservationist/writer; the 26th president of the U.S.; elevated presidential power; created the Rough Riders; won a Nobel Peace Prize

"Raw is a good place for an artist. It's where the truth comes out."

– Keith Urban, Grammy-winning Australian-American singer/songwriter/musician/producer; recorded 9 platinum albums; two-time ACM Entertainer of the Year; music education promoter

"Unannounced changes in life's itinerary are like dancing lessons from God."

– Kurt Vonnegut, award-winning American writer/social critic; known for offbeat science fiction and cutting satire in books like 'Slaughterhouse Five' and 'Cat's Cradle;' was a POW in Germany

"At 49, I can say something I never would have said when I was a player, that I'm a better person because of my failures and disgraces."

– Bill Walton, HOF American basketball star/TV analyst; fan of the counter-culture; known for hyperbolic/cultured quotes during basketball telecasts; many injuries, including spine failure

Sagittarius 6

It's something about the way a Sagittarius 6 looks, and that can be taken two ways. On the one hand there tends to be a physical originality to the Sagittarius 6, an eccentric appearance that however brazen or outlandish somehow suits them perfectly. On the other hand, there is often something special about their eyes, as if they are looking at something far away that only they can see and that is making them smile, or is at least making them shake their head in bemused epiphany.

Generally unfazed by emotional uncertainty, as is the signature state of the sixth lunation phase, the Sagittarius 6 is simply a beacon of positive potential. In this incarnation, there is no bound circumference to the field of human possibility. The higher up, the further out there, the better it gets.

What one has here, in sum, is an authentic optimist. A Sagittarius 6 eschews an accepted ways of doing things, institutional largesse, and the spotty grace of a Man Upstairs. They simply believe that life is driven by their own perspective and a positive attitude, so why not make a bit of a happy life transport device out of that.

Self-motivated, self-actualized, optimistic about tomorrow's outcomes, the Sagittarius 6 in the embodiment of what some spiritualists describe as the power of intention. Even in the face of overwhelming opposition, there is an inescapable bopper bag mentality. With so much 'up' in the world, the Sagittarius 6's just can't find it in them to stay 'down.'

"What's "God"? Well, you know, when you want something really bad and you close your eyes and you wish for it? God's the guy that ignores you."

– Steve Buscemi, Golden Globe/SAG/Emmy-winning American actor/ filmmaker; known for playing oddball characters; lauded for work on TV series 'Boardwalk Empire;' a former fireman

"I really believe there is the possibility of something great that can happen in the right hands."

– Alfonso Cuaron, Oscar-winning Mexican filmmaker; won best director Oscars for 'Roma' and 'Gravity;' directed 'The Prisoner of Azkaban' without having read any of the Harry Potter books

"The positive thinker sees the invisible, feels the intangible, and achieves the impossible."

– Winston Churchill, venerated British politician/army officer/writer; famously the Prime Minister of the United Kingdom during WWII; won a Nobel for literature; was a prolific artist

"Anything that's not positive, I don't have the energy to focus on it."

– DMX, award-winning American rapper/actor; only artist to have had five albums debut at #1; marked by considerable legal troubles; aspires to be a pastor and has released a Gospel album

"It's never too late–never too late to start over, never too late to be happy."

– Jane Fonda, Oscar-winning American actress/model/political activist/ entrepreneur; has had 50+- year acting career; famed for anti-war activism; known as a fitness video trendsetter

"Anybody can do anything, it's up to them. All it takes is the right intentions."

– Jimi Hendrix, Grammy HOF American rock musician; arguably the most influential rock guitarist of all time; self-taught, he played his guitar upside-down and could not read music

"Painters get up and paint. Writers get up and write. I like to get up and act. It's not a big deal. It makes me happy."

– Samuel L. Jackson, award-winning American actor/producer/activist; the highest grossing actor in film history; breakthrough film was 'Pulp Fiction' in a role written for him; former drug addict

"When you first get a hill in sight, look at the top of it only once. Then imagine yourself at the bottom of the other side."

– Florence Griffith Joyner, HOF American track star; Olympic gold medalist; considered fastest woman of all-time based on 100m /200m world records; known for flashy personal appearance

"I used to think that prizes were damaging and divisive, until I got one, and now they seem sort of meaningful and important."

– Bill Nighy, award-winning British actor; discovered passion for acting in elementary school; well-known on British TV, his career breakthrough came at age 54 in the film 'Love Actually'

"Some things get better with age. Like me."

– Keith Richards, HOF English musician/singer/songwriter/author; best known as co-founder of the Rolling Stones; famed for surviving an elaborately decadent lifestyle; a former Boy Scout

"I truly believe in positive synergy, that your positive mindset gives you a more hopeful outlook, and belief that you can do something great means you will do something great."

– Russell Wilson, star American pro football quarterback; a six-time Pro Bowl selection and a Super Bowl champion; the NFL's highest-paid player; visits a children's' hospital every week

"If you're going to deal with reality, you're going to have to make one big discovery: Reality is something that belongs to you as an individual."

– Frank Zappa, Grammy-winning American musician/composer/producer; led the Mothers of Invention; identified with nonconformity, musical virtuosity and cultural satire; anti-censorship

Capricorn 6

So to be fair, not every Capricorn 6 is suffused with a god complex. Not all of them...but a lot more than one might expect in a random population.

Consider that all Capricorn Suns aspire to the top of the tribal totem pole. In the sixth lunation phase, one in which emotions such as confusion and doubt and regret and modesty have minimal impact, the Capricorn 6 claim upon cultural status reaches right up to the heavens. There simply are no self-sabotaging emotional impediments to reaching the top.

This situation tends to engender one of two life paths. Either the Capricorn 6, having mastered the psychological aspects of ascension, speaks of God as an intimate. Or, conversely, a Capricorn 6 may unapologetically and emphatically explain why a Supreme Being would be a rather redundant feature in a Capricorn 6 universe. Either way, it is apparently up to the Capricorn 6 to establish ground rules regarding the human condition in the context of a big picture CEO.

Yes, certainly, this attitude can be somewhat grating to their fellow creatures. Tough! The Capricorn 6 is not here to admire other humans, nor are they actually listening to them except as they may provide a chorus of attribution or affirmation.

Interestingly, given their self-selected place in the chain of being, there tends to be a deep streak of hedonism in the Capricorn 6 phase. This might be related to any number of psychological factors that might be explained better in someone else's book. In the end, though, why shouldn't gods, or anti-gods, be able to do anything they damn well want?

"I'm not apologizing to anyone. I'll apologize when hell freezes over."

– Mel Gibson, Oscar-winning American actor/filmmaker; known for damaged hero roles in films like 'Lethal Weapon' and 'Mad Max;' made the controversial film 'The Passion of the Christ'

"It's the charisma of the evangelist that the audience believes in and comes to see."

– Marjoe Gortner, renowned American Pentecostal preacher/actor; at age four promoted as "the world's youngest ordained minister;" an Evangelical star; lived 'secret' hippie life in L.A.

"And it is long since I have learned to hold popular opinion of no value."

– Alexander Hamilton, celebrated American "Founding Father;" author of The Federalist Papers and first U.S. treasury secretary; founded the N.Y. Post; political intransigence led to his death

"God may exist, but science can explain the universe without the need for a creator."

– Stephen Hawking, exalted English theoretical physicist/cosmologist/ author; recipient of the world's most significant scientific honors; fretted about mankind's "greed and stupidity"

"I like pretending to be God and basically determining the fate of my characters."

– Jay McInerney, award-winning American novelist/journalist/screenwriter; achieved fame with his first book 'Bright Lights, Big City' about modern cocaine culture; an esteemed wine writer

"God is a fiction invented by people so they do not have to face the reality of their condition."

– Michel Onfray, award-winning French philosopher/author; anti-Platonic/ non-idealist; champions materialism; works include 'The Atheist Manifesto' and 'The Hedonist Manifesto'

"It's always very nice to be somebody rather grand."

– Maggie Smith, Oscar/BAFTA/Tony/Emmy/SAG award-winning English actress; known for a witty/poignant air of authority in works like 'Harry Potter' and 'Downton Abbey;' a British Dame

"The best emotions to write out of are anger and fear or dread. The least energizing emotion to write out of is admiration. It is very difficult to write out of because the basic feeling that goes with admiration is a passive contemplative mood."

– Susan Sontag, award-winning American writer/filmmaker/philosopher/teacher/activist; known for provocative/learned essays on modern culture; an ardent/influential human rights activist

"I think what happens is when something becomes successful then a lot of people take credit for it in such ways that it takes credit away from you."

– Eddie Vedder, award-winning American musician/singer-songwriter; best known as the lead singer of the rock/grunge band 'Pearl Jam;' characterized by intense POV's; an ardent surfer

"All power is within you; you can do anything and everything. Believe in that, do not believe that you are weak; do not believe that you are half-crazy lunatics, as most of us do nowadays. You can do anything and everything, without even the guidance of any one. Stand up and express the divinity within you."

– Swami Vivekananda, renowned Indian-born Hindu monk; was the chief disciple of the famed 19th-century mystic Ramakrishna; introduced Vedanta principles throughout the world

"Jesus Christ knew he was God. So wake up and find out eventually who you really are. In our culture, of course, they'll say you're crazy and you're blasphemous, and they'll either put you in jail or in a nut house (which is pretty much the same thing). However if you wake up in India and tell your friends and relations, 'My goodness, I've just discovered that I'm God,' they'll laugh and say, 'Oh, congratulations, at last you found out'."

– Alan Watts, influential British philosopher/author/lecturer/radio personality; popularized Eastern philosophy in the West; he was a spiritual spokesperson for the 1960's counterculture

"I may be a senior, but so what? I'm still hot."

– Betty White, Emmy/Grammy award-winning American actress/comedian; longest TV acting career in history; best known for 'The Golden Girls;' received SAG Life Achievement Award

 Aquarius 6

It is traditional in astrological study to classify Aquarius as the sign of the humanitarian. At the core this means that the average Aquarius Sun individual has a unique capacity for tempering self-regard and respecting that the issues of other people are worthy of consideration and empathy. In the sixth lunation phase, a lifetime in which individuals are generally at peace with their own emotional makeup, an Aquarius tends to be outwardly directed and sincere about establishing a constructive role in community.

Interestingly, the basic insight that tends to drive the Aquarius 6 is that most people, places and things have an innate disposition towards being commonplace. The animus of the Aquarius 6 is a compulsion to find worthwhile links between the elements of the ordinary and to give them a little positive publicity. Even when the personal talents and accomplishments of an Aquarius 6 are quite extraordinary, there is inevitably a subtext having to do with a high regard for the situation of the 'average' people who live down the block.

In this context of what would appear to be a generous orientation towards others, it is interesting to note that an Aquarius 6 is rarely adorned with unadulterated praise. Perhaps there is something about humanity that must smear a little mud on anyone who would pass themselves off as authentically invested in the common welfare. Given life's stresses and humanity's darker inclinations, a general acceptance of someone who is sincerely into the condition of others is sometimes just too much of a strain on credulity.

In the end, though, the Aquarius 6 is the one to look at when it comes to a gentle reminder that life has its communal bright spots. It may be something as simple as a popular song or a tale of space travel or a memorable home run, but these are folks who give us something to share and smile about. It would seem ungenerous to complain.

"I'm hoping someday that some kid, black or white, will hit more home runs than myself. Whoever it is, I'd be pulling for him."

– Hank Aaron, HOF American baseball player/executive/businessman; one of the greatest MLB sluggers of all time; awarded the Presidential Medal of Freedom and NAACP Springarn Medal

"Don't try to do everything on your own. There are a lot of people out there in the universe who wish you well and want to be your friend. Let them help you. You don't have to carry it all on your own."

– Buzz Aldrin, highly decorated American engineer/astronaut/pilot/author; best known as the second man on the Moon; a distinguished combat pilot; had difficulties dealing with fame

"I don't think there's one right way to do anything. There's no one best way to be a woman. There's no best way to be a mentor. I'm just trying to be me and be authentic and live my truth and be as inclusive and interested in other human beings as possible. I'm an actor by training, which means that I study human beings and human behavior. That's what I try to do and what I love to do."

– Elizabeth Banks, Emmy-winning American actress/ director/writer/ producer; known for roles in 'The Hunger Games' and 'Pitch Perfect;' with husband co-wrote a book on fantasy football

"I'm glad that the lyrics reach people and make them understand that we're all the same, really."

– Phil Collins, Oscar/Grammy-winning English drummer/singer/songwriter/ producer/actor; lead singer for R&R HOF band Genesis; #1 in Top 40 hits in the 80's; wrote a book about the Alamo

"Only the gentle are ever really strong."

– James Dean, award-winning American actor; achieved fame as the personification of troubled adolescence in 'Rebel without a Cause;' a racing enthusiast who died in a car crash at age 24

"The truth is you leave this world with nothing. What you are is a temporary administrator, and you must administer well the wealth in your care and generate more. The surplus can be used to do many things for people."

– Carlos Slim Helu, distinguished Mexican business executive/engineer/ investor/philanthropist; the world's richest Latin American; his foundations are major supporters of job skills education

"I can't hang out as loose as I used to, but I can still go down Jefferson Avenue and look in the faces of winos, pimps and junkies, all the things I'm made of."

– Rick James, Grammy-winning American singer/songwriter/musician/ producer; recorded R&B/pop/funk; iconic hit was 'Super Freak;' led a wild and troubled drug-fueled lifestyle

"If we took the time to learn more about different places and people, perhaps we would have more empathy for each other."

– Alicia Keys, Grammy-winning American singer/musician/songwriter/author/entrepreneur; a classically trained pianist; a school valedictorian; cofounder of the Keep A Child Alive charity

"Literature is the art of discovering something extraordinary about ordinary people, and saying with ordinary words something extraordinary."

– Boris Pasternak, Nobel-laureate Russian poet/novelist/literary translator; best known for the romantic novel 'Dr. Zhivago' which led to a Nobel Prize despite book being banned in the USSR

"All of us, whether or not we're celebrities, every one ought to spend part of their life making someone else's life better."

– Jerry Springer, iconic English-born American TV host/lawyer/actor/producer/musician; best known for a scandalous tabloid TV show that ran 27 years; once served as mayor of Cincinnati

"The people I admire most are those who struggle for everyone."

– Vanessa Redgrave, Oscar/Tony/Emmy-winning British actress/activist; an acclaimed actor best known for an inflammatory anti-Zionist Academy Award speech; a human rights crusader

"Travel enables us to enrich our lives with new experiences, to enjoy and to be educated, to learn respect for foreign cultures, to establish friendships, and above all to contribute to international cooperation and peace throughout the world."

– Jules Verne, internationally popular French novelist/poet/playwright; forged the path of adventure science fiction; falsely judged as juvenile, his work was oft mishandled in translation

Pisces 6

Making collectivized observations about Pisces pushes at the limits of intelligibility. Their essence is mystery. Their consciousness, at least in terms of human capacity, is essentially limitless.

In the sixth lunation phase, freed from the doubt that attends most spiritual evolution, the Pisces Sun tends to embrace an awareness that truly flows to the limits of flow. Mere intellectual freedom is not the issue here. More to the point is that the Pisces 6 inhabits a universe that is strange and vast beyond description, and exploring life's potential is entirely a matter of emotional freedom and an unfettered spirit.

Lest this sound overly dreamy or hyperbolic, be assured that Pisces 6 are capable of great achievements in the public domain. Yet Pisces 6 accomplishment can rarely be described as the function of linear progression. Boundaries of perception are obliterated by a Pisces 6 orientation, and consciousness expanded in ways that change what it means to perceive.

The ultimate point, although to a Pisces 6 having a point is very akin to owning a castle in the air, is that an embrace of certainty is for the deluded. If there is love, if God exists, they inhabit a realm so vast that there is no coherent way to track them down. All that there is, according to the Pisces 6 way if looking at things, is immersion in the ocean of being and belief that a purity of intent will lead to something like grace.

To be sure (haha!) a Pisces 6 is treading in deep consciousness and, as a human being, is quite capable of getting caught by an undertow or being knocked about by the big waves. Still, their mantra is a consistent injunction to keep on swimming. Who knows what strange treasure may lie in the next ripple of time?

"A person knows when it just seems to feel right to them. Listen to your heart."

– Johnny Cash, Grammy Legend/HOF American singer-songwriter/guitarist/ actor/author; a 'country' artist with multi-genre success; sold over 90M records; known for free prison concerts

"Everything is determined, the beginning as well as the end, by forces over which we have no control. It is determined for the insect, as well as for the star. Human beings, vegetables, or cosmic dust, we all dance to a mysterious tune, intoned in the distance by an invisible piper."

– Albert Einstein, Nobel laureate German-born theoretical physicist; likely the leading scientist of the 20th C; famed for the Theory of Relativity; enjoyed smoking and the violin; avoided socks

"Management is not a science, it is an art."

– Michael Eisner, distinguished American businessman/author/philanthropist; for 21 years served as Chairman/CEO of the Walt Disney Company; led Disney's animation revitalization

"So often in life, things that you regard as an impediment turn out to be great good fortune."

– Ruth Bader Ginsburg, celebrated American attorney/jurist/educator; the second woman ever appointed to the U.S. Supreme Court; known for her progressive outlook; an ardent opera fan

"Our dreams are firsthand creations, rather than residues of waking life. We have the capacity for infinite creativity; at least while dreaming, we partake of the power of the Spirit, the infinite Godhead that creates the cosmos."

– Jackie Gleason, award-winning American/comedian/actor/writer/ composer/conductor; "The Great One;" famed as bus driver Ralph Kramden on 'The HoneyMooners;' believed in aliens

"The more I go inside, the more there is to see."

– George Harrison, Grammy HOF British musician/singer-songwriter/producer; lead guitarist of The Beatles; devoted to Eastern spiritual practices; invented the megastar rock benefit concert

"Stick around long enough, you'll get some grace."

– Spike Lee, Oscar/Emmy-winning American film director/producer/writer/actor; work centered on controversial social issues, particularly racism; identified with Brooklyn and the N.Y. Knicks

"I'm a Pisces, and they say that Pisces are very sensitive."

– Adam Levine, Grammy-winning American singer/songwriter/musician/actor; sex symbol; rose to fame in Maroon 5; a judge on 'The Voice;' ADHD sufferer; fan of dogs/tattoos/Scrabble/yoga

"Why does it rain? Why am I so sexy? I don't know."

– Shaquille O'Neal, all-time great pro basketball player/TV host/actor/musician/policeman; larger-than- life personality; self-chosen nicknames include "Superman" and "The Big Aristotle"

"Remember that the most beautiful things in the world are the most useless; peacocks and lilies for instance."

– John Steinbeck, Nobel-laureate American author; his socially perceptive novels are realistic, imaginative and compassionate; won a Pulitzer/National Book Award/Medal of Freedom

"I bake all the time, but I don't like to eat the cookies when they're done. I just like the dough."

– Sharon Stone, Golden Globe/Emmy-winning American actor/producer/model/humanitarian; known for her sultry sex appeal; a crusader in funding for AIDS research; a Christian Buddhist

'I don't entirely approve of some of the things I have done, or am, or have been. But I'm me. God knows, I'm me."

– Elizabeth Taylor, Oscar-winning British-American actress/businesswoman/humanitarian; a Hollywood legend; famed for her beauty and a scandalous love life; an HIV-AIDS crusader

7th Lunation Phase/Last Quarter Moon

Moon is 271 to 315 degrees ahead of the Sun

Keyword: Liberation

According to the spiritual conceit of eight types of incarnation, one reaches an apotheosis in the 6th lunation phase. As already described, the 6th lunation phase is a lifetime of expressing one's fully realized soul. It is certainly fair to ask, with regard to the 7th lunation phase, what one does for an encore.

A large part of the answer has to do with the fact that a 7th lunation phase person carries an implicit understanding of what it is like to have a fully realized soul and a memory of having expressed it completely in a previous lifetime. It's rather like having spiritual coin in the bank or, more prosaically, it's a cosmic variation on "been there, done that." One is free to the extent that one no longer has the need to pretend an angst-filled bewilderment about life's purpose or to dwell in the fields of self-justification.

For the LP7 individual, life is often something like pursuing a post-graduate degree. Some in this crowd will gravitate to culturally relevant interests and use the gifts of strength and prescience to extend philosophies into institutions; others will turn artistic gifts into sweeping revelations and unforgettable performances. Certainly many will just want to get on their motorcycles in a conscious commitment to wanderlust and adventure. Almost all will get the joke that life is way too absurd to wrangle successfully into a neat little container, and they will take a lot of satisfaction in celebrating the paradoxical and making the rest of us laugh.

Interestingly, many LP7s will develop a quest-like attitude towards life. These are the serious ones who are listening to their own drumbeat and who eventually come to the conclusion that their life has (an often unexpected) focus. The beauty of the LP7 life is that if this focus thing doesn't work out, one can always get back to the entirely satisfactory life path of highways and Harleys. Perhaps more than any other souls, these are the ones who are consciously free to be something of their own design...or not.

 Aries 7

In any incarnation an Aries will be known by their enthusiasm for whatever matter is at hand. Thus, even the evolved and liberated Aries 7 can seem pretty much like the Aries of any other lunation phase. They all manifest drive as a personality keynote.

Dig beneath the surface of an Aries 7, though, and one discovers the kind of depth that defies a blanket judgment of "energetic." Here there is much more going on than enthusiastic activity. Liberated from personal doubt and reflective self-restraint, the Aries 7 is a being capable of pouring every bit of their attention into the unique split-seconds of their existence.

Metaphorically, if not actually, it is helpful to think of an Aries 7 as a skilled warrior engaged in a running (and frequently joyful) battle with existence. They are always looking for an opening and a moment to pounce. They delight in keeping their opponents off-balance and at arm's length, and have not the slightest bit of temerity about throwing the first punch.

When one considers the personalities and agendas of all the people in the world, it is unsurprising that the Aries 7 is frequently thought of as villainous, or at the very least a kind of human irritant. In truth, the Aries 7 rarely minds the characterization. Why would they be apologetic about the passionate focus that has been granted as a birthright or the fearless drive that allows them to rumble with the best?

As an Aries 7 might put it, "let's ride."

"I don't know if I was the baddest. People kind of saw me in that light."

– Kareem Abdul-Jabbar, American HOF pro basketball player/author/actor/humanitarian; six-time NBA MVP; NCAA banned dunking because of him; Presidential Medal of Freedom recipient

"Be afraid of nothing."

– Joan Crawford, Oscar-winning American actress; known for 'Mildred Pierce;' famed for her bitter rivalry with Bette Davis; memorialized as an abusive mother in 'Mommie Dearest'

"People accuse me of being arrogant all the time. I'm not arrogant, I'm focused."

– Russell Crowe, Oscar-winning New Zealand-born actor/producer/musician; celebrated 'Gladiator' wrap with a 4,000-mile motorcycle ride; a famous brawler; owns a pro rugby team

"People don't understand the kind of fight it takes to record what you want to record the way you want to record it."

– Billie Holiday, Grammy HOF American jazz singer; nicknamed "Lady Day;" famed for her soulful improvisational song-styling; harsh life included abuse, heartbreak and heroin/alcohol addiction

"It's generally more fun playing the villain."

– Charlie Hunnam, award-winning English actor/model/screenwriter; known for hardened outcast and "psycho" roles; rose to fame as gang leader Jackson Teller on 'Sons of Anarchy'

"I'm very, very, very interested in martial arts."

– Keegan-Michael Key, Emmy-winning American actor/writer/producer; rose to fame on Comedy Channel's 'Key & Peele;' famously the "anger translator" for President Obama

"If people think I'm a laid-back guy, that's their mistake."

– Peyton Manning, champion American pro football quarterback/media personality; nicknamed "The Sheriff" for ability to quickly read defenses and adjust plays; record four-time NFL MVP

"I love sex.... It should be animalistic, it should be sadistic, it should at times be masochistic.... There are few rules and moral conventions."

– Jayne Mansfield, Golden Globe-winning American actress/singer/model; a great sex symbol of the 1950's/60's; a Playboy Playmate; a classically trained pianist/violinist; died in car crash at 34

"Every time I start thinking the world is all bad, then I start seeing people out there having a good time on motorcycles. It makes me take another look."

– Steve McQueen iconic American actor; nicknamed "The King of Cool;" his loner-hero vibe made him an icon of pop culture; had a reputation for nasty feuds with his colleagues

"If you no longer go for a gap that exists, you are no longer a racing driver."

– Ayrton Senna, Brazilian Formula One racing champion; known for combative intensity; won 41 races; widely considered the top Grand Prix driver of all time; died in a crash he predicted

"I'd love to do a character with a wife, a nice little house, a couple of kids, a dog, maybe a bit of singing, and no guns and no killing, but nobody offers me those kinds of parts."

– Christopher Walken, Oscar-winning American actor/singer/dancer/director/writer; known best for playing weird/sinister characters; famously associated with the SNL "More Cowbell" sketch

"Snatching the eternal out of the desperately fleeting is the great magic trick of human existence."

– Tennessee Williams, Pulitzer/Tony-winning American playwright; famed for sultry classics including 'Cat on a Hot Tin Roof' and 'Streetcar Named Desire;' Medal of Freedom recipient

 Taurus 7

In earlier Taurus phase descriptions, the image of man confronting mountain has been invoked. Though there is an undeniable resoluteness in Taurus from phase to phase, there is a particular evolution in the Taurus 7 incarnation. Here, from the vantage point of a life being lived by a successfully tested soul, there is a diminution of the confrontational part of the life equation, and a whole lot of emphasis on a spirit that has achieved the de facto status of mountain.

As always it is appropriate to acknowledge that we are still concerning ourselves with real human beings here. Thus, a liberal sprinkling of hardship and imperfection comes along with whatever else one may find in the characterization of souls living in this phase. What makes the difference in a Taurus 7 life, however, is the cogent reality that there is virtually nothing in one's personal experience that is of necessity dismissed, regretted, or held at a safe arm's length.

Often, the Taurus 7 is an individual who has been sorely tested by the culture and has found the culture lacking. Their will is directed towards enduring, surviving, and hopefully improving upon anything that confronts them. They are saturated with strength of character and resolute to a degree that invokes comparison to geological features and events.

Sometimes there is a tendency to label any Taurus as a simple soul, and indeed The Bull is properly identified with the sensory experiences on the earth plane. The Taurus 7 is the reminder, though, that the ability to endure reality can ultimately lead to enlightened places. Here it is worth acknowledging that the holy ones tend to climb up and congregate on the peaks.

"You have to be tenacious, you have to be focused, you have to have a real vision, and be extremely passionate about it."

– Jessica Alba, award-winning American actress/entrepreneur; rose to fame as a super-soldier in the dystopian TV show 'Dark Angel;' pro-natural/anti-toxin co-founder of The Honest Company

"All the good stuff is on the other side of tired."

– Andre Agassi, HOF American tennis pro/author/philanthropist; eight-time Grand Slam champ; made to play tennis by a dad with anger issues; 8th-grade dropout; runs educational foundation

"To see and know the worst is to take from fear her main advantage."

– Charlotte Bronte, famed English novelist/poet; best known for 'Jane Eyre' and the diabolical anti-hero Heathcliff; she and famed sisters forced to battle chauvinistic literary society

"When you spend a great deal of time in darkness, in solitary confinement, where everything blends into one, if you're fortunate, you'll begin to see things more vividly than you've ever seen them before."

– Rubin Hurricane Carter, Canadian-American boxer/humanitarian/author; spent 20 years in prison for a wrongful murder conviction; after exoneration he fought for the wrongly convicted

"Democratic societies are unfit for the publication of such thunderous revelations as I am in the habit of making."

– Salvador Dali, massively influential Spanish artist; a master of Surrealism; known for his bold eccentricity; attracted to fascism; claimed he was his older dead brother reincarnated

"The revolution is not an apple that falls when it is ripe. You have to make it fall."

– Ernesto 'Che' Guevara, famed Argentine political operative/theorist/guerilla/physician; a major figure of the Cuban Marxist revolution; a ubiquitous symbol of counter-cultural rebellion

"If my world were to cave in tomorrow, I would look back on all the pleasures, excitements and worthwhilenesses (sic) I have been lucky enough to have had. Not the sadness, not my miscarriages or my father leaving home, but the joy of everything else. It will have been enough."

– Audrey Hepburn, Oscar/Tony/Emmy/Grammy-winning British actress/humanitarian; a true screen legend; sophisticated/elegant; held her efforts for UNICEF as her greatest achievement

"Someday I hope you get the chance to live like you were dying."

– Tim McGraw, Grammy-winning American country singer/composer/actor/philanthropist; has had ten #1 albums; earned a college baseball scholarship; created a veterans health foundation

"Fear of success is one of the new fears I've heard about lately. And I think it's definitely a sign that we're running out of fears. A person suffering from fear of success is scraping the bottom of the fear barrel."

– Jerry Seinfeld, Emmy-winning American comedian/actor/writer/producer/director; a hugely influential pop icon, best known for playing a semi-fictional version of himself in TV's 'Seinfeld'

"I could still be in prison. Hell, for all I did I could be headed to the gas chamber. This is all icing."

– Danny Trejo, award-winning American actor/humanitarian; best known for playing hyper-villainous roles in films such as 'Machete' and 'Con Air;' a reformed drug addict and criminal

"It had long since come to my attention that people of accomplishment rarely sat back and let things happen to them. They went out and happened to things."

– Leonardo da Vinci, Italian genius, the ultimate Renaissance man; interests included drawing, painting, invention, sculpture and architecture; painted The Last Supper and The Mona Lisa

Don't give them what you think they want. Give them what they never thought was possible."

– Orson Welles, Oscar/Grammy-winning American actor/director/ writer/ producer; his 'Citizen Kane' is held as one of history's greatest films; also famed for 'War of the Worlds' radio panic

 Gemini 7

A Gemini in any lunation phase will find something revelatory in uncertainty. A Gemini 7, largely liberated from any urge towards self-restraint or self-recrimination, will drive ambiguity as if it were a souped up vehicle on a convoluted rally course. Attacking life's twists and turns, and observing no speed limit, the Gemini 7 will unabashedly...perhaps even a bit proudly... streak through life's changefulness towards a checkered flag or a checkered understanding or a checkered reputation, not entirely caring which is what.

There's simply no way around it always being a freedom of thought thing with the Gemini 7. There are no viable one-size-fits-all codes of conduct. If the truth be told, a Gemini 7 views intellectual autonomy as an inalienable right, and skilled improvisation as life's only reliable survival mechanism.

While such an attitude might be judged by many as lacking in grace, a Gemini 7 might reasonably beg to differ. Their thing is not that only *they* have a right to be free in their own heads. They also think that *you* are so entitled.

Thus, many a Gemini 7 is an earnest crusader on behalf of the culturally marginalized and downtrodden. They earnestly bridle whenever people are objectified or are being sold a bill of goods. They honestly believe that the world functions optimally when everyone gets to call it the way they see it, and the Gemini 7 is willing to back that view up with action.

Okay, so yes, this Gemini 7 attitude can present obvious problems. People who see things differently don't always resolve their differences with a frank discussion and a conciliatory back rub. But that's not Gemini 7's problem.

While others are pondering a course of action, they've already circled the next straightaway.

"I regret that I didn't realize that actually they've got no power over you at school — it's all just a trick to indoctrinate you into being a conditioned, tame, placid citizen. Rebel, children, I urge you, fight the turgid slick of conformity with which they seek to smother your glory."

– Russell Brand, idiosyncratic English comedian/actor/author/activist; host of TV's 'Big Mouth;' life story includes ADHD/bipolarism/drug addiction; enjoys soccer/veganism/sexuality

"There were times when I blundered and got the dreaded look from the lads. But that was a good sign. It showed I'd attempted something I'd not tried before."

– John Bonham, award-winning British musician/songwriter; founding member of Led Zeppelin; arguably the G.O.A.T. of R&R drummers; once motorcycled through the halls of the L.A. Hyatt

"Sometimes when a movie is really alive you can see that they were just making decisions on the spot. They weren't bound to anything, they were working with ideas that the actors and situations presented."

– Michael Cera, award-winning Canadian actor/ producer/singer/songwriter; known for nerdy-sensitive roles in 'Superbad,' 'Juno,' and 'Arrested Development;' first album titled 'True That'

"Be honest about what you see, get out of the way and let the story reveal itself."

– Anderson Cooper, Emmy-winning American journalist/TV personality/ author; lead anchor at CNN; born into privileged society; faked press passes to launch career; served a CIA internship

"The least amount of judging we can do, the better off we are."

– Michael J. Fox, Emmy-winning Canadian actor/comedian/author/producer/ humanitarian; best known for 'Back to the Future' and 'Family Ties;' a renowned Parkinson's sufferer/activist

"When I was little, like Maleficent, I was told that I was different–and I felt out of place, and too loud, too full of fire, never good at sitting still, never good at fitting in. And then one day I realized something, something I hope you all realize. Different is good."

– Angelina Jolie, Oscar-winning American actress/filmmaker/humanitarian; expelled from school at age 14 for rebelliousness; known for complex personal relationships; active in refugee causes

"We will not win our rights by staying quietly in our closets."

– Harvey Milk, seminal American politician/activist; first openly gay elected official in California; unapologetically outspoken; martyred in office; Presidential Medal of Freedom recipient

"Clowns get such a bad rap now. At some point, someone decided that clowns were scary, or could be scary. They've been so abused in popular culture. It sounds funny—and it is funny, to a certain extent—to stick up for clowns."

– John C. Reilly, award-winning American actor/comedian/singer/screenwriter/producer; known for roles communicating everyman sincerity; an outspoken humanist; clown painting collector

"I always like to challenge myself. I never want to be put into a box."

– Lionel Richie, Oscar/Grammy-winning American singer/songwriter/actor/producer/activist; has sold over 100M records; co-wrote 'We Are the World;' cancer activist; can't read music

"All creative writers need a certain amount of time when they're creating something where nobody should criticize them at all–at all. Even if the criticism is valid or good, they should just shut up, and let that person create, because at a certain point you have to make it your own–not the world's but your own."

– Gena Rowlands, Emmy-winning American actress; had a six-decade career in movies, theater and television; known for work with husband John Cassavetes and her role in 'The Notebook'

"It's time we stop worrying, and get angry you know? But not angry and pick up a gun, but angry and open our minds."

– Tupac Shakur, iconic American rapper; defined the young urban anti-hero; first solo rapper inducted into the R&R HOF; complex lyrics showcased anger and empathy; murdered at age 25

"Self respect is impossible without liberty."

– Harriet Beecher Stowe, prolific American author/abolitionist/philanthropist; her 'Uncle Tom's Cabin' was vital to the anti-slavery movement; devoted to schools for emancipated slaves

Cancer 7

There is an odd kind of liberation that emerges in the Cancer 7 lunation phase. Ordinarily and rightfully known for how strongly they attach to people, places and things, this is a Cancer that tends to inhabit a less fixed reality. In this seventh lunation lifetime, Cancers—-free in their own spirits, albeit still a bit loony as is their birthright—metaphorically surrender to the tidal aftermath of the broken wave that crested at full Moon.

Tumbling around in the sands of time, Cancer 7's are very hard to describe collectively. Their lives are a mixture of masterful sensitivity and loony liberation. To the outsider they often seem as creatures that alternately inhabit spheres of natural profundity and total insanity.

The Cancer 7 is fully aware that their balance is somehow off, although they are mostly inclined to privately celebrate their active imaginations and true quirkiness. What they really find hard to bear is the hard scrutiny of others, who tend to have an awful lot of behavioral expectations and never seem to quite get what is going on in this non-linear soul. How do you explain to nosy and judgmental outsiders that the core of one's reality is a trippy time stream and a fluid imagination... and why *should* one have to explain that?

Freed from grave foundational concerns, the Cancer 7 is inclined towards being a bit of a gypsy. Contrary to many of their Sun sign kin, a Cancer 7 tends to have a happy attitude about the unpredictable, a state of consciousness that they manifest by readily flashing a little sexy self-esteem and happily dissolving into any character that calls them. You just can't beat surfing Moonbeams.

"I'm kind of proud of myself. I've been able to keep a certain grace about me, even in the times of disgrace and craziness."

– Pamela Anderson, iconic Canadian-American actress/model/author/activist; famed as a buxom blonde sex symbol; identified with Playboy Magazine and 'Baywatch;' passionate vegan

"People don't know my real self, and they're not about to find out."

– Yul Brynner, Oscar/Tony/Grammy-winning Russian-born American actor; forever famous as the king in 'The King and I,' a role he stage-acted 4,000+ times; cultivated a fake exotic persona

"The further you get away from yourself, the more challenging it is. Not to be in your comfort zone is great fun."

– Benedict Cumberbatch, BAFTA/Emmy-winning British actor; known for powerful savant roles such as Dr. Strange and Sherlock Holmes; was once an English teacher in a Tibetan monastery

"You spend your whole life trying to get known and then you spend the rest of it hiding in the toilet."

– Bob Fosse, Oscar/Tony/Emmy-award winning American dancer/choreographer/director; projects included 'Pippin and 'Cabaret;' identified with "jazz hands;" serious anxiety sufferer

"Beyond its entertainment values, 'Baywatch' has enriched and in many cases helped save lives."

– David Hasselhoff, popular American actor/singer/producer/businessman; "The Hoff;" known for good-natured self-deprecating machismo; TV shows included 'Knight Rider' and 'Baywatch'

"It's so weird that I went to rehab. I always said that I would die before I went to rehab. But I thought, 'I'm going to stay here tonight.' And I stayed there for a month. It was great."

– Lindsay Lohan, award-winning American actress/singer-songwriter/businesswoman/fashion designer/producer; known for 'Parent Trap' and 'Mean Girls;' has a checkered personal history

"I'm not an actor because I want my picture taken. I'm an actor because I want to be part of the human exchange."

– Frances McDormand, Oscar/Emmy/Tony-award winning American actress/activist; known for plain characters with revealed depths; stresses imagination; embraces her age; morally fierce

"I come from the theater, where I got into acting because I love transforming. I love nothing more than to be unrecognizable."

– Nick Offerman, award-winning American actor/writer/comedian/producer/carpenter; best known as Ron Swanson in 'Parks and Recreation;' passionate woodworker; Cubs/Bears fan

"Everything we think of as great has come to us from neurotics. It is they and they alone who found religions and create great works of art. The world will never realize how much it owes to them and what they have suffered in order to bestow their gifts on it."

– Marcel Proust, award-winning French writer; his book 'In Search of Lost Time' is the longest known novel in history (1.2M words); Bohemian; gay in a difficult era; lived with his parents

"The capacity for passion is both cruel and divine."

– George Sand, controversial French novelist/essayist; a notoriously amorous individual, her "rustic novels" explored complexities in attachments; preferred men's attire, smoked cigars

"Pretending is a very valuable life skill."

– Meryl Streep, Oscar/Emmy-winning American actress/philanthropist; called "the best actress of her generation;" her range is reflected in 21 Oscar nominations; Medal of Freedom recipient

"The constant attention is what is difficult."

– Natalie Wood, Golden Globe-winning American actress; professional actor from the age of 4; known for 'Rebel Without a Cause' and 'West Side Story;' terrified of water, drowned at sea

 Leo 7

A Leo 7 life presents a bit of a conundrum. Like other members of the Leo Sun tribe, these are individuals who can and do shine very brightly. The most noteworthy among them are in fact possessed of such brilliant personalities that the lesser among us may be tempted, in their presence, to avert our eyes.

So what is the issue? The basic and absolutely compelling truth of the Leo 7 is that they are aware of an ego that is dealing with the rapidly approaching evolutionary advent of a post-personality reality. In this present incarnation they have extraordinary self-awareness of *who* they are, but they are fascinated by not really knowing in terms of cosmic essence, *what* they are.

Thus, the keyword in a Leo 7 life tends to be *genuineness*. Liberated from the shackles of self-doubt and emotional repression, like all the other 7th lunation phase souls, Leo 7's have no inherent blocks to expressing anything that ultimately make them feel real. This can mean anything from preserving one's roots, to counting one's treasure, to abandonment to Spirit, but whatever one's personal predilection it will come from a place of deeply heartfelt consideration.

Ironically, one sometimes knows the Leo 7 best when they are on hiatus. Occasional rest and anonymity are conditions that appeal mightily to these fiercely questing souls. As befits their feline archetype, the Leo 7 finds a way leap impossibly tall walls of awareness but the effort requires a lot of napping.

Ultimately, though, one returns to the puzzle inherent in a brilliant presence contemplating the inevitability of its own extinction. What is the "I" supposed to be as it nears the end its evolutionary road? If it is the obligation of a human soul is to bequeath a legacy to future generations, just how does one do that and what the heck is that supposed to be?

A poignant humor sometimes lurks around the life of a Leo 7 who would really like to know what the world is going to be without him. This is a difficult proposition and life is short. Thank goodness for mirrors.

"As soon as we left the ground, I knew I had to fly."

– Amelia Earhart, record-setting American aviation pioneer/author; first woman to fly solo across the Atlantic; launched one of the first celebrity clothing lines; disappeared during flight

"The key to success is not through achievement, but through enthusiasm."

– Malcolm Forbes, famed American businessman/journalist; publisher of 'Forbes' Magazine; known for lavish lifestyle and vigorous self-promotion; an Army machine gunner; motorcyclist

"There's only one effectively redemptive sacrifice, the sacrifice of self-will to make room for the knowledge of God."

– Aldous Huxley, award-winning English writer/philosopher; pacifist/mystic; best known for the satirically dystopian 'Brave New World' and the psychedelic classic 'The Doors of Perception'

"They say such nice things about people at their funerals that it makes me sad that I'm going to miss mine by just a few days."

– Garrison Keillor, Grammy/Peabody-winning American author/humorist/radio personality; best known as creator/host of 'A Prairie Home Companion,' took a 3-year break to enjoy anonymity

"The future rewards those who press on. I don't have time to feel sorry for myself. I don't have time to complain. I'm going to press on."

– Barack Obama, American attorney/politician/author; 44th president of the USA; 1st African-American president; 1st African-American to edit the Harvard Law Review; avid comic book fan

"You have to sing every day so you can build up to being, you know, amazingly brilliant."

– Mick Jagger, HOF/Grammy-winning English singer/songwriter/actor/film producer; renowned as co-founder/frontman of the Rolling Stones; considered by many as "the ultimate rock star"

"Do not compare, do not measure. No other way is like yours. All other ways deceive and tempt you. You must fulfill the way that is in you."

– Carl Jung, eminent Swiss psychologist/psychiatrist/journalist; pioneer of personality complex exploration/universal archetypes/the Collective Unconscious; interested in occultism/aliens

"I'm dead sober. This is just me."

– Jennifer Lawrence, Oscar-winning American actor; rose to fame as Katniss in 'The Hunger Games;' world's highest paid actress 2015/16; a tomboy deemed "too rough to play with girls"

"I want to make my own life a masterpiece."

– Benito Mussolini, infamous Prime Minister of Italy; founder of the Fascist party; absolute dictator known as 'Il Duce;' contemptuous of democracy; hanged by mob at the end of WWII

"This is the true joy in life: being used for a purpose recognized by yourself as a mighty one, being a force of nature instead of a feverish, selfish little clod of ailments and grievances, complaining that the world will not devote itself to making you happy."

– George Bernard Shaw, Nobel-laureate Irish playwright/critic/polemicist/activist; authored more than 60 plays, none produced before age 38; a fervent Socialist; vital and free-spirited

"If it had been any different, if I had been born just one minute later, or been in the wrong place at the right time or vice versa, the life that I've lived and come to love would not exist. And that is a situation that I would not want to consider in the slightest."

– Slash, award-winning British-American rock musician/environmentalist; famed as Guns 'n Roses lead guitarist; shoplifted his famous top hat; loves reptiles/elephants/horror films

"You only live once, but if you do it right, once is enough."

– Mae West, iconic American actress/singer/writer/comedian/sex symbol; the queen of the bawdy double entendre; career spanned seven decades; wrote 9 of the 13 films she starred in

Virgo 7

It would probably be something of an overstatement to describe a Virgo 7 life as a celebration of imperfection. Even the ones who sometimes put on party hats are sensibly inclined to keep human shortcomings, their own and those of others, in sober perspective. Let's just say that in the Virgo 7 lunation phase one encounters a righteous, sometimes enthusiastic, appreciation for the fact that people are less than gods.

Liberated in the seventh lunation phase, Virgos are eager to investigate the demarcation line between self-glorification and self-awareness. Rarely blinded by the light of their own egos, Virgo 7's are far more concerned with personal integrity than they are with their own magnificence. Knowing that one of the key things all humans have in common is an aptitude for failing, a Virgo 7 is intent upon making plenty of room for vulnerability, sometimes by offering a helping hand and sometimes by making a joke of it.

Virgo 7's tend to conclude that what it's all about is tolerance of human shortcomings and a simultaneous desire to improve. Where they can become prickly is in their expectation that what works for them should also work for you. They somewhat compulsively pick at their own flaws, but they tend to be very sensitive about being called out by people who they feel should be working on their own problems.

At the root of their personalities, Virgo 7's tend to embrace simple self-contained principles. Candor, good health habits, and a willingness to practice one's craft may not seem like much of a magic formula, but most Virgo 7's will put these to work with quite a positive effect. They rarely have a lot of patience for the unsubstantiated and they are unapologetic about their affections.

It might be fair to summarize the Virgo 7 life as one in which appreciating the cloud is every bit as useful as coveting the silver lining it protects. Whether dealing with their own situations or with their culture at large, they get the value of an umbrella. On the other hand, as befits a life in the seventh lunation phase. they also kind of get a thrill just being out in the rain.

"I support anyone's right to be who they want to be. My question is: to what extent do I have to participate in your self-image?"

– Dave Chappelle, Grammy/Emmy-winning American comedian/actor/writer/producer; best known for his satirical sketch comedy TV show; famed for rejecting $50M deal over "integrity"

"You Moon the wrong person at an office party and suddenly you're not 'professional' anymore."

– Jeff Foxworthy, award-winning American comedian/actor/media personality/entrepreneur; famed for folksy "redneck" material; the face of Golden Corral buffets; a philanthropic activist

"I want to sing simple things for the simple lives of simple people."

– Julio Iglesias, Grammy-winning Spanish singer/songwriter; #1 all-time Spanish-speaking singer with 300M+ records sold in 14 languages; played pro soccer with Real Madrid; law school grad

"I was always a self-conscious person."

– Elia Kazan, Oscar-winning Greek-American director/producer/writer/actor; an historically iconic film & stage director; known for brooding modern dramas; reputation clouded by politics

"The word 'potential' used to hang over me like a cloud."

– Randy Johnson, HOF American baseball pitcher; "The Big Unit;" 4-time winner of the Cy Young award; 2nd all-time with 4,875 strikeouts; famously guarded personality; always felt "freakish"

"I've never felt like I needed to change. I've always thought 'If you want somebody different, pick somebody else'."

– Melissa McCarthy, Emmy-winning American actress/comedian/writer/producer/fashion designer; won three People's Choice awards as favorite film comedienne; was a Goth in school

"That's the goal, to survive your gift."

– Itzhak Perlman, Grammy/Emmy-winning Israeli-American violinist/conductor/music teacher; a superstar classical artist; polio survivor; Medal of Freedom/Kennedy Center Honors recipient

"Try to be wrong once in a while, it'll do your ego good."

– Keanu Reeves, award-winning multi-national actor/musician; famed as a brooding action hero in films such as 'The Matrix' 'and 'John Wick;' sad personal life; widely admired for his decency

"I've been called a moron since I was about four. My father called me a moron. My grandfather said I was a moron. And a lot of times when I'm driving, I hear I'm a moron. I like being a moron."

– Adam Sandler, award-winning American actor/comedian/screenwriter/producer/musician; rose to fame on SNL; known for giant hits/big flops; has won nine People's Choice awards

"I try to extract something positive from every situation, even if it's just learning not to make the same mistake twice."

– Claudia Schiffer, iconic German supermodel/actress/fashion designer/producer/entrepreneur; holds all-time record for magazine cover appearances (1,000+); a UNICEF Goodwill Ambassador

"Man is an evasive beast, given to cultivating strange notions about himself."

– Upton Sinclair, Pulitzer-winning American author; wrote 90+ books, mostly political/social tracts; famous for 'The Jungle,' a muckraking work directed at the meat processing industry

'I think without question the hardest single thing to do in sport is to hit a baseball. A .300 hitter, that rarest of breeds these days, goes through life with the certainty that he will fail at his job seven out of ten times."

– Ted Williams, HOF American baseball player/manager; one of baseball's all-time great hitters; two-time winner of the Triple Crown; 19-time all-star; a surly perfectionist with many demons

Libra 7

The seventh lunation phase can be fairly characterized as a time of liberation. The walls of doubt and inhibition are pretty much gone, and one is free to express one's nature with little cosmic opposition. One can easily see how this might present a conundrum for the Libra Sun, whose main focus in life tends to be an artful celebration of moderation and bringing things into balance.

What the Libra 7 life tends to demonstrate is that a manifestation of harmony is anything but a laissez-faire endeavor. In fact, what the Libra 7 incarnation has most urgently to teach is that cheek-turning and the general accommodation of others may be the hardest thing in the world. Anything but naïve about human failings, the Libra 7 courageously presses on to confront human behavior with an attitude of inclusiveness and acceptance, even when the most rational course might be to punch someone in the mouth.

Certainly names such as Gandhi, Desmond Tutu and Eleanor Roosevelt, Libra 7's all, more than adequately make the point about the nature of uninhibited peace-seeking in a conflicted world. People are good and people are bad. From a place of preternatural strength one chooses to love all.

On the granular personal level it is helpful to note that the Libra 7 tends to explore and embrace complexity before distilling it into simple realizations and behaviors. The artist will adore pulp entertainment. The sage will write children's books.

Perhaps most of all the Libra 7 understands that mankind can be thoroughly roiled and ridiculous. But there is also that greater more significant level on which we are all connected. In the Libra 7 worldview, hopefully—-and from a place of fearlessness—that will be in peace.

"It's nice to be important, but it's also important to be nice. Never forget that."

– Sacha Baron Cohen, award-winning English actor/comedian/screenwriter/director/producer; known for sharp social satire in faux-ethnic roles; is both a Cambridge grad and a trained clown

"I think the Earth and everything around it is connected–the sky and the planets and the stars and everything else we see as a mystery."

– Marion Cotillard, Oscar-winning French actress/singer-songwriter/musician/environmentalist; only winner of an Oscar in a French-speaking performance (as Edith Piaf in 'La Vie en Rose')

"Spider-Man's probably my favorite. You see, Batman is a billionaire and there's nothing really cool about a billionaire saving the world. But

Spider-Man is Peter Parker, a conflicted character who puts on a suit and saves the world. I love that."

– Zac Efron, award-winning American actor/singer; known for heartthrob roles; fame came via 'High School Musical;' anime fan; car restorer; Tom Cruise taught him to ride a motorcycle

"A coward is incapable of exhibiting love; it is the prerogative of the brave."

– Mahatma Gandhi, world-renowned Indian leader famed for political non-violence; notably not a Nobel Peace Prize recipient, although India now bestows an annual peace prize in his name

"When you're mad at someone, it's probably best not to break his arm with a baseball bat."

– Evel Knievel, iconic American daredevil; best known for motorcycle distance jumping; 433 broken bones documented; kidnapped the wife he was married to for 40 years; sold insurance

"When I was a kid, some of the guys would try to get me to hate white people for what they've been doing to Negroes, and for a while I tried real hard. But every time I got to hating them, some white guy would come along and mess the whole thing up."

– Thelonious Monk, Grammy HOF American jazz pianist/composer; a father of bebop/modern jazz; extraordinarily close to family & friends; relished games; binge-watched 'Laurel and Hardy'

"The world needs less destruction."

– Bob Odenkirk, Emmy-winning American actor/comedian/writer/director/producer; famed for his role as a glib lawyer on 'Breaking Bad' and 'Better Call Saul;' was an SNL writer for 5 years

"For our own success to be real, it must contribute to the success of others."

– Eleanor Roosevelt, venerated American political figure/diplomat/activist/ author; longest-tenured/uniquely activist U.S. First Lady; winner of the U.N. Prize in the Field of Human Rights

"It pays to know the enemy–not least because at some time you may have the opportunity to turn him into a friend."

– Margaret Thatcher, highly-honored British stateswoman; the "Iron Lady;" served as the UK's first female PM from 1979-1990; strongly Conservative; helped to develop soft-serve ice cream

"One of the sayings in our country is 'Ubuntu'–the essence of being human. 'Ubuntu' speaks particularly about the fact that you can't exist as a human being in isolation. It speaks about our interconnectedness. You can't be human all by yourself, and when you have this quality – 'Ubuntu'–you are known for your generosity. We think of ourselves far too frequently as just individuals, separated from one another, whereas you are connected and what you do affects the whole World. When you do well, it spreads out; it is for the whole of humanity."

– Desmond Tutu, Nobel Peace Prize laureate South African cleric/theologian/ rights activist; known best for work against apartheid policies; Gandhi Peace Prize recipient

"Everyone surrounding you has gone through similar things; the search for love or the desire to have a family or the loss of a child."

– Alicia Vikander, Oscar-winning Swedish actress; known for films dealing with deep treatments of human love/sexuality such as 'The Danish Girl' and 'Ex Machina;' studied chess and ballet

"Keep love in your heart. A life without it is like a sunless garden when the flowers are dead. The consciousness of loving and being loved brings warmth and a richness to life that nothing else can bring."

– Oscar Wilde, award-winning Irish playwright/poet/author; celebrated for his flamboyant wit and style; famously charged/ imprisoned for being homosexual; wrote children's books

 Scorpio 7

It is probably a comfort to others that a Scorpio 7 is not always destined to be a terrorist or something akin to the 'Terminator' T-1000 robot. To be truthful, Scorpio energy does tend to get a little hell bent under the conditions of a seventh lunation lifetime. But there is something more going on here than Scorpio ferocity unbound.

What one actually witnesses in a Scorpio 7 lifetime is that blind passion counts for little without self-control and an objective. While most Scorpios are ready to take on conflict, versus a solitary challenger or the most sacred institutional norms of society, the Scorpio 7 is not one to simply throw blind punches. There is strategy involved in the Scorpio 7 way, and it can be deathly cunning in its execution.

To be sure the average Scorpio 7 is fairly obsessed with having an impact, although they are strategic masters of pretending otherwise and feigning dispassion. Scorpio 7's who act or entertain often not-so-secretly relish making the audience feel some discomfort. The ones more inclined towards a political life are usually found fighting 'against' rather than 'for' anything, as they do not like their intensity modulated and cannot bear being subject to anyone else's rules.

Indeed the key to a Scorpio 7 lifetime is that the rules that bind others to a sort of socially proscribed behavior are considered either irrelevant or the vaguest of suggestions once the battle is judged to be imminent. Scorpio 7's do not believe that solutions to stressful situations (aka to the Scorpio 7 as "life") conform to neatly proscribed patterns. Winners don't get blindsided by expectations, their own or others; they just figure out where they are going and arrive.

Interestingly, one often reads about dropping out of school, substance abuse, and sexual profligacy with even some of the most lauded of Scorpio 7's. Their behavior reflects the depths of their feelings and, even when doing the sort of things for which others may judge them, they keep in their hearts the incontrovertible belief that they can handle it.

Frankly, the Scorpio 7 can damn well handle just about anything.

"You may be as vicious about me as you please. You will only do me justice."

– Richard Burton, Golden Globe/Tony/Grammy-winning Welsh actor, famed for his baritone voice and dark gravitas; Hamlet and King Arthur were key roles; an alcohol-fueled "hell raiser"

"I will leave an impression."

– Sean "Puffy" Combs, Grammy-winning American rapper/singer/producer/ entrepreneur/ record executive/actor; born in a public housing project; estimated to be worth $735M in 2015

"I told my psychiatrist that everyone hates me. He said I was being ridiculous–everyone hasn't met me yet."

– Rodney Dangerfield, Grammy-winning American comedian/actor/ producer/writer/musician; known by catchphrase "I don't get no respect;" suffered chronic depression; smoked weed daily

"If I fail, at least I will have failed my way."

– Jodie Foster, Oscar-winning American actress/director/producer; breakout role was as 12 year-old prostitute in 'Taxi Driver;' known for intense films like 'Silence of the Lambs' and 'Contact'

"No one changes the world who isn't obsessed."

– Billie Jean King, all-time great American tennis player/activist; winner of 39 Grand Slam events; a crusader for equal pay/gay rights; recipient of the Presidential Medal of Freedom

"I'm proud that I was one of the first ones out, singing loud and proud."

– K. D. Lang, Grammy-winning Canadian country/pop singer-songwriter; famously lesbian; known for her androgynous look; breakout hit was "Constant Craving;" a devoted Buddhist

"Don't be afraid. Be the kind of person your mother warned you about."

– Lorde, Grammy-winning New Zealand singer-songwriter; breakout hit was 'Royals;' has a condition known as synaesthesia that lets her see sounds as colors; a high school dropout

"I don't mind assholes. It's the dork I don't trust. The dork is the one who's trying to be whatever he thinks you want him to be. I trust the asshole cause you know where he's gonna stand."

– Matthew McConaughey, Oscar-winning American actor/producer/ philanthropist; breakout film was 'Dazed and Confused;' notably cool and Texan; People Magazine's "Sexiest Man Alive"

"What matters is not the idea a man holds, but the depth at which he holds it."

– Ezra Pound, iconic American poet/critic; a leading figure of the modernist era; his major work is the 800-page 'Cantos;' a brash personality; infamous as an expatriate/fascist sympathizer

"It's wonderful to hear that I have terrified people."

– Robert Patrick, award-winning American actor; frequently plays dangerous characters; famed as the T-1000 robot in 'Terminator 2;'an active lifelong supporter of the USO; a college drop-out

"It's funny when people say, 'I don't think Julia likes me.' Honey, if I don't like you, you're going to know about it."

– Julia Roberts, Oscar-winning American actress/producer; 'Pretty Woman' made her an iconic star; first woman to earn $20M for a film ('Erin Brockovich'); led a very complicated love life

"Why did the chicken cross the road? Because you didn't f—ing cook it!"

– Gordon Ramsay, award-winning Scottish chef/restaurateur/writer/television personality/food critic; his enterprises have earned 16 Michelin stars; known for his acerbic on-air TV personality

Sagittarius 7

Astrology contends that the planet that rules the affairs of Sagittarius is Jupiter. It is particularly useful to have a mental image of this enormous and dynamic 'gas giant' when considering the wholly liberated Sagittarius 7. Because of all souls, it is the Sagittarius 7 who rises above the hard pack of the world like a colorful and buoyant helium balloon.

It is Walt Disney, a member of this clan, who is credited with creating the concept of "imagineering." This extraordinary mix of mental liberation, resolute observation and a desire to bring quasi-magical things into material fruition constitutes the essence of this lifetime. Of all souls, the Sagittarius 7 is the most capable of building, and then inhabiting, a castle in the air.

Interestingly, one of the cogent collective markers of the Sagittarius 7 is their penchant for examining communication. They tend to live in a perceptive state where language, and the entire world of symbolic notation, is not only descriptive but creative. They strive to find dynamic terminology that accurately matches the extraordinary breadth and depth of all that they are capable of doing and perceiving.

Please do not construe any of this to mean that a Sagittarius 7 is immune to life's sometimes nasty vicissitudes. Their pretentions are sometimes punctured and they do sometimes lose their overt cheerfulness. Even so, the Sagittarius 7 always seems to have a ready and deeply knowing smile, and a predisposition to catching the next updraft.

Ultimately, the Sagittarius 7 appreciates that dreams are for builders as well as romantics. Their visions beckon to a personal and cultural ecstasy that must be woven diligently, unapologetically and without self-sabotage in the spirit of a better day. Shackles—-mental, physical, spiritual—- are just not their style.

"Indulge your imagination in every possible flight."

– Jane Austen, honored English novelist; famed for social commentary in works such as 'Pride and Prejudice' and 'Sense and Sensibility;' admired for her humor and openness to experience

"I don't know what happens to me on stage. Something else seems to take over."

– Maria Callas, Grammy HOF Greek-American operatic soprano; one of the most influential singers in history; lauded for dramatic ability as well as voice; described as "The God-Given"

"If you cannot be a poet, be the poem."

– David Carradine, award-winning American actor/musician/director; starred in thoughtful martial arts projects such as TV's 'Kung Fu' and cinema's 'Kill Bill;' led a renegade personal life

"Either you repeat the same conventional doctrines everybody is saying, or else you say something true and it will sound like it's from Neptune."

– Noam Chomsky, award-winning American linguist/philosopher/critic/author; "the father of modern linguistics;" voted "World's Top Public Intellectual;" a radical critic of U.S. foreign policy

"The ultimate mystery is one's own self."

– Sammy Davis, Jr., Grammy HOF American singer/musician/dancer/actor/activist; began in vaudeville at age 3 and gained fame as an impressionist; NAACP HOF/Kennedy Honors recipient

"The soul should always stand ajar, ready to welcome the ecstatic experience."

– Emily Dickinson; esteemed American poet; famed for her choice of personal self-seclusion and her transcendentalist poems about truth/death/spirit; largely unpublished in her lifetime

"It's kind of fun to do the impossible."

– Walt Disney, world-renowned American entrepreneur/cartoonist/producer; legendary animation pioneer; founder of a vast family entertainment empire; Medal of Freedom honoree

"It will never be possible by pure reason to arrive at some absolute truth."

– Werner Heisenberg, Nobel laureate German theoretical physicist/research scientist; quantum mechanics pioneer; famed for the "uncertainty principle;" resisted nuclear arms development

"You should never feel afraid to become a piece of art. It's exhilarating."

– Nicki Minaj, award-winning American-Trinidadian rapper/singer/songwriter/actress/model; nicknamed "Nicki the Ninja;" her Chinese tattoo translates as "God is with me always"

"I dream for a living."

– Steven Spielberg, Oscar/Emmy/Golden Globe-winning American filmmaker; one of the most popular movie creators in film history; famed for adventure fantasies such as 'E.T.' and 'Jaws'

"I was trying to daydream, but my mind kept wandering."

– Steven Wright, Oscar-winning American stand-up comedian/actor/writer/film producer; known for his deadpan style and cracked philosophical observations; often hailed as "visionary"

"I believe you can speak things into existence."

– Jay-Z, Grammy-winning American rapper/songwriter/producer/entrepreneur/record executive; has sold 50M+ albums; has won 22 rap Grammys (2019); never writes down his lyrics

 Capricorn 7

Most 7th lunation phase lives appear to be relatively divorced from the experience of guilt. These are souls who have put the wrenching emotional tugs engendered by the soul's emergence in previous incarnations into their karmic rearview. Thus, citizens of the 7th lunation phase are pretty unencumbered by misgivings when it comes down to having a healthy relationship with a strong personal will.

Nowhere is this principal better illustrated than in the life of a Capricorn 7, a phase in which people are pretty much just not inclined to wrestle with their consciences. Disposed towards succeeding in the material world, all Capricorns have an orientation towards an authoritative utilitarianism. With the Capricorn 7 one simply gets amplification of the principle that the things that bring one to the top of the social heap are good, while any roadblocks to success are to be ignored, shouted down, moved aside or, if necessary, run over.

Granted, some of the implications here are dark. Capricorn 7's are souls who are more than ready to accept that life is ethically vague. Morality is the vaguest of premises, many of them would argue, and remorsefulness generally misguided. They may not want you to know they are thinking it, but many of them would privately concur that any idealism about human affairs is for suckers and also-rans.

So what becomes captivating in this regard is the star power that the Capricorn 7 phase is able to generate. As the considerable list of Hollywood leading men (and political firebrands) below indicates, there is something about the Capricorn 7 vibe that resonates deeply with the masses. The Capricorn 7 may not always call to our better selves, but we do have a strong admiration of their largely unsentimental clarity and, often, their successes.

As for the rest, the Capricorn 7 appreciates a lot of personal privacy. Behind closed doors some of them are oriented towards pursuits they would rather not have a light shine on, while others are flat-out boring. It's not what they are essentially about and it's none of your business, anyway.

"It's not listed in the Bible, but my spiritual gift, my specific calling from God, is to be a television talk-show host."

– Jim Bakker, infamous American televangelist; co-host with wife Tammy Faye of TV's PTL Club; developer of Heritage City; plagued by fraud and sex scandals; served 5 years in federal prison

"Most chick-singers say 'if you hurt me, I'll die'... I say, if you hurt me, I'll kick your ass."

– Pat Benatar, Grammy-winning American singer-songwriter; best known for defiant rock/pop ballads such as 'Heartbreaker' and 'Love is a Battlefield;' left life as an Army wife to sing in clubs

"I won't admit or deny anything...makes me more interesting."

– Orlando Bloom, award-winning English actor/humanitarian; breakthrough role was Legolas in 'The Lord of the Rings;' enjoys daredevil pursuits; mildly dyslexic; a practicing Buddhist

"All you owe the public is a good performance."

– Humphrey Bogart, Oscar-winning American actor; considered one of the great male icons of classic Hollywood cinema; known for brooding tough guy roles; passionate about sailing/chess

"I think what makes people fascinating is conflict. It's drama, it's the human condition. Nobody wants to watch perfection."

– Nicolas Cage, Oscar-winning American actor/filmmaker; known best for playing complex and darkly manic heroes; odd affections/affectations; contractually bound to not ride motorcycles

"Life's complicated and people do things for a lot of reasons. I think if you live in a black-and-white world, you're gonna suffer a lot. I used to be like that. But I don't believe that anymore."

– Bradley Cooper, award-winning American actor/filmmaker; known best for distressed hero roles; directorial debut was hit 'A Star is Born;' his earliest aspiration was to become a Ninja

"I don't have a seller's remorse about how I've lived. I am cognizant of what I have done, and any of us could maybe draw the line better. But I've tried to live pretty fearlessly."

– Kevin Costner, Oscar/Emmy/Golden Globe-winning American actor/film maker/musician; known best for epics and sports fantasies such as 'Dances with Wolves' and 'Field of Dreams'

"Social justice is collectivism. Social justice is the rights of a group. It denies individual responsibility. It's a negation of individual responsibility, so social justice is totally contrary to the Word of God."

– Ted Cruz, outspoken hard-line conservative American politician/attorney; first Hispanic U.S. Senator from Texas; founder of the Harvard Latino Law Review; vocal opponent of Obamacare

"Here you are, you're a liberal, probably define peace as the absence of conflict. I define peace as the ability to defend yourself and blow your enemies into smithereens."

– Sean Hannity, hard-line conservative American media host/political commentator/author; hosts most-watched cable news program in the U.S.; staunch Trump supporter; hypnotism fan

"It's kind of rebellious to be yourself."

– Kate Moss, award-winning English supermodel/businesswoman; the face of the mid-1990's heroin chic fashion trend; a legendary hard partier; Playboy's 60th Anniversary cover girl

"It is silly to appeal to people's moral sense."

– Hermann Goring, infamous German political/military leader; a central figure in the Nazi Party; Commander of the Luftwaffe/creator of the Gestapo; died by suicide after war trial conviction

"The only rule is there are no rules."

– Aristotle Onassis; eminent Greek business tycoon; created Olympic Airways and the world's largest privately-owned shipping fleet; married JFK's widow Jackie; famously smug

 Aquarius 7

It is the Aquarius 7 who accomplishes one of the neatest tricks of human existence. Here is the individual who, while reaching for (and often gaining) the highest possible high, somehow manages to foster a meaningful and salutary relationship with the entirety of humanity. Often legitimately laying claim to the title of genius, with all the personal uniqueness that term conveys, the Aquarius 7 seems best suited to the role of responsible avatar, rather than the lordly possessor, of transpersonal human potential.

Their secret is that they tend to see life in term of its limitless possibilities rather than its myriad shortcomings. Others may see their optimistic humanism as eccentric, but what is most strange about them is, given the nature of life on our planet, distaste for complaining. They are certainly human, and they certainly have their doubts and setbacks, but their bottom line is that life presents a very ample buffet in which everyone is bound to encounter something delicious if one just maintains an appetite while moving on down the line.

When the Aquarius 7 does come upon that which delights their nature, there really is no stopping them. Whether they find themselves at the age of 3 or 30, these different drummers thereafter tend to produce a remarkably rich and prolific body of work. There is true passion for the awareness of cultural being in the Aquarius 7, and they tend to express a calling as a crafted masterwork of human participation rather than as an outburst of self-referential feeling.

Ultimately, the Aquarius 7 vibe tends to be a magical mixture of science, art, mysticism and hyperactivity. They are at their best the mileposts of evolution. They really tend to be human in the most attractive sense of the word.

"Do what keeps you happy, and don't ever let people box you in."

– Jennifer Aniston, Emmy/SAG/Golden Globe-winning American actress/producer/entrepreneur; broke through as Rachel on TV's "Friends;' one of TV's highest paid actors; a high school outcast

"The most important thing in life is to stop saying 'I wish' and start saying 'I will.' Consider nothing impossible; then treat possibilities as probabilities."

– Charles Dickens, venerated English writer/social critic; created some of the most famous characters in literature including Oliver Twist and Ebenezer Scrooge; epileptic/OCD/spiritual

"I am never wrong when it comes to my possibilities."

– Placido Domingo; Emmy/Grammy-winning Spanish opera singer/conductor/philanthropist; esteemed for role/language versatility; one of the Three Tenors; Presidential MOF recipient

"Do the thing and the power will come."

– Thomas Edison, legendary American inventor/businessman; landmark contributor in the fields of electric power/communication/recording/film; hyperactive/non-verbal child; self-educated

"All I knew is that I never wanted to be average."

– Michael Jordan, HOF American basketball player/entrepreneur/pitchman/philanthropist; considered by many to be basketball's GOAT; six-time NBA Finals MVP; only billionaire athlete

"I just want to give it all that I got. I just don't want to waste it."

– Carole King, Grammy HOF American singer-songwriter/environmentalist; best known for 'Tapestry;' wrote over 100 pop hits; first woman to win Song of the Year ('You've Got a Friend')

"It is the greatest shot of adrenaline to be doing what you have wanted to do so badly. You almost feel like you could fly without the plane."

– Charles Lindbergh, Medal of Honor American aviator/military officer/author/inventor/activist; famed for solo non-stop trans-Atlantic flight; began career as a stunt flyer; an environmentalist

"Complaints are prayers to the devil."

– Bob Marley, R&R HOF Jamaican singer-songwriter/political activist; reggae/Rastafarian/ganja pioneer; Grammy Lifetime Achievement award; BBC named 'One Love' Song of the Millennium

"The wonders of the music of the future will be of a higher and wider scale and will introduce many sounds that the human ear is now incapable of hearing. Among these new sounds will be the glorious music of angelic chorales. As men hear these they will cease to consider Angels as figments of their imagination."

– Wolfgang Amadeus Mozart, venerated Austrian composer; a musical prodigy from the age of 3; composed 50 symphonies and 21 operas among his 600+ works; known for personal volatility

"We are, because God is."

– Emanuel Swedenborg, influential Swedish theologian/scientist/philosopher/mystic; developed theory of earth/spirit "correspondences" in book 'Heaven and Hell;' extraordinarily psychic

"There's nothing wrong with shooting for the stars."

– Justin Timberlake, Grammy/Emmy-winning American singer-songwriter/ actor/entrepreneur; a pop legend; Mickey Mouse Club alum; member of NSYNC; motorcycle buff; OCD/hyperactive

"Create the highest, grandest vision possible for your life, because you become what you believe."

– Oprah Winfrey, Emmy/Tony award-winning American media executive/ actress/TV host/ producer/entrepreneur/philanthropist; one of America's most culturally influential individuals

Strange Coincidence:

– Jennifer Aniston, Thomas Edison and Michael Jordan all had traumatic near-drowning incidents as children that rendered them considerably aquaphobic as adults.

Pisces 7

If one is going to be honest, it's pretty difficult to tell the difference between Pisces natives with regard to their lunation phase. Any Pisces senses that the potential of consciousness, in terms of the human capacity for perception, is essentially limitless. Any time and space currents one may choose to navigate derive from a "greater power" that may be confronted, or even embraced, but never really delimited or controlled.

When a Pisces has reached the seventh lunation phase, the difference is most often to be found in the amplitude of the Piscean spirit rather than its nature. If one is true to the fish iconology of the sign, Pisces 7's are akin to the big ones that constantly get away. Having spiritually negotiated the deep and the distant, and figuratively having freed themselves from a hook or two, the Pisces 7 displays qualities not often predominant in its Pisces brethren...independence, forthrightness, resilience, fearlessness.

Certainly, an orientation towards passionately diving into the experience of consciousness can make the Pisces 7 seem somewhat emotionally and intellectually untethered. Yet one must also consider the Pisces 7's of enormous accomplishment, including the ones who triumph in the purportedly mundane fields of commerce and politics. Common to these is the recognition of the force that one can muster when one discovers a strong current and goes with the flow.

Words beyond this, as they often do with Pisces, fail. Passion and ardor come to mind, along with endorphins and hysteria. Who but a Pisces knows what life is really like in that boundless ocean? Not you, probably. Not me, for sure.

"Put all your soul into it, play the way you feel!"

– Frederic Chopin, acclaimed Romantic-era Polish composer/pianist; famed for his emotional expressiveness; preferred to play in the dark; prestigious piano competition held in his name

"You get addicted to emotions. Our endorphins kick in and it's like a high. On the low end you might love roller coasters. On the high end you might be a bank robber or something."

– Bryan Cranston, Emmy/SAG/GG-winning American actor/director/producer/screenwriter; most famed as Walter White in 'Breaking Bad;' after college he rode a motorcycle cross country

"Success is born out of faith, an undying passion, and a relentless drive."

– Stephen Curry, all-star American pro basketball player; six-time all-star; two-time MVP; three-time NBA champion; holds season record for 3-pointers; a devout Christian; a germaphobe

"The very thing you fear could be the best thing to ever happen to you."

ell; distinguished American businessman/philanthropist; famed nous computer enterprise begun in a dorm room; awards include ntrepreneur of the Year

"All that was neither a city, nor a church, nor a river, nor color, nor light, nor shadow: it was reverie. For a long time, I remained motionless, letting myself be penetrated gently by this unspeakable ensemble, by the serenity of the sky and the melancholy of the moment. I do not know what was going on in my mind, and I could not express it; it was one of those ineffable moments when one feels something in himself which is going to sleep and something which is awakening."

– Victor Hugo, celebrated Romantic-era French poet/novelist/dramatist/ humanitarian; best known for 'Les Misérables' and 'The Hunchback of Notre Dame;' incredibly eccentric/libidinous

"It takes nerves of steel to stay neurotic."

– Herb Kelleher, distinguished American businessman/lawyer; founder/CEO of Southwest Airlines; admired for "maverick" strategies/immersive employee culture; a motorcycle buff

"Dream audaciously. Have the courage to fail forward. Act with urgency."

– Phil Knight, distinguished American business magnate/philanthropist; founder of Nike; first sold running shoes out of his car; has donated nearly a billion dollars to educational institutions

"Passion gives me moments of wholeness."

– Anais Nin, award-winning French-Cuban American writer; fame came from her eight-volume personal diaries; one of the first female eroticists; influenced by surrealism and psychotherapy

"I can fathom anything, man. I love biting off more than I can chew and figuring it out."

– Jordan Peele, Oscar/Emmy-winning American actor/comedian/ writer/ director/producer; known for horror/comedy genres that "appeal to outsiders;" college major was "puppetry"

"Nothing bad can happen to a writer. Everything is material."

– Philip Roth, Pulitzer-winning American author; focused on the interplay of life and art; known for themes of lust/Jewish culture/American values; winner of the National Medal of the Arts

"I am glad that I paid so little attention to good advice; had I abided by it I might have been saved from some of my most valuable mistakes."

– Edna St. Vincent Millay, Pulitzer-winning American poet/playwright/activist; concerned with love/heterosexual relationships from a feminist perspective; a talented musician and linguist

"Make sure you are doing what God wants you to do—then do it with all your strength."

– George Washington, American political leader/general/statesman/ Founding Father; commander of the Colonial armies; 1st president of the United States; an excellent dancer

ation Phase/Balsamic Moon

is 316 to 359 degrees ahead of the Sun

Keyword: Completion

The essence of the 8th lunation phase life cannot be easily described. It is here where a soul has formed itself, lived its purpose, cleaned out the attic and moved itself to the cosmic curb to wait for the moving van. "To move where?" is indeed the salient question.

Both Dane Rudhyar and Marc Roberts write about this phase as a time in which the soul accepts its destiny and creates a living prophecy of the future. For some the mundane is emphasized, but that is in a very broad social sense that concerns itself with a collective cultural destination. For others the path is deeply inward, as one contemplates the bio/spiritual 'next step' in a cosmic chain of being.

To live such a lifetime is to have a constant sense that one is sloughing off old skin for the purpose of being essentially different from what one was in the past. Is the soul headed to a new and unique cycle of human incarnation? Is this life a transition into a post-human existence that no mere human can possibly describe? I don't know.[2]

It is perhaps helpful to note that while the LP8 individual is truly preoccupied with BIG considerations, an observable quirk of this incarnation can be described as dealing with karmic loose ends. In the LP8 lifetime, one frequently encounters intense (sex! money! rock & roll!) episodic events involving people, places and things that are here

2 My LP8 clients want answers to these things that, of course, I cannot possibly provide. Usually I just tell them to watch the Albert Brooks movie 'Defending Your Life.' His exploration of post-death existence gets pretty close to what needs to be communicated here...and Shirley MacLaine's brief cameo as the guide to the Pavilion of Past Lives is alone worth the price of admission.

with great import for a while and then completely gone. The spiritual conceit is to chalk this up to a karmic reconciliation of unresolved energies from past incarnations...and it's now or never to balance the books.

For the rest of it there is only one motto that can possibly do justice here. "Onward!"

 Aries 8

In the 8th lunation phase Aries remains an individual disposed towards action. Here though, at the precipice of the truly unknowable, the Aries takes just a moment to consider a single question: what is the appropriate act of a person who has just about run out of time?

There is little homogeneity among the answers, but the principles that guide an Aries 8 are reasonably easy to detect. The first, which might cause some discomfort to those looking on from the outside, is that an Aries 8 has little tolerance for the notion that life is being guided and controlled by some unseen hand. Whatever the Aries 8 chooses to do, it is rarely in their spirit to attribute to a doctrinal God that has passed down a holy law that demarcates acceptable behavior or the nature of reality.

Far more germane to the Aries 8 life is a belief that whatever one decides to do, one must do it with both personal integrity and enthusiasm. If this is a final step, it is to be taken purposefully and boldly. In so much as there may be divinity in the universe, it is encountered in the result of those actions rather than in the cause.

Lest this sound far too self-involved, it is good to keep in mind that many an Aries 8 comes to the conclusion that the common welfare of mankind should figure into life-purpose calculations. Others see the final lunation phase as an opportunity to right wrongs, both personal and communal. Still others just want to sing or dance or play a tribute to the life force.

In sum, the Aries 8 is a phase in which one takes actions to express one's true nature. Unlike many other Aries' phases this is not just about the nature of the act. It is about the nature of the actor.

"I suppose the story of my life is a search for love, but more than that, I have been looking for a way to repair myself from the damages I suffered early on and to define my obligation, if I had any, to myself and my species."

– Marlon Brando, Oscar/Emmy-winning American actor/director; known for a tumultuous personality/broad cultural influence; declined an Oscar citing the plight of Native Americans

"When the time comes, the journey toward the brilliant white light that marks the barrier between this world and the next will not hold as much fear as it once would have. For in my study of death, I have found the celebration of life."

– Dolores Cannon, celebrated American author/hypnotherapist/past-life regressionist; developed technique of 'Quantum Healing Hypnosis;' famed for Nostradamus contacts

"True wealth is not measured in money or status or power. It is measured in the legacy we leave behind for those we love and those we inspire."

– Cesar Chavez, key American labor leader/community organizer/civil rights activist; co-founder of the United Farm Workers Association; recipient of the Presidential Medal of Freedom

"I have friends who have a normal family, kids and a dog, and I think I would blow my brains out. It's fine for them. But I'm such a free spirit, I feel more alive when I've got somewhere to go."

– Kenny Chesney, award-winning American country music singer/songwriter/record producer/humanitarian; recorded 20 hit albums; a health/fitness fanatic; hates stickiness

"We are going to die, and that makes us the lucky ones. Most people are never going to die, because they are never going to be born. The number of people who could be here in my place outnumbers the sand grains in the Sahara. If you think about all the different ways in which our genes could be permuted, you and I are quite grotesquely lucky to be here. The number of events that had to happen in order for you to exist, in order for me to exist... we are privileged to be alive and we should make the most of our time on this world."

– Richard Dawkins, award-winning English evolutionary biologist/author; an atheist known for his book 'The God Delusion;' an annual award is made in his name for the progress of reason

"I don't look at what I've lost. I look instead at what I have left."

– Betty Ford, distinguished First Lady of the U.S.; revered for her struggle/activism in areas such as breast cancer and substance addiction; recipient of the Presidential Medal of Freedom

"It's like dance is a metaphor for going beyond where you think you can go."

– Jennifer Grey, popular American actress; known for dancing via her breakout role as Baby in 'Dirty Dancing' and later as a winner of 'Dancing with the Stars;' career harmed by rhinoplasty

"It's perfectly clear to me that religion is a myth. It's something we have invented to explain the inexplicable. My religion and the spiritual side of my life come from a sense of connection to the humankind and nature on this planet and in the universe. I am in overwhelming awe of it all: It is so fantastic, so complex, so beyond comprehension."

– Hugh Hefner, award-winning American publisher/editor; a controversial cultural icon; founder of 'Playboy;' an annual award is given in his name for advancement of 1st amendment rights

"I am waiting for a sign that will indicate to me what meaning I must give to my life, but right now my existence is satisfactory."

– Lucy Lawless, award-winning New Zealand actor/singer/activist; famous as the title character in 'Xena: Warrior Princess;' although heterosexual, Xena made her a lesbian icon

"Some people feel like stuff just happens to you and you cope as best you can. Some people feel like we can change what happens not only to ourselves but to other people. That's me; and I like that in anybody."

– Rachel Maddow, Emmy-winning American TV host/liberal political commentator/author; highly-esteemed for insight/clarity/affability; a Rhodes scholar; an AIDS activist; enjoys fishing

"I do twenty minutes every time the refrigerator door opens and the light comes on."

– Debbie Reynolds, award-winning American actress/singer/businesswoman/humanitarian; achieved fame in 'Singin' in the Rain;' recipient of the SAG Lifetime Achievement Award

"When you don't follow your nature there is a hole in the universe where you were supposed to be."

– Dane Rudhyar, award-winning French-American composer/author/painter/novelist/humanistic astrologer; described as a New Age "seed man;" a pioneer of modern transpersonal astrology

Taurus 8

Bullfighting is a repugnant activity to many, and there is no desire to elevate its status here. Still, it is hard to not grant at least some respect to the courage and grace one finds in the bull ring. Those who participate are not facile actors and there is no mistaking that death is on the line.

The preceding may or may not be a useful metaphor, but there is unquestionably something of the *corrida* in the life of a Taurus 8. Think about the prospects for this moment as the final act of the participants. Now focus particularly on the perspective of the bull.

One may postulate such a thing as a smart bull, but by their behavior one gets the idea that the bull is not extraordinarily interested in playing chess. The bull knows, in the way that an animal is true to its essence, that it has muscle and ferocity on its side. There is a challenge, there is a charge, and there is blood and sand.

For a Taurus 8, life is most often lived at this moment of raging consummation. Whatever is attempted is undertaken with fearlessness and a sense of finality. There are few doubts about the capacity to confront whatever must be confronted, and no doubts at all about the power of one's will.

Perhaps what one reads in the soul of a Taurus 8, a bull in its final incarnation, is that they are finished with the delicacy of life. There is little respect for the china shop here. The essence of completed karma and the chasm of indescribable consciousness which they face demand a willingness to engage and spiritually liberate.

There are horrible tyrants on the list of Taurus 8's, essential social philosophers and great artists. There is beauty and there is pain and there is great intuitive skill in the lives of the Taurus 8's. Yet the key may be is that inside every one of them there is an undaunted, however wounded, bull damn well fully prepared to perfect themselves or die trying.

"I have to keep law and order and it means that I have to kill my enemies before they kill me."

– Idi Amin, infamous Ugandan military leader/politician; a cruel despot known as the "Butcher of Uganda," his presidency was a reign of terror; found the taste of human flesh "too salty"

"It punches an audience senseless."

– Cate Blanchett, Oscar/Golden Globe/SAG-winning Australian actress/director/activist; vast resume includes turns as Katherine Hepburn and Bob Dylan; an Armani beauty ambassador

"At some point in your life, if you're lucky, you get to design the way in which things evolve."

– Daniel Day-Lewis, Oscar/Golden Globe/SAG-winning English actor; best known for dark historical portrayals in films such as 'Let There Be Blood' and 'Lincoln;' craftsmanship obsessed

"It has taken me most of my adult life to come to terms with who I am. To do that, I had to break free of attitudes that brought me down."

– Janet Jackson, Grammy-winning American singer/songwriter/actress/dancer; had five straight #1 albums on Billboard; her Super Bowl "wardrobe malfunction" helped to birth YouTube

"Two things fill the mind with ever new and increasing admiration and awe, the oftener and more steadily we reflect on them: the starry heavens above me and the moral law within me."

– Immanuel Kant, eminent Prussian philosopher; a central figure of the Age of Enlightenment; famed for 'Critique of Pure Reason;' his work synthesized rationalism and subjective perception

"Lamborghini is refinement, luxury and perfection."

– Ferruccio Lamborghini, famed Italian industrialist; built his empire on tractors; created his namesake luxury sports car line to challenge Ferrari; the Lamborghini logo is a raging bull

"Workers of the world unite; you have nothing to lose but your chains."

– Karl Marx, world-renowned German philosopher/political theorist/ socialist revolutionary; history's best known socialist thinker; authored 'The Communist Manifesto' and 'Das Kapital'

"Be peaceful, be courteous, obey the law, respect everyone; but if someone puts his hand on you, send him to the cemetery."

– Malcolm X, iconic American Muslim minister/human rights activist; a charismatic Nation of Islam spokesperson disdainful of the white race; a segregationist; assassinated by rival Muslims

"You throw your best punch, otherwise don't do it."

– Don Rickles, Emmy-winning American stand-up comedian/actor/author; best known for insult humor; wryly nicknamed "Mr. Warmth;" claimed never regretting anything he said in his act

"By sealing our work with our blood, we may see at least the bright dawn of universal happiness."

– Maximilien Robespierre, influential French lawyer/statesman; a key human rights activist in the French Revolution; became radical architect of the "Reign of Terror;" executed by guillotine

"If you have a problem with my answer, that's your problem, not my problem."

– Dennis Rodman, award-winning American pro basketball player; nicknamed "The Worm;" famed as a fierce defender; unrepentant exhibitionist; apologist for North Korea's dictator

"It's up to you to perfect that gift that you've been given. Put your spirit into that song. Focus on the words that you are singing. Get into the experience that you are singing about and sing your heart out."

– Stevie Wonder, Grammy HOF American singer/songwriter/musician/ record producer/activist; had first #1 song at age 13; has won 25 Grammys; Presidential Medal of Freedom recipient

Gemini 8

Of all the Sun signs that come to the end of the karmic road in the eighth lunation phase, it is the Gemini 8 who seems least clothed in a cloak of finality. Why is this? Because right up to the very end the Gemini spirit is predicated on the awareness that life offers no consistency, i.e. people, places and things are born to be mutable and unresolved.

So if a Gemini 8 has a guiding star at the precipice of fulfillment, it's one whose brightness is in a constant state of fluctuation. The heavens cast odd shadows and things that at first seem one way soon seem to be something opposite. And yes, it can be quite a challenge to negotiate such a life.

Fortunately for the Gemini 8, happily living in one's head and testing the limits of perspective is the whole game. It's more than okay to see the trick that a fluctuating existence plays on the mind and to be in on the joke. In fact, for most Gemini 8's it is pretty liberating to BE the joke.

Through all, the wisdom that a Gemini 8 has to impart is an injunction to be engaged in the moment while not expecting the moment to last. Happiness is very much related to dexterity in action and, especially, in thought. Why be so hung up on the beach when there is an opportunity for contemplation in every grain of sand?

Ultimately, a Gemini 8 life tends to be one in which nothing is sacred but everything is truly interesting. A Gemini 8 makes ready for the post-karmic chasm by reporting every moment of preparation. In life, they are prone to conclude, the devil is in the details...but so are the angels.

"I was fascinated by a compelling character embroiled in a controversial topic that told the story from a different point of view."

– Bjorn Borg, HOF Swedish tennis pro; won 11 Grand Slam singles titles; fiercely competitive but called "The Martian" for his composed demeanor; retired at 26; planned to auction his trophies

"You can get more with a simple prayer and a Thompson sub-machinegun than you can with a simple prayer alone."

– John Dillinger, legendary American gangster of the Great Depression era; famed for robbing banks and for escaping from prison; a raconteur and national celebrity; gunned down by the FBI

"Sometimes it's not enough to know what things mean; sometimes you have to know what things don't mean."

– Bob Dylan, Nobel-laureate American singer-songwriter/author/visual artist; a folk/pop lyricist legend; honors include Grammy Lifetime Achievement, an Oscar and a Medal of Freedom

"Only those who attempt the absurd will achieve the impossible. I think it's in my basement... let me go upstairs and check."

– M. C. Escher, award-winning Dutch graphic artist; a master of illusion, his fantastical optics were appreciated more by mathematicians than art critics; self-described as a "thinking person"

"History is moving pretty quickly these days, and the heroes and villains keep on changing parts."

– Ian Fleming, renowned British author; creator of James Bond; he was a Commander in British naval intelligence; JFK's fandom led to great fame; annual crime fiction award given in his name

"Sometimes I over-tinker, which is something wrong with my brain chemistry. But in figuring out why I do that, maybe I'll make myself a better person. I doubt it."

– John Goodman, Emmy/SAG/Golden Globe-winning American actor; key roles include Dan on 'Roseanne' and Walter in 'The Big Lebowski; earned a Fine Arts degree on a football scholarship

"Some questions don't have answers, which is a terribly difficult lesson to learn."

– Katharine Graham, Pulitzer-winning American publisher/journalist; famed for heading 'The Washington Post' during Watergate; intimates included Warren Buffet and Truman Capote

"I always had the theory that the most important thing is be happy, enjoy what are you doing, and be fresh mentally."

– Rafael Nadal, all-time great Spanish pro tennis player; "The King of Clay," winner of 81 straight matches on this surface; has won 19 Grand Slam singles titles; a PlayStation addict

"I have a pet lizard named Puff, five goldfish–named Pinky, Brain, Jowls, Pearl and Sandy, an oscar fish named Chef, two pacus, an albino African frog named Whitey, a bonsai tree, four Venus flytraps, a fruit fly farm and sea monkeys."

– Chris Pratt, award-winning American actor/producer; known for quirky portrayals in 'Parks & Recreation,' 'Guardians of the Galaxy,' and 'Jurassic World;' paints; plays guitar; was a stripper

"If I could prescribe a single rule for looking at a work of art it would be to enjoy it. If we're honest with ourselves, we have to admit we enjoy our tears just as much as we enjoy our laughter. The only moments of life that are a bore are when we don't care one way or another."

– Vincent Price, award-winning American actor; best known for his work in horror films; a Yale grad, he also taught there; wrote cookbooks; the visual inspiration for the character Dr. Strange

"I've got a terrible person in me just as much as anybody else, and I think–I like to think I also have a really good person in me."

– Amy Schumer, Emmy-winning American stand-up comedian/actress/author; known for candor about personal life; has kept detailed journals since youth; 'Glamour' Trailblazer of the Year

"It takes a smart guy to play dumb."

– Mr. T, iconic American actor/wrestler/bodyguard/TV personality; tough guy in 'Rocky III' and 'The A-Team;' catch-phrase is "I pity the fool;" featured in Snickers' "Get Some Nuts" campaign

 Cancer 8

The Cancer 8 lives a life that is a testament to emotion. Now this is not meant to be some backhanded judgmental description of these souls as slaves to their feelings. No, for while they do mostly tend to be awesomely sensitive Cancer 8's are not about swaying to those everyday moods that come blowing along on each breeze.

Like other eighth lunation phase beings coming to term with their karmic essence a Cancer 8 is in a powerful time of reckoning. Here the essence of a human life as a cauldron of strong feelings must come to full boil for the purpose of being served up to the rest of humanity as an archetype. The uniqueness of a Cancer 8 life is in guiding what may be called an ultimate feeling to the surface.

Essentially the Cancer 8 asks constantly the question: if you knew you were going to disappear forever, what is the last thing to which you would attach? Not surprisingly for many the answer is "love," but this is not the only answer. People who operate without guile at the emotional level may answer this question with "money," or "nature," or "work," or "hate" or even "dessert."

A Cancer 8 very much brings inspiration and imagination to their life quest. Their consideration of life's meaning is wholly grounded in the primacy of the individual as a subjective participant. But it really all boils down to having an extraordinarily intense feeling about something...

...and answering the question "what do I do with this?"

"Elegance is not catching somebody's eyes; it's staying in somebody's memory."

– Giorgio Armani, award-winning Italian fashion designer; known best for classic menswear; a huge influence in modern Hollywood couture; lines include perfumes, restaurants, hotels

"I need you. I need you to hate, so I can use you for your energy."

– Curtis Jackson (50 Cent), Grammy-winning American rapper/songwriter/actor/television producer/entrepreneur; his violent/drug-fueled street life is chronicled in 'Get Rich or Die Tryin'

"I am a cage, in search of a bird."

– Franz Kafka, highly influential German/Bohemian novelist/short story writer; a master of the absurd; famed for 'The Metamorphosis;' he fantasized getting rich writing tourist guidebooks

"I'm the kind of person who would rather get my hopes up really high and watch them get dashed to pieces than wisely keep my expectations at bay and hope they are exceeded. This quality has made me a needy and theatrical friend, but has given me a spectacularly dramatic emotional life."

– Mindy Kaling, award-winning American comedian/actress/writer/director/producer; was Kelly Kapoor on 'The Office;' 1st Indian-American to have own network show; romantic film obsessed

"I would surrender my being to see you whole once more."

– Khloe Kardashian, award-winning American media personality/model/activist/entrepreneur; gained fame as a reality TV star; the "most relatable" Kardashian; invented selfie "duck lips"

"The ultimate lesson is learning how to love and be loved unconditionally."

– Elisabeth Kubler-Ross, venerated Swiss-American psychiatrist/author; famed for nine books on dying including the classic 'On Death and Dying;' conceptualized the "five stages of grief"

"Singleness of purpose is one of the chief essentials for success in life, no matter what may be one's aim."

– John D. Rockefeller, iconic American capitalist/philanthropist; the richest person in modern history; monopolized oil prior to anti-trust laws; annually celebrated the date of his first job

"You can overcome anything, if and only if you love something enough."

– Lionel Messi, all-time great Argentine pro footballer; growth-stunted as a child; three-time World Soccer Player of the Year; six-time Ballon d'Or recipient; named "Messiah" by the media

"If nothing saves us from death, at least love should save us from life."

– Pablo Neruda, Nobel -laureate Chilean poet/journalist/diplomat/politician; famed both as a writer of love poetry and as a Communist; winner of the Lenin and Stalin Peace prizes

"There's nothing worse than being disappointed in somebody."

– Jessica Simpson, award-winning American singer/actress/fashion designer/ author; a teen pop phenomenon whose 1st album sold 4 million copies; biggest hit was 'I Wanna Love You Forever'

"It is not enough to be industrious; so are the ants. What are you industrious about?"

– Henry David Thoreau, admired American essayist/poet/philosopher; one of the great 19th C Transcendentalists; wrote 'Walden'/'Civil Disobedience;' advocated life in harmony with nature

"My problem is desserts. I am obsessed with desserts."

– Sofia Vergara, award-winning American-Colombian actress/ model/ producer; three-time top earning American TV actress; famed as Gloria in 'Modern Family;' was an "ugly duckling" child

 Leo 8

Contemplation comes pretty naturally to any eighth lunation phase soul. It's an incarnation in which there is a recognition of all that has been experienced and settled for good on karma's path. All that remains is a final expression of one's nature on the brink of eternity.

For a Leo 8, who has presumably spent many lifetimes in the exaltation of personal identity, the awareness that lingers often becomes somewhat poignant. To a certain extent there is a diminution of the blazing light that challenges all darkness. Suddenly, at the edge of the void, the Leo 8 comes face to face with the proposition that being luminous and being in control are not exactly the same things.

Of course, the Leo 8 may still roar with the best of his leonine tribe. An honest and potent expression of "who I am" is the king's goal. But who is one, really?

In seeking an answer to this question, what many Leo 8's discover is that life's extraordinary vicissitudes take one farther away from a valid answer. The 'secret' awareness of a Leo 8 incarnation is that in adjusting to reality one tends to grow past one's truest self. Identity is paramount, in other words, before the Great Spirit exercises its preeminence.

What one thus tends to get with a Leo 8 is someone whose exaltation of self leaves them acting a lot like an adolescent, or maybe a teenager. Regardless of the requirements of the Void, the Leo 8 ultimately places the rising of the sap and the buzz of the bees above a final immersion in greater consciousness. A super-abundance of solemnity about life's meaning is strictly for squares.

Just don't chalk it down to naiveté or expect them to tone down. The Leo 8 has burned lot of spiritual effort getting to this point. If their final answer is that life is a high school dance, who are you to say it is not?

"I think it's always best to be who you are."

– Halle Berry, Oscar/Emmy/Sag-winning American actress/model; only African-American to win the Best Actress Oscar; was a Bond girl, Catwoman, and an X-Man; a Miss America runner-up

"I wish to sing of my interior visions with the naive candor of a child."

– Claude Debussy, award-winning French composer; an Impressionist but hated the term; recipient of the Prix de Rome but hated the Residence requirement; wrote 'Claire de Lune'

"When I do something, it is all about self-discovery. I want to learn and discover my own limits."

– Larry Ellison, renowned American businessman/philanthropist; co-founder of Oracle; a self-made multi-billionaire; a world-class yachtsman; "the world's most avid trophy-home buyer"

"This is a business that I have always had the last laugh in. It has nothing to do with acting; it has to do with good karma."

– George Hamilton, Golden Globe-winning American actor/entrepreneur; best known for his debonair playboy style and signature suntan; his autobiography is titled 'Don't Mind If I Do'

"We are in danger of developing a cult of the Common Man, which means a cult of mediocrity."

– Herbert Hoover, distinguished American engineer/businessman/humanitarian; 31st president of the U.S.A., his first elected office; a self-made millionaire; linked to Great Depression onset

"I will not be an ordinary man, because I have a right to be extraordinary."

– Peter O'Toole, Golden Globe/BAFTA-winning British actor; a great bon vivant and raconteur; known for star turns in historical epics; holds record for Oscar nominations without a win (8)

"Every time we teach a child something, we keep him from inventing it himself. On the other hand, that which we allow him to discover for himself will remain with him visible for the rest of his life."

– Jean Piaget, prize-winning Swiss psychologist; his theory of cognitive development explains how children build intelligence; his first scholarly papers were rejected as "adolescent"

"I can only say that whatever my life and work have been, I'm not envious of anyone–and this is my biggest satisfaction."

– Roman Polanski, Oscar-winning French-Polish film director/producer/writer/actor; his work tends to be dark and unsettling; infamous for statutory rape conviction and flight from justice

"There are so many different walks of life, so many different personalities in the world. And no longer do you have to be a chameleon and try and adapt to that environment–you can truly be yourself."

– Hope Solo, Gold Medal-winning American soccer player; won two Golden Gloves at the Women's World Cup; first keeper with 100 shutouts; a blunt critic of soccer's gender pay-gap

"You know, I am a Leo. Lion is a giant part of me."

– Patrick Swayze, iconic American actor/dancer/singer-songwriter; known for playing the virile yet sensitive guy in films such as 'Dirty Dancing' and 'Ghost;' was a Disneyland Prince Charming

"There's nothing I despise more than people trying to be something that they're not."

– Charlize Theron, Oscar/Golden Globe/SAG-winning South African actress/model; gained fame as a serial killer in 'Monster;' a Playboy/Victoria's Secret sex symbol; does her own stunt work

"Somebody who's designing something for himself has at least got a market of one that he's very close to."

– Steve Wozniak, iconic American engineer/programmer/philanthropist/ entrepreneur; best known as co-founder and "brains" of Apple; member of the Inventor HOF; a college dropout

 Virgo 8

It is a Virgo's lot in life to seek flawlessness. The burden of their quest is to be extraordinarily perceptive about imperfection. Where others may relish the salutary properties of the ointment, the Virgo can't help but consider the fly.

The Virgo 8, at the end of karma's road, does not suddenly run into the perfection that they would be the first to admit almost certainly does not exist. Perhaps more than any other soul, the Virgo 8 must deal with the fruitlessness of reaching any sort of absolute condition. Rather than achieving a goal the Virgo 8 becomes a fierce testament to the value of attempting a goal.

Frankly, it's not always a pretty thing to watch. Virgo 8's bring a strident imperfectability to everything and there is often a fair amount of blood, sweat and tears along the way. Real pain is a natural outcropping of a life in which a goal that beyond reach is sought by a seeker who is congenitally unable to be satisfied.

In truth, it seems many a Virgo 8 makes their life about pain. These souls express a desire to function as teachers/models to the rest of us. Their lesson plan runs along the lines of: pain is unavoidable; but surmounting it is the key to the dignity of the human race.

In the end it is reasonable to accept the Virgo 8 soul as life's imperfect perfectionist. Their portion is to live ambitious lives in which they are both hero and anti-hero and back again. They covet being brought low as the only route to possibly rising up.

"Take your medicine," the Virgo 8 shouts while heading off in the general direction of eternity. "It's good for you."

"Cycling is so hard, the suffering is so intense, that it's absolutely cleansing. The pain is so deep and strong that a curtain descends over your brain....Once; someone asked me what pleasure I took in riding for so long. 'PLEASURE????,' I said. 'I don't understand the question.' I didn't do it for the pleasure; I did it for the pain."

– Lance Armstrong, iconic American pro athlete; only seven-time winner of the Tour de France; titles stripped due to doping; a cancer survivor; his foundation has raised $470M to fight cancer

"People have different goals, when you start out making a movie. If the goal is darkness and destruction and despair, it's not like, 'Hey, let's go to set, and then let's hit the bar afterwards. Let's jaunt into London and pick up some Chinese food.' No, you go home from set and you go fight at the gym, and then you go to sleep. You stay in it. You never excuse yourself, you never take it easy on yourself, you never eat good food."

–J on Bernthal, award-winning American actor; known best for playing the rugged hero/anti-hero in dark dramas such as 'The Walking Dead' and 'The Punisher;' has a real life trigger too

"Pain is one of life's great lessons. You need to know how you'll react to the negatives in your life. Only then will you learn from the pain, and the next time it happens, you can speed up your healing process."

– Terry Bradshaw, HOF American pro football QB/actor/TV personality/author/singer; first pick in 1970 NFL draft; four-time Super Bowl champion; suffers from ADD, depression, memory loss

"We're all human beings. Experience is experience, let's just be honest. Let's not try and dissect suffering into a race, or whatever you want to call it. We're all human beings, one way or another. All races have gone through times that are challenging; that's part of being a human."

– Idris Elba, NAACP/Golden Globe/SAG-award winning English actor/ writer/ producer/musician; acclaimed as self-destructive DCI John Luther; fulfilled lifelong ambition to fight professionally

"Entertainment has to come hand in hand with a little bit of medicine. Some people go to the movies to be reminded that everything's okay. I don't make those kinds of movies. That, to me, is a lie. Everything's not okay."

– David Fincher, Golden Globe/Emmy/Grammy-winning American director/ producer; known for dark thrillers like 'Fight Club' and 'Gone Girl;' an obsessive who reshoots scenes dozens of times

"Whatever life throws at me I'll take it and be grateful for it as well."

– Tom Felton, award-winning English actor/musician; best known as dark wizard Draco Malfoy in the 'Harry Potter' films; he fantasized about Draco coming back a hero and saving everyone

"And as long as people have problems, the blues can never die."

– B. B. King, Grammy/R&R HOF American singer-songwriter/guitarist/record producer; a pioneer of modern electric blues; famously rescued his guitar, Lucille, from a burning building

"I'm a perfectionist, so I always feel there's room for improvement."

– Ludacris, Grammy/SAG-winning American rapper/actor/producer/ humanitarian; plays tech expert Tej Parker in the 'Fast & Furious' films; his charity foundation supports urban youths

"Reach for it. Push yourself as far as you can."

– Christa McAuliffe, American teacher/astronaut; known to her students as "The Field Trip Teacher;" 1st American civilian astronaut; perished in the Space Shuttle Challenger disaster

"Sometimes painful things can teach us lessons that we didn't think we needed to know."

– Amy Poehler, award -winning American actress/comedian/writer/producer/director; Emmy-winning SNL alum; a Golden Globe winner for 'Parks and Recreation;' a thoughtful feminist

"Tell me what you are doing with your suffering, and I will tell you who you are."

– Tariq Ramadan, renowned Swiss-Muslim theologian/writer/educator; a leading Islamic influencer in the Western world; distinguished Oxford U career disrupted by rape allegations

"Where I come from, being a hard man is being able to take a good beating and then get back up again and carry on fighting."

– Mickey Rourke, Golden Globe-winning American actor/screenwriter/boxer; a legitimate tough guy; highly checkered career history; praised in wrenching 2008 comeback as 'The Wrestler'

 Libra 8

From the outside Libra 8's are not a particularly homogeneous group. In terms of personal predilections they are amalgam of humanity that includes athletes and actors, thinkers and tinkerers, statesmen and saints. What they all do appear to have in common, though, is the human ability to manifest a connection to grace, no matter how ephemeral or transitory.

When one considers this assertion it is important to notice not only the principle of "grace" but also that of "connection." Truly, a Libra 8 is often on a path that that leads to the awareness that orients a being meaningfully and totally within the breadth of the universe. More often than not, though, they will experience this state not as the epiphany of a solitary soul discovering and exalting itself, but as an expression of being that reveals the inter-connectedness, and even the interchangeability, between and among beings.

To put it as simply as possible, the Libra 8 ultimately believes in love and they want to hold your hand.

As one considers these Libra 8 beings at the end of their karmic cycle what lingers, sandwiched in between the far more scratchy Virgo and Scorpio soul paths, is the delicacy of their life statement. It is difficult to be so centered in awareness that one is always surmounting life's divisive tendencies, but it is the prospect of transcendent loving and peaceful reconciliation that lights the Libra 8 soul.

Sometimes it seems that a high-functioning Libra 8 is one step removed from a true investment in reality, as if living in a quasi-dream state. Perhaps this state of consciousness facilitates their leap into the void as if they are buoyed by an exceptional lightness of being. For their sake as well as ours let's just not wake them, okay?

"The opposite of a correct statement is a false statement. But the opposite of a profound truth may well be another profound truth."

– Niels Bohr, Nobel-laureate Danish physicist/philosopher; made essential contributions to the fields of atomic structure and quantum theory; held that a thing could be two things at once

"If you have your full attention in the moment, you will see only love."

– Deepak Chopra, award-winning Indian-American doctor/author/ humanitarian; a luminary in the New Age fields of holistic medicine/personal transformation; advocates "lightness of being"

"I'm a storyteller, I'm not a literary writer, and I don't want to be a literary writer. People say to me, 'Oh, when are you going to write something different?' What? I don't want to write anything different. I'm writing relationships between people, all different colors, all different sizes, all different sexual orientations, and that's what I want to do."

– Jackie Collins, celebrated English romance novelist; all of her 32 novels have been 'NY Times' bestsellers; sold 500 million books in 40 languages; famed for pushing conventional boundaries

"The ideal way to approach a character is to find something in yourself that relates in some way."

– Jesse Eisenberg, award-winning American actor/author/playwright; played Facebook founder Mark Zuckerberg in 'The Social Network;' fosters cats; runs a communal wordplay website

"Perhaps they were right putting love into books. Perhaps it could not live anywhere else."

– William Faulkner, Nobel-laureate American author; two-time Pulitzer winner; his famed novel 'The Sound and the Fury' tells the same story through the eyes of four different narrators

"I love doing what I do."

– Brett Favre, HOF American pro football QB; three-time NFL MVP; at retirement he held/shared 402 NFL records including most consecutive starts (321); had a love/hate relationship with fans

"In a burning building I would save a cat before a Rembrandt."

– Alberto Giacometti, era-defining Swiss sculptor/painter; influenced by Surrealism, realism and existentialism; best known for human figures; his 'Walking Man' was auctioned for $141M

"I couldn't live without something that touches my heart. No one should."

– Donna Karan, award-winning fashion creator/entrepreneur; known for her eponymous style label and the trendy DKNY; she ran afoul of PETA and eventually discontinued the use of fur

"Eternity; it is the sea mingled with the Sun."

– Arthur Rimbaud, award-winning French poet/adventurer; his work is noted for hallucinative imagery and modernistic alienation; quit poetry at age 19; his life was enormously paradoxical

"The world says they'll never make it, love says they will."

– Tanya Tucker, Grammy-winning American singer-songwriter; country music's "wild child;" had first hit, 'Delta Dawn,' at age 13/nine hit albums before 20; experienced career revival at age 61

"We respect the dignity and the rights of every man and every nation. The path to a brighter future of the world leads through honest reconciliation of the conflicting interests and not through hatred and bloodshed. To follow that path means to enhance the moral power of the all-embracing idea of human solidarity."

– Lech Walesa, Nobel Peace Prize-laureate Polish hero; first democratically elected president of Poland; co-creator of Solidarity, the first independent labor union in a Soviet bloc nation

"I'm Serena Williams on the court, but away I have so many different names. I call myself Butterfly."

– Serena Williams, all-time great American tennis pro/entrepreneur; has won more Grand Slam singles titles than any person in history; four-time Olympics gold medalist; has own clothing line

Scorpio 8

In any incarnation a Scorpio wages an obsessive battle between extraordinary self-control and the need for fierce expression of rather primal feelings. Having arrived at the terminus of the karma highway, a Scorpio 8 confronts the ultimate showdown of this character bifurcation. At some point, not unsurprisingly and as often as not and with an extraordinary amount of enthusiasm, Scorpio 8 tends to go boom.

To outsiders the most obvious badge a Scorpio 8 wears while they work out this frisson in their souls is an unholy amount of sex-appeal. This is a quality that goes far beyond one's physical attributes and, rather, permeates to the soul level. The Scorpio 8's compelling vibe is the marker of a being fully aware that it is gambling with personal oblivion while being totally turned on by the ultimacy of the stakes.

To be candid, the Scorpio 8 does not seem to be primarily operating on the level of discrimination and intellect. Their choice making apparatus, such as it is, seems to be far closer to that of a wild animal unpremeditatedly hunting life's resources and stimulations. Their ultimate eradication may always be lurking, but if one gets to chose between predator and prey while here...well, instinct says to ratchet up one's native cunning and drop the other guy.

Considering their inner battle with opposed behavioral traits and given the stakes of their engagement with transient existence, one unsurprisingly encounters plenty of Scorpio 8 tales of severe depression and anxiety. Scorpio 8's don't easily fit into a world of mundane concerns. They drop out a lot and stir pots that prefer to cradle congealed contents.

But, oh lord, Scorpio 8's do leave us with an ultimate and authentic sense of heart pumping resolution predicated upon blind passion. Their lives are guidebooks to the magic of willpower...damn the conflicts and consequences and messy setbacks. The Scorpio 8 trip into the void is a purifying howl.

"One thing I can say about our band is this. If you got something good to lay on us, enlighten us, but if you got something bad to lay on us, you can get your teeth knocked clean down your throat man."

– Duane Allman, Grammy-winning American guitarist/'Southern rock' pioneer; founder of the Allman Brothers Band; died in a bike crash at age 24; Lynyrd Skynyrd's 'Free Bird' is a tribute

"If I had a philosophy, it's that I support the beautiful side of anarchy."

– Bjork, award-winning Icelandic singer/songwriter/musician/producer/actress/DJ; known for eclectic/visceral style; swore off acting after clash with director of lauded 'Dancer in the Dark'

"My friends have named me the person they least want to do extreme adventures with because I always seem to be very close to being part of a disaster."

– Leonardo DiCaprio, Oscar-winning American actor/producer/environmentalist/disruptor; known for unconventional/stark hero roles; a legendary bad boy and a major philanthropist

"It never occurs to me that there are things I can't do."

– Whoopi Goldberg, Oscar/Emmy/Tony/Grammy-winning American actor/comedian/author/TV personality; winner of the Mark Twain Prize; dyslexic; a former junkie and a phone sex operator

"Whatever you are made of, be the best of that."

– Anne Hathaway, Oscar/Golden Globe/SAG/Emmy-winning American actress/activist; lauded as Fantine in 'Les Misérables;' at first cast in princess roles; hoped to be a nun; a feminist mentor

"Opinions are like orgasms...mine matters most and I really don't care if you have one."

– Sylvia Plath, Pulitzer-winning American poet/novelist/short-story writer; known for confessional poetry; wrote the feminist classic 'The Bell Jar;' clinical depression led to suicide

"My goal is to always come from a place of love ...but sometimes you just have to break it down for a motherfucker."

– RuPaul, Emmy-winning American drag queen/actor/model/singer/songwriter/TV personality; best known for TV reality series 'RuPaul's Drag Race;' was kicked out of high school for truancy

"You will eat my rear rockets and like it! Ohhhh yeahhh!"

– Randy Savage, American pro wrestler/actor/rapper; "Macho Man;" won 20 titles; ranked among the top wrestlers in history; voted 'Most Popular' and 'Most Hated' in successive years

"You're only human. You live once and life is wonderful, so eat the damned red velvet cupcake."

– Emma Stone, Oscar/Golden Globe/SAG-winning American actor; breakout films include teen classics 'Superbad' and 'Easy A;' famed for 'LaLa Land;' suffered severe anxiety as a child

"I'm shooting a commercial for safe sex. How ironic, because I don't have that."

– Tila Tequilla, popular American television & social media personality/singer; won an AVN award for "Best Celebrity Sex Tape;" working on a gospel album; actively 'alt-right' politically

"I just love it when people say I can't do it, there's nothing that makes me feel better because all my life, people have said that I wasn't going to make it."

– Ted Turner, American business luminary/philanthropist/yachtsman; "Captain Outrageous;" the founder of CNN; numerous media honors include TV HOF; a 'Playgirl' "sexiest man"

"You know you're in love when you wear condoms while having sex with other women."

– Owen Wilson, award-winning American actor/producer/screenwriter; known for efforts with Wes Anderson and Ben stiller; famed as Hansel in 'Zoolander;' severe depression sufferer

Sagittarius 8

One might reasonably expect the zodiac's philosopher, Sagittarius, to be a liberated and enlightened soul in a phase of full evolution. Yet, unlike a Sagittarius from the untethered seventh phase, a Sagittarius 8 lives a life that is imbued with a finality regarding purpose. Even the most buoyant of souls must face the end of the karmic path with something like sobriety.

Having established this, it is still true that the one word most apt in describing the Sagittarius 8's orientation towards existence is 'optimism.' This, though, is an optimism that is earned rather than appropriated, birthed by an honest experience of life's full possibilities. The Sagittarius 8 endeavors to pass all the ups and downs of existence through an experiential filter, almost inevitably pronouncing the purified essence to be way better than merely potable.

So it is that a Sagittarius 8 tends to live a life marked by its cultivated orientation towards positive outcomes and personal generosity. A felicitous wisdom comes more easily to these souls than others, and what they want to share is that everyone should be happy about being alive. Failure and pain are real experiences, of course, but they are most valuable in orienting oneself towards a better tomorrow.

Likely the magic in a Sagittarius 8 soul is zest or, if one prefers a more flowery description, the Zen of pursuit. Critics and obstructionists and other worldly obstacles, the Sagittarius 8 will argue, only damage the spirit of those who are willing to surrender to negativity. Luck is the residue of intelligent design and an infallible belief that everything is going to work out okay in the end.

For the rest, Sagittarius 8's really do care about leaving the world a better place and improving the lives of others. Their sassy trademark approach is to get up in to your face with a crystal clear observation at which they dare you not to laugh. Think bigger, take chances and have more fun, they will tell you, not because you are simple-minded but because you are full of grace and wise.

"I wish you music to help with the burdens of life, and to help you release your happiness to others."

– Ludwig van Beethoven, immortal German composer/pianist; bridged the Classical and Romantic eras; his nine symphonies have been called "the cornerstone of Western civilization"

"Good tired can be a day that you lost, but you don't even have to tell yourself because you knew you fought your battles, you chased your dreams, you lived your days and when you hit the hay at night, you settle easy, you sleep the sleep of the just and you say 'take me away'."

– Harry Chapin, Grammy HOF American singer/songwriter/producer/humanitarian; famed for 'Cat's in the Cradle;' a world hunger activist; ASCAP humanitarian award is given in his name

"You can't live a positive life with a negative mind."

– Miley Cyrus, award-winning American singer/songwriter/actress/philanthropist; successful in pop/country/hip hop genres; rose to fame as 'Hannah Montana;' famously free-spirited

"Money is like manure. You have to spread it around or it smells."

– J. Paul Getty, historically prominent petrol-industrialist/collector/philanthropist; in his lifetime he was the world's richest person; his eponymous foundation is home to a $10B art collection

"I'm all about fashion, cheeseburgers and bright-red lipstick."

– Scarlett Johansson, award-winning American actress/singer; one of the highest grossing and highest paid actors in history; genres range from intimate dramas to superhero blockbusters

"Choose the positive. You have choice, you are master of your attitude, choose the positive, the constructive. Optimism is a faith that leads to success."

– Bruce Lee, award-winning Hong Kong-American actor/director/martial artist/philosopher; iconic films include 'Fists of Fury' and 'Enter the Dragon;' popularized Kung Fu in the West

"Make sure your life is a rare entertainment! It doesn't take anything drastic. You needn't be gorgeous or wealthy or smart, just very enthusiastic!"

– Bette Midler, Grammy/Golden Globe/Tony/Emmy-winning American singer/songwriter/ actress/comedian/film producer; "The Divine Miss M;" known for her inspiring joie de vivre

"You should embrace who you are, and make the best person that you can be, not what somebody else wants you to be."

– Raven-Symone, award-winning American actress/singer/songwriter/ producer; known for her portrayal of the psychic/sassy Raven Baxter in multiple TV series; was a Disney 'Cheetah Girl'

"Thinking about the devil is worse than seeing the devil."

– Branch Rickey, American baseball player/manager/executive; famed for the signing of Jackie Robinson; crusaded for MLB expansion; annual community service award is given in his name

"The Lord is my Rock. He has always been there, always present at good times and bad; and to me when I feel His presence, my life is full."

– Aaron Rodgers, American pro football QB/actor/spokesperson; two-time NFL MVP; best TD to INT pass ratio in NFL history; received no scholarship offers to play in college; ultra-competitive

"I think there's nothing worse than inertia. You can inert and study your navel and gradually you'll fall off the chair. I think the key is to keep flying."

ɔtt, prolific Emmy/Golden Globe-winning British filmmaker; famed cts-driven classics 'Alien' & 'Blade Runner;' known for 'Thelma & ted to Sci-Fi HOF

"Anyone who doesn't sing and dance at every opportunity is missing out on the joy of life."

– Dick Van Dyke, Emmy/Tony/Grammy award-winning American actor/ comedian/writer/singer/ dancer/writer; famed for classic TV sitcom and roles in musical films; rejects aging limitations

 Capricorn 8

There is a fabulous paradox in the Capricorn 8 life that can only be deeply appreciated, never reconciled. It has to do with the fact that a Capricorn is by nature a climber whose focus is unwaveringly placed on the prize at the top of the mountain. Here, though, at the end of the karmic path where one's nature reaches its apotheosis, one must accept a finality in part predicated upon the comprehension of the human existential truth "here...but no further."

So it is that the Capricorn 8 life is most often a deeply aware quest in which one's being is absolutely committed to attaining the unattainable. What makes these souls so compelling is that they are preternaturally uncompromised by this state of affairs. They innately accept that whatever the ultimate outcome of their journey may be one must be loyal to purpose, and that the devil is particularly interested in those that give faint effort and are willing to lag behind.

Made of ambition and resilience, Capricorn 8 shortfalls are absolutely indistinguishable from what every other being might easily qualify as great success. Certainly, a study of Capricorn 8 lives parses the difference between aspiration and attainment. Yet in these beings the two are absolutely intimate acquaintances.

The ultimate key is that a Capricorn 8 has a very real appreciation of the role of time in human affairs. Capricorn 8's are not closed off from the awareness that the clock will eventually run out, but they never function on the principle that it will run out tomorrow. Tomorrows exist for sighting an effective route, making a good plan and for putting one foot ahead of the other.

"See you at the top," is the Capricorn 8 mantra. This might ultimately be an illusion, they are well aware, but they still mean it.

"What we need to do is always lean into the future; when the world changes around you and when it changes against you–what used to be a tail wind is now a head wind–you have to lean into that and figure out what to do because complaining isn't a strategy."

– Jeff Bezos, quintessential American/entrepreneur/investor/philanthropist; best known as the founder/CEO of Amazon; the world's richest man; declared "Greatest Living CEO" by HBR

"I think every year I become happier because I become more confident and more comfortable in my own skin."

– Zooey Deschanel, popular American actress/model/singer-songwriter/director/producer; best known for TV series 'New Girl;' described as a "super-girly feminist;" aspired to be a princess

"Regrets are a waste of time. They're the past crippling you in the present."

– Federico Fellini, Oscar-winning Italian film director/screenwriter; won four 'best foreign film' Oscars; uniquely combined fantasy and earthiness in films such as 'La Dolce Vita' and '8-1/2'

To understand the heart and mind of a person, look not at what he has already achieved, but at what he aspires to."

– Kahlil Gibran, esteemed Lebanese-American writer/poet/artist; known for the wisdom classic 'The Prophet;' Arab American Institute 'Spirit of Humanity' awards are presented in his name

"Never get married in the morning, because you never know who you'll meet that night."

– Paul Hornung, HOF American football player/TV analyst/businessman; "The Golden Boy;" charismatic; won Heisman Award/NFL MVP; prolific scorer as runner/kicker; 4-time NFL champ

"If you live in an oppressive society, you've got to be resilient. You can't let each little thing crush you. You have to take every encounter and make yourself larger, rather than allow yourself to be diminished by it."

– James Earl Jones, Tony/Grammy/Emmy-award winning American actor; famed for his booming deep voice, particularly as Darth Vader and Mufasa; is a stutterer; a Kennedy Center Honoree

"When you're out of will power you call on stubbornness, that's the trick."

– Henri Matisse, eminent French painter/draftsman/sculptor/printmaker; considered the greatest colorist of the 20th C; criticized for his "wild" style; built a museum for his own works

"Rivers know this: there is no hurry. We shall get there someday."

– A. A. Milne, award-winning English author/playwright/poet; the creator of 'Winnie-the-Pooh;' disliked being typecast as a children's writer, but enjoyed his status in literary history

"Every day has the potential to be the greatest day of your life."

– Lin-Manuel Miranda, Pulitzer/Grammy/Tony/Emmy-award winning American composer/ lyricist/singer/rapper/actor/producer/playwright; created & starred in 'Hamilton'

"One day a long time from now you'll cease to care anymore whom you please or what anybody has to say about you. That's when you'll finally produce the work you're capable of."

– J. D. Salinger, iconic American writer; his coming-of-age classic 'Catcher in the Rye' still sells 250,000+ copies per year; disliked celebrity & ego, kept writing for 50 years without publishing

"I just want people to remember me a hundred years from now. I don't care that they're not able to quote any single line that I've written. But just that they can say, 'Oh, he was a writer.' That's sufficiently an honored position for me."

– Rod Serling, Emmy/Hugo/Golden Globe-winning American screenwriter/playwright/television producer/narrator; famed as the creator/host of 'The Twilight Zone;' a combat veteran and pro boxer

"The greatest thing about tomorrow is I will be better than I am today."

– Tiger Woods, preeminent American golfer/spokesperson/entrepreneur/philanthropist; holds many all-time golf records including most PGA wins; story includes disgrace and comeback

Aquarius 8

The Aquarius 8 lives at the final outpost of human potential as applied to the substantive experiential world. An urge exists in these souls to create a meaningful and enduring human postscript to all life journeys, while simultaneously anticipating an existence that cannot be confined by any reasonable understanding of being, time and space. Frankly, it's the sort of situation that gets a little overwhelming sometimes.

Metaphorically and/or literally, it's not unfair to report that the Aquarius 8 is prone to getting high. On one level this means getting so close to something in the domain of human existence that may be called Truth that one is likely to become virtually incandescent. On another, it indicates that there are demons in the thin air that can bring the highest aspirations phenomenally crashing to the ground.

It really goes both ways with Aquarius 8, success and failure. Yet what these souls take out of their experiences is far more of a revelation than a material payoff or penalty. Both boosted and bound by their humanity, it is the Aquarius 8's lot in life to appreciate that the essential resolution of the human condition is not arrival but evolution.

Throughout all, the Aquarius 8 life is most often an experiment regarding the tensile strength of the human spirit. Certainly there are limits to human potential, but it is an Aquarius 8's lot in life to bend and mold and grow and, most importantly, innovate past any easy application of finality to the human species quest for growth. Aquarius 8's are rightfully celebrated as champions for taking on what can only be described as an embrace of the greater good.

Ultimately, perhaps we appreciate the Aquarius 8 most for the poignancy that often permeates their lives. However high they may rise, they are not getting out of this incarnation with any less finality than the rest of us. But as we identify with Aquarius 8 aspiration to push the envelope and exist on a higher plane, we tend to appreciate the best of our own humanity.

"The trick is in knowing what you want to do, and then resolving to do everything you have to do to get there."

– John Belushi, Emmy-winning American actor/comedian/singer; famed as an original 'SNL' cast member; known for unhinged ringleader roles in films like 'Animal House;' died of drug OD

"We will go forward...we will never go back."

– Michael Bloomberg, award-winning American businessman/politician/ philanthropist/author; Eagle Scout; Harvard MBA; founder of Bloomberg LP; 3x mayor of NYC at a salary of $1/year

"It is our duty to give meaning to the life of future generations by sharing our knowledge and experience; by teaching an appreciation of work well done and a respect for nature, the source of all life; by encouraging the young to venture off the beaten path and avoid complacency by challenging their emotions."

– Paul Bocuse, eminent French chef/restaurateur; described as the "Pope of Haute Cuisine;" named CIA "Chef of the Century;" renowned for innovating a lighter/fresher classical cuisine

"The world will not be inherited by the strongest; it will be inherited by those most able to change."

– Charles Darwin, eminent English naturalist/geologist/biologist; famed for concept of evolution; Darwin Awards given for dumb/fatal risk life and limb, thereby improving the human genome

"The music is key. It has the power to transport you. I go from being a slightly insecure, shy kind of a person offstage, to this super-confident, motivated, entity onstage."

– Neil Diamond, R&R HOF/Grammy/Golden Globe-winning American singer-songwriter/actor; sold over 125M records; won Songwriters HOF lifetime achievement award; dislikes songwriting

"I get it now; I didn't get it then. That life is about losing and about doing it as gracefully as possible... and enjoying everything in between."

– Mia Farrow, Golden Globe-winning American actress/model/activist; starred in 'Rosemary's Baby;' 1st American in the Royal Shakespeare Company; three celebrity marriages ended badly

"I was at a meeting two years ago in Beijing, and I passed a bunch of women who were marching in a protest. Their signs were probably saying something I wouldn't have agreed with at all. But I was so glad to see women marching. And it's happening all over the world."

– Betty Friedan, pioneering American feminist writer/activist; author of 'The Feminine Mystique;' co-founder of NOW; renowned for a feminism that was not anti-men or anti-family

"Behind the cloud the Sun is still shining."

– Abraham Lincoln, revered American statesman; the 16th U.S. president; preserved the Union in time of Civil War; landmark programs ran from emancipation of slaves to graduated income tax

"There's beauty everywhere. There are amazing things happening everywhere, you just have to be able to open your eyes and witness it. Some days, that's harder than others."

– Sarah McLachlan, Grammy-winning Canadian singer-songwriter; known for yearning ballads like "Arms of an Angel;" won multiple Juno Awards; a member of the Canadian Music HOF

"Heart in champions has to do with the depth of our motivation and how well your mind and body react to pressure–that is, being able to do what you do best under maximum pain and stress."

– Bill Russell, HOF pro American basketball player/activist; best under pressure, he holds NBA record of playing on 11 championship teams; Medal of Freedom recipient for civil rights work

"By attempting the impossible one can attain the highest level of the possible."

– August Strindberg, groundbreaking Swedish playwright/novelist/social activist; a pioneer of naturalism in works such as 'Miss Julie' and 'The Father;' annual August Prize honors his name

"Just before you break through the sound barrier, the cockpit shakes the most."

– Chuck Yeager, decorated American USAF officer/test pilot/author; the man who broke the sound barrier; autobiography is titled 'Press On!;' Aviation HOF/Medal of Freedom honoree

 Pisces 8

If you have done me the honor of reading through this entire manuscript it should by now be abundantly clear that this little project of mine is hardly a work of rigorous scholarship. I make no representations as to its scientific or historical accuracy, nor do I maintain that any truth manifested here to be anything but artistic. If you like it, please consider it akin to a catchy song rather than an exposition of cosmic infallibility.

The above qualification, while adhering to every statement in this book, is somehow most relevant in considering Pisces 8. For here, at the terminus of this evolutionary conceit, we must consider the souls who may have actually dipped a toe in some sort of oceanic transcendence. Not to put too fine a point on it, the Pisces 8 individual seems to be somehow intimate with God.

Okay, okay, I don't have to get on such a high horse about this. It would probably be reasonable to simply describe Pisces 8's as really different from other people. In the truest sense of the word they are characters, liberated by cosmic possibility to wholly and unrepentantly manifest some spirit-based essence without any of the doubts or filters encountered by most of the rest of us.

And yet I can't get away from that God thing. The creation of this book has provided innumerable moment of personal frisson and synchronicity, but one of my favorites has to do with assembling the famous people attached to this Pisces 8 section. While working I found that, according to the indispensible provider of birth information

Astrotheme, one of the individuals who qualifies as a Pisces 8 is Jesus Christ.

Now, hold on a second. I have no idea when Jesus Christ was born, although clearly we celebrate on the Capricorn date December 25th, and why should that not be fine with me? The point here though, whatever the temporal justification that the Astrotheme folks may be working from, is that Jesus Christ *should be* a Pisces 8, every bit as much as Charles Barkley.

"I never knew what I wanted except that it was something I hadn't seen before."

– Robert Altman, award-winning American film director/screenwriter/producer; made offbeat naturalistic movies such as 'Mash' and 'The Player;' Independent Spirit award given in his name

"I only act from my heart."

– Bad Bunny, Grammy-winning Puerto Rican singer/rapper; known for Latin trap & reggaeton work; stage name derives from school punishment in which he was forced to wear bunny ears

"I'm never embarrassed."

– Charles Barkley, Emmy-winning American HOF pro basketball player/TV analyst/media celebrity/writer; Olympic gold medal winner/NBA MVP; celebrated for candor & charisma

"There's something about a catharsis that is very important."

– Glenn Close, SAG/Emmy/Tony-winning American actress/singer/producer; seven-time Oscar and three-time Grammy nominee; best known as the psychotic mistress in 'Fatal Attraction'

"Man, just believe in yourself, be able to dream, and know that there's going to be valleys and peaks. Always stay centered, and know that God is the key, the beginning and end of everything you do."

– Common, Oscar/Grammy/Golden Globe-winning American rapper/actor/writer/humanitarian; featured in 50+ movies; socially conscious; his memoir is titled 'Let Love Have the Last Word'

"I bleed like nobody else."

– Rick Flair, WWE HOF pro American wrestler/manager; nicknamed "Nature Boy;" known for a flamboyant angry persona and lavish ring robes; a six-time winner of Wrestler of the Year

"Whether I was in my body or out of my body as I wrote it I know not. God knows."

– George Frideric Handel, acclaimed German-British Baroque composer; wrote in many formats but best known for oratorio 'Messiah' and the 'Hallelujah Chorus;' popular in his own lifetime

"If you're lucky enough to use something you see in a dream, it is purely original. It's not in the world–it's in your head. I think that is amazing."

– Alexander McQueen, award-winning British fashion designer/couturier; known for shocking fantasy creations; his fashion shows were media sensations; 4X Fashion Designer of the Year

"No great work of art is ever finished."

– Michelangelo, revered Renaissance Italian sculptor/painter/architect/poet; one of history's most influential artists; sculptor of David and La Pieta; painter of the Sistine Chapel ceiling

"As human beings, our job in life is to help people realize how rare and valuable each one of us really is, that each of us has something that no one else has-or ever will have-something inside that is unique to all time."

– Fred Rogers, Emmy/Peabody-winning American television personality/writer/producer; a TV icon; famed for 'Mr. Rogers Neighborhood;' a musician and pastor; recipient of Presidential MOF

“Talent is a burden not a joy. I am not of this planet. I do not come from you. I am not like you.”

– Nina Simone, Grammy HOF American singer/songwriter/musician/rights activist; known for emotional/style intensity; vested in a wide range of music genres; was a H.S. valedictorian

“My real fantasy if I was to drop out would be to live in a mobile home and be a hippie and drive around festivals and have millions of children–children with dreadlocks and nose rings–and play the flute.”

– Rachel Weisz, Oscar-winning British-American actress/model; nicknamed “English Rose;” breakthrough film was ‘The Mummy;’ a Cambridge University grad; married to James Bond

Celebrity Roster

Aaliyah (Capricorn 5)
Aaron, Hank (Aquarius 6)
Abdul, Paula (Gemini 5)
Abdul-Jabbar, Kareem (Aries 7)
Abrams, J.J. (Cancer 3)
Acker, Amy (Sagittarius 4)
Adams, Ansel (Pisces 4)
Adams, Douglas (Pisces 4)
Adams, Scott (Gemini 3)
Adele (Taurus 5)
Affleck, Ben (Leo 2)
Agassi, Andre (Taurus 7)
Aguilera, Christina (Sagittarius 4)
Ailey, Alvin (Capricorn 5)
Alba, Jessica (Taurus 7)
Albright, Madeleine (Taurus 2)
Alcott, Louisa May (Sagittarius 2)
Aldrin, Buzz (Aquarius 6)
Ali, Muhammad (Capricorn 1)
Allen, Paul (Aquarius 2)
Allen, Woody (Sagittarius 2)
Allman, Duane (Scorpio 8)
Altman, Robert (Pisces 8)
Amin, Idi (Taurus 8)
Andersen, Hans Christian (Aries 1)
Anderson, Gillian (Leo 5)
Anderson, Pamela (Cancer 7)
Andrews, Julie (Libra 1)
Angelou, Maya (Aries 4)
Aniston, Jennifer (Aquarius 7)
Ann-Margret (Taurus 1)
Apatow, Judd (Sagittarius 2)
Applegate, Christina (Sagittarius 3)
Arden, Elizabeth (Capricorn 3)
Armani, Giorgio (Cancer 8)
Armstrong, Lance (Virgo 8)
Armstrong, Louis (Leo 6)
Armstrong, Neil (Leo 3)
Armstrong-Jones, Antony (Pisces 2)
Arquette, Patricia (Aries 3)
Arthur, Bea (Taurus 5)
Ashe, Arthur (Cancer 3)
Asimov, Isaac (Capricorn 3)
Atlas, Charles (Scorpio 3)
Auden, W. H. (Pisces 3)
Austen, Jane (Sagittarius 7)
Bacall, Lauren (Virgo 5)
Bacon, Kevin (Cancer 6)
Bad Bunny (Pisces 8)
Badu, Erykah (Pisces 1)
Baez, Joan (Capricorn 3)
Bailey, Alice A. (Gemini 3)
Bakker, Jim (Capricorn 7)
Baldwin, Alec (Aries 4)
Baldwin, James A. (Leo 1)
Bale, Christian (Aquarius 2)
Ball, Lucille (Leo 4)
Ballmer, Steve (Aries 4)
Balzac, Honore de (Taurus 5)
Banks, Elizabeth (Aquarius 6)
Banks, Tyra (Sagittarius 3)
Bardem, Javier (Pisces 4)
Bardot, Brigitte (Libra 6)
Barkley, Charles (Pisces 8)
Barnum, P.T. (Cancer 1)
Barr, Roseanne (Scorpio 5)
Barrymore, Drew (Pisces 3)
Baryshnikov, Mikhail (Aquarius 5)
Basinger, Kim (Sagittarius 1)
Bassett, Angela (Leo 1)
Baudelaire, Charles (Aries 3)
Baum, Joe (Leo 2)
Beauvoir, Simone de (Capricorn 2)
Beck, Jeff (Cancer 1)

Odenkirk, Bob (Libra 7)
O'Donnell, Lawrence (Scorpio 3)
Offerman, Nick (Cancer 7)
O'Hara, Maureen (Leo 2)
O'Keeffe, Georgia (Scorpio 1)
Oldenburg, Claes (Aquarius 5)
Oldman, Gary (Aries 1)
Oliver, John (Taurus 1)
Olivier, Laurence (Taurus 3)
Olsen, Mary-Kate (Gemini 2)
Onassis, Aristotle (Capricorn 7)
Onassis, Jackie Kennedy (Leo 6)
O'Neal, Shaquille (Pisces 6)
Onfray, Michel (Capricorn 6)
O'Reilly, Bill (Virgo 5)
Osteen, Joel (Pisces 3)
Oswald, Lee Harvey (Libra 2)
O'Toole, Peter (Leo 8)
Pablo Picasso (Scorpio 1)
Pacino, Al (Taurus 6)
Page, Jimmy (Capricorn 4)
Page, Larry (Aries 6)
Paglia, Camille (Aries 4)
Palin, Michael (Taurus 1)
Palmer, Arnold (Virgo 2)
Paltrow, Gwyneth (Libra 6)
Parker, Charlie "Bird" (Virgo 4)
Parker, Dorothy (Virgo 3)
Parton, Dolly (Capricorn 5)
Pasternak, Boris (Aquarius 6)
Pasteur, Louis (Capricorn 4)
Patrick, Robert (Scorpio 7)
Patterson, James (Aries 1)
Pavarotti, Luciano (Libra 4)
Peele, Jordan (Pisces 7)
Pegg, Simon (Aquarius 3)
Pei, I.M. (Taurus 2)
Pele (Libra 6)
Pelosi, Nancy (Aries 5)
Perlman, Itzhak (Virgo 7)
Perot, Ross (Cancer 1)
Perry, Katy (Scorpio 1)
Perry, Tyler (Virgo 1)
Pesci, Joe (Aquarius 2)
Peterson, Adrian (Aries 1)
Pfeiffer, Michelle (Taurus 3)
Phelps, Michael (Cancer 4)
Philbin, Regis (Virgo 4)
Piaget, Jean (Leo 8)
Pierce, Paul (Libra 1)
Pine, Chris (Virgo 5)
Pink (Virgo 5)
Pitbull (Capricorn 3)
Plath, Sylvia (Scorpio 8)
Poehler, Amy (Virgo 8)
Polanski, Roman (Leo 8)
Pollack, Sydney (Cancer 6)
Pollock, Jackson (Aquarius 3)
Pope Francis (Sagittarius 2)
Pope John Paul II (Taurus 1)
Portman, Natalie (Gemini 3)
Potter, Beatrix (Leo 5)
Pound, Ezra (Scorpio 7)
Pratt, Chris (Gemini 8)
Presley, Elvis (Capricorn 1)
Price, Leontyne (Aquarius 3)
Price, Vincent (Gemini 8)
Prince (Gemini 6)
Prince Harry, Duke of Sussex (Virgo 6)
Proust, Marcel (Cancer 7)
Pryor, Richard (Sagittarius 1)
Puck, Wolfgang (Cancer 4)
Queen Elizabeth II (Taurus 3)
Queen Victoria (Gemini 1)
Quintanilla, Selena (Aries 6)
Radcliffe, Daniel (Leo 6)
Ramadan, Tariq (Virgo 8)
Ramone, Joey (Taurus 4)
Ramsay, Gordon (Scorpio 7)
Rather, Dan (Scorpio 6)

Acknowledgments

Thank you to my perfect wife, Ann, who has the extraordinary grace and kindness to let me do this and call it earning a living.

Thank you to my brilliant son, Jesse, for all the pride and joy he has brought to my life and, in particular, for the lunation phase calculator he so effortlessly produced for this project. That calculator can be found at www.the96incarnations.com by the way.

Thank you to my friend Ken Beller for his wisdom and encouragement, and his willingness to always do more than I ask...and for knowing what I should ask even when I don't.

Thank you to Nick Caya and his team at Word-2-Kindle for so professionally caring about a stranger's work and making the self-publishing process flow so smoothly.

Thank you to the astrological community...my teachers, my colleagues, and my clients...who have made this incarnation such an extraordinary trip for me.

Thank you to Tim Berners-Lee for inventing the World Wide Web so that the world might be flooded with enough random data to assemble this book.

Thank you to God for creating the Sun and the Moon and the stars, as well as for giving life to all of us regular folk who might conceivably get to be shiny objects in our next lives.

Made in the USA
Las Vegas, NV
23 October 2021